The Mind's Affective Life

CH00751754

The Mind's Affective Life is an innovative examination of the relationship between feeling and thinking. Our thoughts and behaviour are shaped by both our emotions and reason; yet until recently most of the literature analysing thought has concentrated largely on philosophical reasoning, and has neglected emotions.

This book is an original and provocative contribution to the rapidly growing literature on the neglected affective dimensions of our thinking. Drawing on contemporary psychoanalysis, philosophy, feminist theory and recent innovations in neuroscience, the author argues that in order to understand thought we need to consider not only its emotional and rational aspects but also the complex interaction between them. Only through such a rich and subtle understanding of thought processes can we hope to avoid what the author identifies as a significant contemporary problem for individuals and cultures: the suppression or denial of intolerable states of feeling.

The Mind's Affective Life will appeal to and inspire students and experts alike in the fields of philosophy, psychoanalysis, psychotherapy and women's studies. It will also be of great interest to anyone concerned with the relation between the cognitive and emotional dimensions of the mind.

Gemma Corradi Fiumara is Associate Professor of Philosophy at the University of Rome and a training member of the Italian Psychoanalytic Society.

The Mind's Affective Life

A Psychoanalytic and Philosophical Inquiry

Gemma Corradi Fiumara

First published 2001 by Brunner-Routledge
27 Church Road, Hove, East Sussex BN3 2FA

Simultaneously published in the USA and Canada
by Taylor & Francis Inc
325 Chestnut Street, Philadelphia PA 19106

Brunner-Routledge is an imprint of the Taylor & Francis Group

© 2001 Gemma Corradi Fiumara

Typeset in Times by Keystroke, Jacaranda Lodge, Wolverhampton
Printed and bound in Great Britain by TJ International Ltd, Padstow,
Cornwall, UK

Every effort has been made to ensure that the advice and information in
this book is true and accurate at the time of going to press. However,
neither the publisher nor the author can accept any legal responsibility or
liability for any errors or omissions that may be made. In the case of drug
administration, any medical procedure or the use of technical equipment
mentioned within this book, you are strongly advised to consult the
manufacturer's guidelines.

British Library Cataloguing in Publication Data
A catalogue record for this book is available from the British Library

Library of Congress Cataloging in Publication Data
    Corradi Fiumara, Gemma.
      The mind's affective life : a psychoanalytic and philosophical inquiry /
    Gemma Corradi Fiumara.
        p.   cm.
    Includes bibliographical references and index.
    ISBN 1-58391-153-7 – ISBN 1-58391-154-5 (pbk.)
        1. Psychoanalysis and philosophy. 2. Emotions and cognition.
    3. Emotional intelligence. I. Title.

    BF175.4.P45 C67 2001
    150'.1 – dc21   00-053351

ISBN 1-58391-153-7 (hbk)
ISBN 1-58391-154-5 (pbk)

For Linda and Michele Fiumara

Contents

Introduction

While affects co-operate with reason to make it functional, they can also distort it to the point of rendering it useless or self defeating. It is therefore essential to focus on the intersections, synergies, and conflicts which exist between emotion and intelligence, feeling and thinking. This central topic is approached through different paths and perspectives, indicated in the titles of the chapters and paragraphs that compose the book.

We cannot envisage the relationship between affective life and rational theorising in terms of 'inside' and 'outside': we argue that affects inhabit and fuel the illusively empty interiority of our epistemologies – while ultimately remaining external to the intellectual productions that would confer cognitive legitimacy onto them. This paradoxical, obscured texture of our culture needs to be made visible for our evolving rationality to become more integrated and inclusive. The book tries to indicate ways of developing our emotional intelligence; it aims, in fact, at an account of how emotions serve to construct both interpersonal relations and reality.

Our mind's life presents paradoxical aspects because it is at once dependent upon affects while considering itself autonomous in generating knowledge. In fact, reigning world views appear both to rely upon *and* disavow the role of affects in their epistemic constructions. There would be no enclaves of 'pure', homogeneous rationality if they were not sustained by the connecting forces of ignored emotional resources. Moreover, our affective capacities seem to meet the challenge of life's problems so efficiently as to relieve abstract thought from these burdens. Such 'lesser' functions of our mind and culture almost protect the intellectual games of the 'higher' levels by steadily coping with relational vicissitudes on their behalf. It is unlikely that any epistemology will face alarming problems of pluralism of views, and of its psychic genesis, as long as the more affective ways of knowing laboriously perform these tasks. Of course, attempts to resolve these unavoidable tensions are unwittingly played out in our society with a great variety of results.

Contemporary views drawing on our psychoanalytic culture exemplify challenges to existing enclaves of homogeneous rationality which are inexorably made more problematic and even recognised as defensive forms of insulation from our affective life. But then, the exploration of affects in psychoanalysis is also related to clinical accounts generated through some particular theory, while the problematic connection between affect and theory itself is not frequently examined. The emotion-intellect link is thus one of the main problems; it is in fact a central question of psychoanalysis as a theory, and of philosophy as a practice.

In an attempt to explore the mind's affective life, contributions from the domain of psychoanalysis are of course used, as the analytic relation seems the ideal place for the study of affects. As is known, psychoanalytic research is affect-centred, focused on the mediating forces that intervene between drive and defence, between conscious and unconscious life. There is implicit evidence that psychoanalysis is a study of the mind that considers affectivity as a central working concept inseparably linked to cognition, in an obstinate, holistic view of our human experience. In fact, mental events can be seen as two-sided – one side looks in the direction of propositional, logical processes, while the other points to affectual, unconscious dynamics. The meaning of mental events may separately exist on each side, but a fuller significance actually derives from their continued interaction. Moreover, different creatures constantly concur and share in psychic vicissitudes, thus reciprocally contributing to both sides of mental events.

The book is also an attempt to explore the affective components of apparently non-affective human enterprises. For this purpose contributions emanating from the enlightening literature of feminist epistemologies are utilised; their innovative arguments are in fact hospitable to questions which imply the embodied, pulsating existence of the questioners. Certain aspects of culture, as is known, conspire with silencing strategies such as exclusion, repression, denial and foreclosure; our subjectivity should thus be rethought in ways that would make it possible to theorise our affects' voices. The silencing of emotions also needs to be understood as something more than simple exclusion; we should in fact look for the symptomatic silences or readable absences which ultimately reveal that a style of denials is at work. A general attitude of avoidant denials, moreover, seems to tacitly transform illuminating distinctions into innumerable divisive and oppositional paradigms. These are so pervasive as to become almost inconspicuous – and, ironically, even canonic; just think of binarised, adversarial 'opposites' such as body and mind, emotion and reason, subject and object, conscious/unconscious, digital/analogic, literal/metaphoric, and logical/empirical. In the present work there is an attempt to show that a typical oppositional juxtaposition – 'affective versus cognitive life' – is in fact an obscuring pseudo-dualism. We should rethink oppositions in such a way that they can be viewed as life-enhancing differences; only in this way may we escape the constraints which compel us to supervise 'boundaries' of all kinds. We can no longer reason with a sort of implicit outlook which requires the oblivion, or silencing, of one of the terms. This book, however, does not go against any particular way of viewing our psychic organisation; it basically strives to show aspects of our mind's life which might remain inconspicuous unless we develop a special awareness of them, and a more familiar vocabulary for their exploration.

Philosophers often defend the existence of knowledge as an autonomous category which cannot be reconnected to the interplay of libidic and aggressive derivatives; and yet, as long as knowledge is conceived as being independent from affective components, it is ultimately unreasonable to envisage its evolutionary vicissitudes. Drawing on a variety of sources, the book attempts to demonstrate that affective factors cannot be severed from intellectual achievements, and it also strives towards a rethinking of the different forces which are tacitly at work in our minds.

Chapter 1

The fragility of 'pure reason'

The island of 'pure reason' and the sea of passions

In a revealing passage of his first *Critique*, Kant seems to eloquently express both a concern for the purity of reason *and* an interest in whatever is left out of it. An emblematic figure in the affirmation and 'idealisation' of reason, Kant indirectly recognises our intense curiosity for whatever terrain *surrounds* the circumscribed enclosure of our conscious and coherent mind: 'We have . . . traversed the whole domain of the pure understanding, . . . and assigned to everything in it its proper place. This domain, however, is an island and enclosed by nature itself within limits that can never be changed. It is the country of truth (a very attractive name), but surrounded by a wide and stormy ocean, the true home of illusion, where many a fog bank and ice that soon melts away tempt us to believe in new lands, while constantly deceiving the adventurous mariner with vain hopes, and involving him in adventures which he can never leave, and yet can never bring to an end.'[1]

As soon as one tries to talk about anything outside 'the island of truth', anything exceeding the conscious, rational mind, we seem bound to use a metaphoric language of 'fog banks' and 'melting icebergs'. Yet, what primarily transpires is both a fascination for the surrounding ocean *and* a clear intent to discourage any venture which might take place outside canonic domains. Following this Kantian similitude, we may say that the irresistible attraction for the 'stormy ocean of illusions' could be interpreted as a paradoxical recognition of the value and potential of exploring whatever exceeds the boundaries of 'pure reason', as a concern for its profound origins. Indeed, why should he warn us against something that no one would be interested in pursuing? There is in fact an incoercible interest for what constitutes the receptacle, terrain, or surroundings of whatever 'pure reason' seems to prevail in a given epoch. Contemporary views of rationality deriving from psychoanalytic culture are among the constant examples of challenge to existing islands of pure reason and to their 'natural' boundaries, which are inexorably made more problematic, and often recognised as defensive forms of insulation from the stormy ocean of our affective life. Moreover, it seems inadequate to think constantly about the relation between affective life and 'rationality', only in terms of 'inside' and 'outside'. Such a spatial view proves too simplistic, in that affects simultaneously inhabit philosophy's illusively empty interiority, while remaining exterior to the productions that would confer legitimacy and voice onto them.

Why should we begin evoking our rationalist tradition on the way to an exploration of the mind's affectual texture? Why not start right away with human emotions? The problem is that in our Western culture anything that has to do with the mind is frequently considered simply 'rational', and somehow quite thinkable. It is therefore necessary, at the beginning, to acknowledge our pervasive rationality – almost second nature to us – in order to let our affective life emerge more clearly in the only context in which it can manifest itself: the mainstream of our contemporary epistemologies. It is, I believe, the best way to proceed if we are to avoid the risk that rationality may silently presume to be independent from its affective components. On the other hand, the fact that instincts and affects can only begin to operate psychically at the level of mental ego functions – and are thus dependent on reasoning – is more readily accepted and comprehensible.

Reigning epistemologies, in fact, appear to somehow both rely upon *and* disavow the role of affects in their epistemic constructions and in the affirmation of rationality. There would be no Kantian 'islands' of homogeneous pure reason if they were not sustained and allowed for by the innumerable connecting functions of our affective and metaphoric resources. Certain not so 'pure' areas of culture and mental functioning seem to meet the challenge of life problems so efficiently as to relieve epistemic domains of abstract thought from these burdens. Such 'lesser' areas of our culture almost protect the lucid intraepistemic games of the 'higher' levels by steadily coping with coexistential vicissitudes and 'foreign affairs' on their behalf. It is unlikely that any epistemology will begin to cope with alarming problems of external relations and of its own affective depths, as long as the more hermeneutic and affect-prone disciplines will laboriously perform this function. If the 'lesser' human languages were to monitor the inclination to be hyper-functional and to solve problems for the sedate and solemn 'pure reason' is possible that also the more 'insular', lucid, and serious intellectual domains of culture might have to confront their hypo-functional policies. Perhaps official philosophy resists recognition of its dependence upon resources that it draws from the mind's affective life. Certain areas of philosophy systematically tend to eschew a number of difficult questions on the grounds that they are peripheral or not quite to the point; obtruding emotional issues, in fact, are usually 'described' as tangentially connected to truth claims, insufficiently clear, unfocused, inappropriately articulated, excessively controversial, or sub-rational. According to Le Doeuff, since the activity of separation and division is philosophically productive (as the proper 'field', or Kantian island, is created by its exclusions), philosophy ultimately creates itself through what it represses – almost as if the 'psychoanalytic' function of repression were essential to its practices. It should be interesting, then, to districate the corporate cohesion of rationality so as to allow our affective life to speak out from the centre of our culture, rather than letting it mutely function in there.[2]

Most inquiries in a variety of fields proclaim an appreciation of dialectical criticism even while they are relentlessly focused on securing consensus and winning adhesions. They ultimately appear to base their cultural enterprises upon a conviction that consensus is a powerful 'instrument' and that, if properly constituted, it might even provide for the *quality* of rational solutions to problems – almost as if consensus were an essential component of rationality. Indeed, why should reason, logic and truth-oriented argument ever fail to win consensus? Thus the paradox of strenuous search for qualified consensus, in conjunction with the alleged purity and putative autonomy of rational truth, seems to elicit enough curiosity about the cherished idea of our human 'pure reason', and of its contemporary variants.

Of course, agreement among epistemic subjects across geographical and historical domains is not something that customarily happens in our world. The variegated specificities of cultures and experiences make the goal of generalised consensus in cognitive or evaluative issues rather ideal and unrealistic.[3] Only by abstracting from embodied contingencies, and by shifting to the level of idealisation, could we expect or even, ultimately, require consensus. To insist tacitly on cognitive homogeneity is perhaps comparable to maintaining that in ideal circumstances subjects would necessarily reach agreement, as if truth were essentially irresistible. To reach out insistently for ideal circumstances seems profoundly interwoven with an idealisation of our all too human rationality.

The generic suggestion that truth and correctness should be able to elicit consensus sounds of course quite appropriate in our culture. But the 'truth' in matters of human endeavours can in fact be made evidentially secure only in ideal insulated circumstances, and not in general, under the imperfect conditions in which we necessarily conduct our cognitive affairs.[4] Truth as such would ultimately command agreement in and of itself only from those subjects whose epistemic situation is 'suitably' favourable, those willing to inhabit any Kantian islands of 'pure understanding'. In the contingencies of our language and subjectivity, consensus would be too much to expect – or to ask for. But then, we are easily seduced by the generality and 'objectivity' of rational judgements because we probably perceive them as potentially implementing admirable 'universal' principles. Consensuality, moreover, is not something that we could demand here and now, for 'truth' and general agreement only seem to converge in a remote, ideal locus. A locus that we can speculate about in terms of a desire for the agreement that would be reached by ideally rational inquirers functioning in ideally favourable circumstances.[5] But, again, idealisation is ultimately the result of a laborious emotional experience and not only part of a reasoning process.[6] In this outlook, therefore, we should somehow distinguish between our 'ideals' and our 'idealisations'. An ideal as such may belong to the practical order, as it is something that can function as a guideline in our actual proceedings, providing a goal of appropriate endeavour; an ideal may represent a state of things whose implementation – even if only in part – is to be positively evaluated and which should, by its very nature, be seen as desirable. An idealisation, on the other hand, is inherently different, for it involves the projection of profound affective components that disregard limits or limitations of various kinds; an idealisation is, accordingly, the affective production and expression of a hypothetical state of things – something that ultimately represents the result of profound psychic yearning.

The story of Babel,[7] for instance, evokes the nostalgia for an ideal, original condition which has had to be relinquished in the process of developing more complex constructions. Such an ideal antecedent state may be regarded as a condition of total, unequivocal communication. The myth proclaims the need for an emancipatory separation as a condition for the development of what might be more powerful forms of world control. Yet the suspicion remains that the laborious quest for truth at the core of our philosophical games might be thought of as capable of ultimately 're-establishing' an ideal condition of total communication in our technological era; such an ideal might explain our inexhaustible search for truth conditions and standards of meaning. Our longing for a 'lost' condition of unequivocal language might be what sustains our persistent search for standards of accurate representation and objectivity. Should the flourishing research on truth conditions reach a cluster of conclusive convergences, the result might be sufficient to virtually reproduce a pre-Babelic structure of consensual communication.[8]

Rescher suggests that the 'consensus theory of truth', with respect to the ideal situation or case, is not something that rests on the nature of consensus, but rather on our affective attachment to the notion of an ideal rationality; by 'ideal rationality' we could mean a condition of 'identical circumstances' in which 'ideally rational' inquirers will proceed in the same way and onto the same conclusions, 'But it is rationality and not consensus that is doing the work for us here', he concludes.[9] What matters for rationality is not that agents finally come to accept something in common, but indeed *how rationally* they come to do so. In the final analysis we seem to rescue our celebrated Western logos not through consensuality as such, but through the ideal *process* by which consensus should come about.[10] And it is here that some quality of idealisation must perforce be introduced as a further item imported from inner emotional dimensions which are perplexingly regarded as heterogeneous to our rigorous rational enterprises; it is almost as if the affective components which are expelled from the 'island of pure understanding' were at the same time consistently utilised to sustain the idealised quality of the non-contingent rationality which is propagated. And the unavoidable vociferations which accompany the lucid parsimony of the 'ideal' rationality at any given moment, eventually exhibit the insistent 'irrational', which is customarily excluded as sub-rational or corporeal, as affectual or banal. If we could seriously listen to the dense and intricate sound of voices that one can hear during the intervals of scientific meetings, in the pause between classes, or in the corridors of courts, one could perhaps get in touch with the acumen of concerned creatures intent upon seeking connections with whatever is excluded by pure reason: human beings trying to reconnect an 'unlivable' idealised rationality with their own affective lives.

In order to explore further the necessity to reconnect thinking and feeling, we could also note that some affective atmosphere inevitably shadows our debates. Yet, paradoxically, only the kindlier sort of emotions seem to be identified, duly deplored, and thus latently delegitimised. By contrast, anger, as a serious and legitimate reaction in defence of purity and consistency, is not usually recognised as a 'deplorable' emotion, and remains an acceptable part of mainstream discourse. It almost seems that in argumentative interactions we ultimately seek to produce arguments so powerful that they just cannot be refused, so cogent that they reverberate into the very life of the interlocutor and cause an 'illness' unless they are accepted. Nozick remarks that perhaps philosophers 'need arguments so powerful that they set up reverberations in the brain: if the person refuses to accept the conclusion, he *dies*. How is that for a powerful argument? . . . A "perfect" philosophical argument would leave no choice.'[11] The lucid elegance of scholarly anger is an integral part of our cultural games; as such it is rarely identified or deplored. Abundant testimony could be provided for expressions of intense 'righteous' rage at the highest levels of inquiry; and a derivative of righteous rage is of course the legitimisation of splitting and control.[12] The 'solution' does not lie in further purifying reason, or guarding it from contaminating threats; we should rather recognise the projective quality of theoretical purity, the illusive belief that passionate action only occurs in that 'stormy ocean' surrounding rationality, and the possibility that the Kantian island of pure reason is not as free from foggy affects as it purports to be. The 'pure' epistemic subject, moreover, might come to automatically function as the ethical subject because by thinking in the pursuit of truth, according to the most accredited rational methods, he appears to resist unreason, and is thus 'entitled' to legislate. The constitutive act of the rational sovereign subject ultimately establishes it as an ethical and theoretical norm, as a subject tacitly entitled to righteous anger or disdain; and these affects, of course, are as intense as they are inconspicuous, or unidentified.

Representatives of alternative epistemologies often claim that philosophy has managed to disguise its inherent 'power' by propagating an image of the human subject as a conscious, rational, self-transparent entity. Braidotti, for instance, suggests that 'the instigation of rationality as the founding myth of Western philosophy and regulating principle of human affairs' entails a joint process of abstraction and violence; while playing a normative role it both disguises the power it exercises and makes it ubiquitous.[13] By conflating abstraction and coercion, canonic rationality can play an essential role in the perpetuation of the hegemonic model of thought that is applied to disparate fields. Even a discipline such as psychoanalysis, which patiently and implacably explores these occult dynamics, is itself prone to them. In psychoanalytic culture, in fact, comparable paradoxes are tacitly at work. On the one hand psychoanalysis can be viewed as a recuperative effort for those qualities of human life which are ignored, silenced or smothered in the obstinate march of rationality, thus inclining on the side of the unconscious. On the other, it can be viewed as intent to colonise, or domesticate the wilder sides of life for 'scientific' and 'therapeutic' purposes. As remarked by Ferrell, 'psycho-analysis itself harbours ambivalence to which its churches, its heretics and feuds attest.'[14] The scholarly and theoretical part of psychoanalytic culture is just as recalcitrant as any other epistemology to a recognition of its own composite and paradoxical nature; and, perhaps, a generalised transference phenomenon is also at work in it. In McDougall's view, the experience of personal analysis and case supervision, together with the close teacher–pupil relationship that characterises the transmission of psychoanalytic knowledge, are all marked by strong positive and negative affects which, if not recognised, may readily be used in near-perverse ways. They probably contribute to the subtle animosity that usually accompanies theoretical divergences. 'The sanctification of concepts and the worship (or denigration) of their authors appear . . . to be sequels of unresolved transference ties.'[15] In this climate, of course, disciples tend to become apostles. She also suggests that the erroneous belief in the purity of concepts ultimately transforms schools into sects and theories into doctrines: 'Is it not our leading perversion, then, the belief that we hold the key to the truth?'[16] In a synoptic view we could say with Le Doeuff that theorists, philosophers, or innovators ultimately project their desires and anxieties, while also attempting to pass off 'this discourse of desire and defence as a purely rational theoretical discourse'.[17]

The contingency of the subject

While contemporary culture is inclined to regard knowledge more as a derivative of social practices than of individual, rationally guaranteed construction, there is still a tendency to consider the subject as 'definitively bounded and generically endowed'.[18] Mainstream philosophy for the most part adheres to some generic individualism while somehow eschewing the complexities of historical individuality – what Rorty calls 'the contingency of selfhood'.[19] Even an emblematic representative of the unity and autonomy of selfhood obliquely recognises the weight of its contingency. 'The so called principle that everything contingent has a cause' says Kant 'comes no doubt before us with great solemnity and self-assumed dignity.'[20]

Scheman is among those who attempt to explore the latent privilege in the philosophers' generic picture of the self and of 'our' relations to persons, nature and culture;[21] a picture which only describes views ultimately accountable to a small fraction of human beings. Our 'appropriate' standards of inquiry seem to demand that the (knowing) subject be a fixed pole in order for the object to be visible across different subjects, and repeatedly so across geographic and historical circumstances.[22] In this outlook, the objective horizon comes to be defined prior to any experiential observation, thus rendering the view largely non-perspectival. Ferrell suggests that this is attained by disqualifying in advance the question of the identity of the epistemic subject, and by somehow settling the whole matter through a fictional postulate of equivalence among subjects;[23] as soon as this epistemic scenario has inconspicuously become familiar, any intrusion of live and affective subjectivity comes to appear as an alarming imperfection or a disgrace. Ricoeur is among those who regard the idea of pure reason as 'an illusion that conceals the play of forces under the artifice of order. It posits an entirely arbitrary unity, the fiction called "thinking", apart from the bristling multiplicity of instincts. And finally, it imagines a "substratum of subject" in which the acts of thought would have their origin. This final illusion is the most dangerous . . . In this way we take as cause, under the title of "I", what is the effect of its own effect.'[24]

We read about 'patients' or 'analysands' in psychoanalytic literature, we discuss 'subjects' or 'individuals' in philosophically oriented contributions; yet, the inner functions of 'patients' and 'subjects', 'analysands' and 'individuals' are not so distinct and often coincide, even in the variegated perspectives of different methods of research. Although not in therapy, most creatures do patiently mature and somehow explore their inner lives, while those who engage in analysis continue to think and argue. Not being sufficiently free to think and grow can be a major crippling conflict, aggravated by a latent sense of guilt about refusing to homogenise with official sources of knowledge, about resisting the seduction of idealised pure reason. When 'patients' or 'subjects' recognise how this homogenisation can be destructive to contacts with one's own deep subjectivity, they may be freer to overcome some perverse guilt, or sense of persecution, about the effort to be a sane and separate person. This is a tension of separateness which can not, or should not, be resolved. In Scheman's view we need to explore the terrifying extent to which any culture, person, or part of the self has been reduced to the 'dreams' and theories of any reigning epistemology or coalition of theorists; and yet, any marginalised culture, person or part of the self can hold on to its deeply felt, though perhaps unaccountable, untheorisable conviction that it is something *other* than the product of those 'dreams' and theories.[25] Indeed, 'developing a mind of one's own'[26] is generally seen as a primary goal of the psychoanalytic experience. In exploring the issue of the individuality of mind, it is often argued that the therapeutic process should aid analysands to utilise the complex vicissitudes of identification with the analyst only in order to progressively identify with their own experience, and to create a privileged relationship with one's own inner world.[27] This is not just a problem of the patient or of the therapist who tries to analyse him – but a problem of *all* interpersonal or cultural relations.[28]

It is often remarked, in a developmental context, that alongside the infant's need for relatedness, there is the need for a private space.[29] The infant can be fuelled from within, as well as from without. Disengagement has a place of equal importance with engagement. If the private self becomes decentred and one loses contact with it, one also loses a sense of psychic aliveness. A private mental space is the condition for the development of what we may call 'epistemophily', our human *desire* for thinking – a potential capacity which is to be protected from excessive intrusion; this is the space for the generation of personal value and meaning. There is, thus, a high psychic payment exacted when there is an occupation of this site by external projections, or when it is so firmly incapsulated that we have no contact with this private area of the self. Modell reminds us that in some character pathologies there seems to be an unexplainable vindictive rage, as if the self had been totally usurped, or as if it were irremediably besieged. Of course, psychopathology simply illuminates by exaggeration that which is present in all of us.[30]

Terms such as 'patient' or 'thinker', 'citizen' or 'believer', refer to different linguistic instantiations, or discursive levels, that encompass various structural aspects of the self which never quite coalesce. By refusing to be definitively fixed in a fictional unity emanating from outer sources, we can perhaps also monitor the dangers of a mimetic subjection to whomever represents an admired, dominant epistemology. At times, creatures may even be inclined to mute their passion for their profound identity – the ideas and values they nurture – in order to create a spurious harmony with the theorising that they most admire. Their attempt to be like minded with the authorial authorities of knowledge almost requires a breaking of the passionate links that they have with their own inner world. However, doing this has a profound effect, for it impedes making proper contact with one's internal structures. We may thus abandon our sources of affective and cognitive force in order to adhere to the constraining power of whatever coalition of paradigms comes to appear as the 'pure reason' of the moment. By proper contact with one's inner world we should understand a contact that is at the same time clear and passionate; so passionate that it eventually becomes creatively clear. This sort of contact with one's ideas and values also implies something of an exclusionary outlook: it establishes some sort of 'barrier' between oneself and the external emissaries of culture, in so far as one's own inner self and primary convictions inevitably differ from those of cultural authorities.[31]

Perhaps we could say that in the logic of clear and sound philosophy, to be among the enlightened is to be among the sane, and for different creatures to join these ranks demands a willingness to 'simply' *separate* from the difference-bearing aspects of their identity, their most intense particularity, such as a curiosity for one's epistemophily and a lack of interest for the dutiful gloss of any prestigious trend. Thus, 'our' sound and enlightened vocabulary also serves to demonstrate what any lucid and democratic classicity is increasingly eager to propagate: that one does not have to be a standard person ('an able-bodied-middle-aged-fair-complexioned-minimally-religious-man') to embrace elitist attitudes with regard to different others (or of different parts of one's own self).[32] The logic of any current classicity is an outlook that probably anyone can, or 'should', acquire by simply insulating one's profound self. And the inclination to accept these seductions ultimately comes to appear as the most rigorous of attitudes. This is a nameless, inconspicuous, and denuding inclination which could perhaps be called 'co-optosis' – in the sense that as long as one can aspire to be co-opted into whatever privileged ranks, and somehow manages to do so, one can sacrifice authentic personal resources.

With regard to the coordinates of thinking that we are supposed to admire, Scheman remarks that 'epistemological elitism is most attractive (to the elite) and most objectionable (to others) when the non-elite world say something different from what gets said on their behalf, allegedly in the name of their own more enlightened selves.'[33] As some have argued, the frequent 'we' pronoun of our mainstream epistemology does not in fact have a genuinely generic sense. By designating their 'we' as generic, they in fact qualify all other outlooks as different, thereby requiring an act of self-estrangement on the part of all those non-elite inquirers who aspire to be included. Current epistemology seems intent upon democratising its privileged outlook on things, while personal epistemophily pursues itineraries that neither interfere nor compete with epistemology, inasmuch as those involved do not primarily aspire to the cognitive stances it advertises. Also, if some unrecognised person or part of the self provides the indispensable connectives with life at large, the philosophically dominant part will emanate the epistemology that ultimately keeps it separate and serviceable. Thus, by looking critically at the sources of epistemic authority, there appears to be no reason why those who begin to realise that they are modelled by the 'pure reason' of modernity and of it contemporary variants – the 'objects' to their cognitive 'subjects' – should accept the terms of that epistemology as the only path to projects of self-creation and creative inquiry.[34] Through affective contacts with our own inner world we also become more open to facing the thinness of our rational veneer and thus the potential of human regression into mass psychology.[35] Dismissing whatever might threaten their sense of control, the authorial-authoritative agents of knowledge tend to theorise their own subjectivity (which they call generically human) as unitary and transparent to consciousness, as characterised by integrity and consistency. In Scheman's language, 'Not only is such subjectivity a myth; its logic is that of paranoia.'[36]

Although hierarchised as more rational and less subject to passion, the cohesive and transparent selfhood that differentiates itself from 'sub-rational creatures' can be shown to be anything but strong: it epitomises in fact the sort of rational selfhood that succumbs most easily when confronted with the slightest pressure from the vestiges of the reptilian brain that operates alongside cognitive structures in human beings. Even the central theatres of Western rationality, which pride themselves in the rigour of their logic and presume of their complexive power, are periodically shaken by horribly destructive festivals which unfold with total indifference towards 'strong' superior minds, incapable of resisting the archaic mechanisms of our embodied condition. 'Superior' minds who, nevertheless, resume their normal, brilliant logomachies as soon as the period of terror has come to an end. When faced by the incursions of the more primitive dynamics, epistemic subjects appear to be defenceless and, in any case, anything but strong or superior. Such an image of a fictional, non-contingent selfhood is more adequately characterisable by adjectives such as 'powerful', 'cogent', or 'coercive', but not necessarily as 'strong', 'resourceful', or 'vital'.[37]

In struggling with the understanding of the unconscious and working with suffering humans to overcome crippling limitations, psychoanalysis has discovered the power of primitive affects as being essentially threatening at all times: in this perspective, no philosophical approach or 'sound' epistemology could completely free itself from the 'contamination' by these profound forces that motivate human behaviour.[38] In Grosz's view, if the knowing subject is a 'blind spot' in the assessment of knowledge, then our cognitive processes are somehow vitiated by an irreducibly arational component at their core; the knower who produces and relies upon the principles of reason is not himself capable of being included in terms of the sources and motivations of the reason he utilises.[39] If reason is not self-inclusive, then there must be a non-rational kernel within rationality that may subvert its claims of providing methods and systems of judgement for other and lesser forms of knowledge which it inconspicuously tries to hierarchise. Even the generic conviction that our rational selfhood somehow manages to know about affects and desires can be a coercive manœuvre disguised as a policy of integration. An epistemic subject whose authority is defined by his location on one side of a vast spectrum of differences cannot authoritatively theorise that distance away. In the language of Scheman, philosophers' problems are the 'neuroses of privilege'; discipline makes the difference between such problems and psychosis.[40]

But just as exclusionary 'gestures' can operate in separating off certain 'unteachable' subjects, so similar attitudes can operate intra-psychically; they separate those aspects of the caring and curious self that, if acknowledged, would disqualify the subject for admission to the circumscribed lucidity required by a pre-emptive epistemic self-constitution. According to Grosz, at least some of our contemporary culture analyses the strategies of self-definition and evaluation, the way philosophy evades its sources and its none-too-pure history, leaving its desires unacknowledged so that it can maintain its own image of purity *and* the unacknowledged debt it owes to what it must exclude.[41] For, indeed, the intra-epistemic lucidity, literality, and homogeneity of any circumscribed domain can only be maintained because other parts of the self become hyper-functional and dutiful in negotiating all kinds of indispensable contacts, including heterogeneous inter-epistemic relations. This style of work performed by diverse and non-commensurable thinkers does not strive to emulate mainstream research into meaning and truth, but rather to nurture ulterior and compatible forms of inquiry. Thus, caring and curious inquirers challenge the belief in a transparent language and in discursive forms that are open to the pure transcription of thought; they rather aim to expand and multiply the criteria for what can be considered true and meaningful.[42]

Detachment, avoidance of disquieting contacts, and self insulation can actually represent highly valued internal benefits deriving from normative knowledge. As is known, external goods can be regarded as extrinsic or incidental rewards to be gained from engaging in an activity; in fact, the benefits associated with an ordinary activity could be attained through the pursuit of other practices, while the inner benefits inherent to a special activity bear a non-contingent relation to it. These can only be specified in terms of that commitment and can only be recognised by the experience of participating in a specific practice; epistemology – as the exercise of 'pure reason' – could be just one of them. These intrinsic rewards may include the confirmation of the purported non-contingency of selfhood, and of the autonomy of our ways of looking at things. It would be an 'island', indeed. In facing these issues, we are not inquiring into the rewards that might motivate any individual in his practice and which could also be attained by other means; we are interested in those internal benefits that can only be achieved through an elitist practice of philosophy. Rorty ironically remarks that in comparison with this 'universal impress' the disparate contingencies of individual lives come to appear as unimportant: 'The mistake of the poets is to waste words on idiosyncrasies, on contingencies – to tell us about accidental appearances rather than essential reality. To admit that mere spatio-temporal locations, mere contingent circumstances, mattered would be to reduce us to the level of a dying animal . . . One could die with satisfaction, having accomplished the only task laid upon humanity, *to know the truth*, to be in touch with what is "out there". There would be nothing more to do, and thus no possible loss to be feared. Extinction would not matter, for one would have become identical with the truth, and truth, on this traditional view, is imperishable.'[43]

The illusions of the cognitive autonomy of the self can also be exemplified in the tendency to disqualify other diverse identities by tacitly regarding their modes of knowledge as purely natural or practical, 'just the way they are'. As is illustrated in the vast literature of feminist culture, 'feminine nature' often comes to be regarded as just what 'it is'; namely, 'essentially feminine'. Conversely, it would *sound* paradoxical to speak of 'man's nature' or of 'man's way of viewing things', because normal discourse does not usually appear as gender specific, and because this customary obscuration conspires to make it count as general; so profoundly general that even extinction would not really matter, for it would ultimately coincide with some imperishable truth. But then, the fact that gender specificity is so frequently vulnerable to obscurity could be used as a seminal paradigm for the *innumerable* obscured particularities of the human condition, and for the recognition that even within gender identity countless differences can be identified. The idealisation of the thinking subject – or its unrecognised contingency – tends to coalesce with complementary paradigms which essentialise 'natural' qualities, such as the intuitive 'nature' of women's minds, the 'innate' warmth of Italians, or the 'inborn' sense of rhythm of Blacks. This is the other side of the illusive autonomy and cohesiveness of the knowing subject. The tendency to consider certain human capacities as purely natural is often illustrated by the attribution of essential good qualities to certain human groups: a romanticised approach closer to contempt than to respect, which is ultimately an attitude that can pervasively obscure the laborious appreciation of our conditional identities.

Hierarchised knowledges

Recent contributions in epistemology generally include some preliminary delegitimisation of common uses of the word 'know', in the sense of 'knowing how' (to do something), before proceeding to examine the 'serious', and epistemically 'relevant' meanings of the word 'know' in the sense of 'knowing that' (something is the case). Assenting to propositions or attributing epistemic characterisations to them, remains at the 'heart of contemporary epistemology' – remarks Alcoff.[44] It seems that knowledge is viewed as an eminently (or exclusively) intellectual enterprise whereby 'knowing how to be' or 'knowing how to do' are tacitly hierarchised as 'lesser', sub-epistemic modes of our cognitive lives. It is almost as if knowledge could shape the people that it 'possesses'. Overwhelmed by the problems of truth, we may weaken our capacities of insight, and risk selective blindness. In Wittgenstein's view, 'Philosophers constantly see the methods of science before their eyes, and are *irresistibly* tempted to answer questions in the way science does. This tendency is the real source of metaphysics, and leads the philosopher into complete darkness.'[45]

As is known, it is rather typical of any current epistemology to claim general validity by constantly trying to subsume issues that might exceed its paradigms into the dominant type of 'distanced control', and to render that goal either invisible or apparently inevitable:[46] almost a way of hierarchising itself as the paradigmatic way of knowledge. And critique, of course, is possible and welcome, but generally within the confines of its own *pax epistemica*. But then, in Scheman's synoptic view, the very attitude of any critique would seem to require a stable logical ground to stand on: 'Part of the requirement of such ground would be a universally valid epistemology, and the irony is that part of the oppressiveness of the hegemonic construction of knowledge is its claim to be providing precisely that.'[47] Mainstream philosophy seems thus primarily concerned with knowledge in the sense of information; and this sense comes to be regarded as the one that is basic to human cognition and which is required for 'serious' cognitive ventures. An inquirer is normally considered to be interested in the question of what conditions are necessary and sufficient for a person to have knowledge or, more precisely, to know that something is the case. In the language of Rorty, we could say that the Western philosophical tradition 'thinks of human life as a triumph just insofar as it breaks out of the world of time, appearance, and idiosyncratic opinion into another world – into the world of enduring truth.'[48] This triumphal and pervasive outlook would probably view as scandalous – or totally ignore – the attitude of using personal affect, feelings, or emotions as instruments of knowledge. By contrast, within the psychoanalytic tradition, the joint vicissitudes of transference and counter transference constitute the axis of the process itself and are often used as a valuable source of knowledge of one's mind and of interpersonal relations. But then, the whole of psychoanalytic culture could be entirely disregarded as an implausible source of 'proper' knowledge.

There are, of course, legitimate uses for an abstract and intellectual conception of reason, especially for the purpose of characterising certain logical operations. But the point is that it is risky to tacitly take such a limited view as an inconspicuously general model of reason. Perhaps the situation comes down to this: if philosophy is generically defined and confined by the logic of its customary rationality, then our affective lives may either produce a mimicry of the rationalistic genre, or else they may speak elsewhere, in other humanistic disciplines, that is in genres less hostile to them. If philosophy is more than this, more than a project of self-legitimisation, then our affective lives can find ways of contributing to further forms of knowing, and to further ways of articulating human desire.

An unduly narrowed conception of knowledge might be informed by a myth which restricts the cognitive faculties to the domain of thinking and leaves them ultimately unrelated to the capacity to do certain things, to be a certain way, or to try to develop a mind of one's own. Decades ago, Ryle's latent aim was already to criticise the intellectualist legend by way of an effort to demonstrate that *all* knowing is basically a kind of knowing how, a sort of capacity, or disposition.

His principal insight is that pure concepts of cognition, or forms of 'knowing that', do not constitute the core of mental conduct because, in fact, 'the consideration of propositions is itself an operation the execution of which can be more or less intelligent, less or more stupid.'[49] The Rylean argument goes on to demonstrate that to describe a person by an 'intelligence' epithet is not to ascribe to a creature a group of propositions but rather the 'ability . . . to do certain sorts of things'.[50] In the Rylean perspective we can almost perceive a reversal of the intellectualist hierarchisation of human knowledges, which somehow emanates from the primacy of 'knowing that'.

A vague adherence to a unity-of-science and unity-of-knowledge outlook may not only engender a hierarchisation of human faculties, but also structures of tacit epistemic censorship whereby accredited 'knowers', typically speaking out of nowhere, tend to oversimplify the enormously variegated and evolving complexity of human culture. As Code suggests, experience is considered second-class in comparison to knowledge: 'The standard is upheld rhetorically by a distinction between knowledge and experience, in whose terms knowledge is valued more highly than experience and confers authority, where experience cannot. This "distinction" has the effect of discrediting putative claims to knowledge that fall outside the purview of a narrowly stipulated scope of the term, for which knowledge properly so-called must transcend the particularties of experience.'[51] Such an elitist view can only function in a linguistic world which ultimately excludes a philosophy of listening, attentive to the innumerable different stories of coping with life, nature and knowledge.[52] It is only through a careful reading of mainstream epistemology that the rifts, flaws and hiatuses within it can be utilised to reveal spaces where these texts exceed themselves, where they say more than they mean, thus ultimately opening spaces for different outlooks. Theory is no longer theoretical – and inclines to ideology – when it loses sight of its own conditional nature and circulates as a form of epistemic inquisition. In fact, theory is only oppressive when it perpetuates existing power relations, when it tacitly presents itself as the single voice of knowledge.[53] In Grosz's view the tendency of a single paradigm (or a limited number of them) to govern current forms of knowledge could indicate that power, rather than rationality, has largely been at work in developing current classicities.[54] The pragmatic style of frequent redefinitions of the 'knowing subject' seems to express the central idea that a new image of both knowledge and subjectivity is becoming necessary. 'In the classical age, discourse is that translucent necessity through which representation and beings must pass' remarks Foucault.[55] The voice of such discourse, however, prevents us from seriously listening to those who primarily know how to do, how to be, how to develop, and who are only tangentially involved in 'knowing that'.

The visual metaphor which dominates Western epistemology typically offers paradigms for the autonomous 'knowing subject' and for an outlook of detached mastery. The general idea of knowledge is portrayed as all-seeing in the sense that not only does it try to represent reality, but it attempts to perceive itself in the process of seeing the world, thus expanding into an immense 'reflective power'.[56] This generalised claim, however, finds its legitimacy not in the illusory transparency of its perception of itself, but probably in the linguistic capacity to powerfully articulate such a claim. In the words of Hacking, 'Linguistic imperialism is better armed than the military.'[57] This attitude also reveals philosophy's endemic reverence towards the inevitable hegemony of whatever happens to be a sufficiently enunciative and self-proclaimed rationality. In regarding our intuitive modes as correctives, Adorno remarks that 'Intuitions prevent reason from reflecting upon itself as a mere form of reflection or arbitrariness, in order to prepare an end for arbitrariness.'[58]

Even though 'knowing that' refers to truth, 'knowing how' does not simply refer to success – because even a skilled person can and does sometimes fail; this primarily indicates that the logic of the two kinds of knowing is different. The possibility of failure does nothing to detract from the epistemic value of a skill, just as 'being justified' remains a valid cognitive and epistemic appraisal despite the fact that it does not necessarily entail truth.[59] It is therefore doubtful that we can define 'knowing how' in terms of 'knowing that' in such a way that the former is diminished in its cognitive value or ultimately rendered peripheral with respect to a self-proclaimed centrality rooted in different forms of 'knowing that'.[60]

NOTES

1. Immanuel Kant, *Immanuel Kant's Critique of Pure Reason*, trans. F. Max Müller, New York and London: The Macmillan Company, 1907, second edition; 'The transcendental doctrine of the faculty of judgement or analytic principles', Chapter 3, p. 193.
2. Michelle Le Doeuff, *The Philosophical Imaginary*, trans. C. Gordon, Stanford, CA: Stanford University Press, 1989.
3. Nicholas Rescher, *Pluralism. Against the Demand for Consensus*, Oxford: Clarendon Press, 1995, p. 43.
4. Ibid., p. 54.
5. Ibid., p. 54.
6. The topic of idealisation is variously discussed in psychoanalytic literature. See, for instance, Sigmund Freud, 'On narcissism' (1914), in *Standard Edition*, vol. 14, pp. 69–102; and 'The ego and the id' (1923), in *Standard Edition*, vol. 19, pp. 3–68.
7. The story appears in *Genesis* 11: 9.
8. A comparable issue is discussed in Jacqueline Amati Mehler *et al.*, 'The Babel of the unconscious', *The International Journal of Psychoanalysis*, vol. 71, 1990, pp. 569–83.
9. N. Rescher, *Pluralism*, p. 55.
10. For a comparable discussion of this issue see Robert Nozick, *Philosophical Explanations*, Oxford: Clarendon Press, 1981, pp. 4–6.
11. Ibid., p. 4.
12. The veneration of truth seems indeed to invite and justify variegated expressions of anger only mitigated by the elegance of terms.
13. See Rosi Braidotti, *Patterns of Dissonance. A Study of Women in Contemporary Philosophy*, Cambridge, UK: Polity Press (in association with Basil Blackwell), 1991, p. 278.
14. Robyn Ferrell, *Passion in Theory: Conceptions of Freud and Lacan*, London and New York: Routledge, 1996, Warwick Studies on European Philosophy, edited by Andrew Benjamin, p. 97.

15. Joyce McDougall, *The Many Faces of Eros. A Psychoanalytic Exploration of Human Sexuality*, London: Free Association Books, 1995, p. 234.
16. Ibid., p. 233.
17. Michelle Le Doeuff, 'Women and philosophy', in T. Moi (ed.) *French Feminist Thought*, Oxford, UK and Cambridge, US, Blackwell, 1987, p. 197.
18. Naomi Scheman, *Engenderings. Construction of Knowledge, Authority and Privilege*, London and New York: Routledge, 1993, p. 247.
19. Richard Rorty, *Contingency, Irony and Solidarity*, Cambridge: Cambridge University Press, 1989.
20. I. Kant, *Immanuel Kant's Critique of Pure Reason*, 'The transcendental doctrine of the faculty of judgement or analytic principles', Chapter 3 (Transcendental Analytic), 'On the ground of distinction of all subjects into phenomena and noumena', p. 198.
21. N. Scheman, *Engenderings*, p. 247.
22. See R. Ferrell, *Passion in Theory*, p. 200.
23. Ibid., p. 100. The agents of epistemology are contingent and multiple, ranging from the micro-community of the infant-mother dyad to the macro-community of our so called Western culture; as such they evolve, dissolve and recombine through the variety of purposes which prevail. Thus the studies of how knowledge is generated should begin from the contingencies of community, self and culture, and more specifically from the sort of affects, feelings and emotions which confer meaning to such contingencies. At this point we could accept that as contingent, evolving subjects sustained by our micro- and macro-cultures, we need not coincide with some quasi-caricature of the ideal knowing subject.
24. Paul Ricoeur, *Oneself as Another*, trans. by K. Blamey, Chicago and London: The University of Chicago Press, 1992, p. 15.
25. N. Scheman, *Engenderings*, p. 69.
26. Robert Caper, 'A mind of one's own', *International Journal of Psychoanalysis*, vol. 78(2), 1997, pp. 265–78.
27. Ibid., p. 274.
28. Ibid., p. 274.
29. Arnold Modell, *The Private Self*, Cambridge, MA and London: Harvard University Press, 1996, p. 71.
30. Ibid., p. 75.
31. R. Caper, 'A mind of one's own', pp. 265–78.
32. N. Scheman, *Engenderings*, p. 96.
33. Ibid., p. 76.
34. Ibid., p. 105.
35. For a discussion of this issue see Gemma Corradi Fiumara, *The Other Side of Language. A Philosophy of Listening*, London and New York: Routledge, 1990, p. 68.
36. N. Scheman, *Engenderings*, p. 105.
37. For a discussion of this topic see 'A differentiation between the concepts of power and strength', and 'On the accepted meaning of "strong" and "weak" in Western culture', in G. Corradi Fiumara, *The Other Side of Language. A Philosophy of Listening*, pp. 62–71.
38. Otto Kernberg, 'Modernity and its discontents. A discussion of the paper by Sergio Paulo Rouanet', *International Psychoanalysis. The Newsletter of the International Psychoanalytical Association*, vol. 6(2), 1997, p. 25.
39. Elisabeth Grosz, 'Bodies and knowledges: feminism and the crisis of reason' in L. Alcoff and E. Potter (eds), *Feminist Epistemologies*, London and New York: Routledge, 1993, pp. 192–3.
40. N. Scheman, *Engenderings*, p. 96.
41. E. Grosz, 'Bodies and knowledges: feminism and the crisis of reason', p. 165.

42. Ibid., p. 165.
43. R. Rorty, *Contingency, Irony and Solidarity*, p. 26.
44. Linda Alcoff and Vrinda Dalmiya, 'Are "old wives' tales" justified?', in L. Alcoff and E. Potter (eds), *Feminist Epistemologies*, p. 226.
45. Ludwig Wittgenstein, *The Blue and Brown Books*, edited and with a preface by R. Rhees, Oxford: Basil Blackwell, 1958, p. 58.
46. N. Scheman, *Engenderings*, p. 124.
47. Ibid., p. 124.
48. R. Rorty, *Contingency, Irony and Solidarity*, p. 29.
49. Gilbert Ryle, *The Concept of Mind*, London: Hutchison, 1949, p. 31.
50. Ibid., p. 28.
51. Lorraine Code, *What Can She Know? Feminist Theory and the Construction of Knowledge*, Ithaca, NY and London: Cornell University Press, 1991, p. 222.
52. See G. Corradi Fiumara, *The Other Side of Language. A Philosophy of Listening.*
53. Trin Min-ha, *Woman, Native, Other*, Bloomington, IN: Indiana University Press, 1989, p. 42.
54. E. Grosz, 'Bodies and knowledges: feminism and the crisis of reason', p. 210.
55. Michel Foucault, *The Order of Things*, London: Tavistock Publications, 1970, p. 311.
56. This thesis is advocated by Rosi Braidotti in both *Patterns of Dissonance. A Study of Women in Contemporary Philosophy*, Cambridge: Polity Press, 1991, and in *Subjects, Embodiment and Sexual Differences in Contemporary Feminist Theory*, New York: Columbia University Press, 1996.
57. Ian Hacking, *Why Does Language Matter in Philosophy?* Cambridge: Cambridge University Press, 1975, p. 149.
58. Theodor W. Adorno, *Against Epistemology*, trans. W. Domingo, Oxford: Basil Blackwell, 1982, p. 47.
59. L. Alcoff and V. Dalmiya, 'Are "old wives' tales" justified?', in L. Alcoff and E. Potter (eds) *Feminist Epistemologies*, p. 234.
60. Ibid., p. 234.

Chapter 2

From philosophy to epistemophily

Latent functions of knowledge

One of the disquieting problems of our culture is that epistemic subjects inconspicuously tend to become normative agents.[1] Whether reflective knowledge is generated in a disciplined philosophical élite, in a pioneering psychoanalytic milieu, or among revolutionary theorists of history, the emerging figures ultimately come to appear as eminently suited to exercise cognitive power;[2] it is the sort of power which also 'legitimately' produces distinct 'objects' for our subsequent inquiries. From this perspective, the creation of epistemic agency coincides with the construction of some privileged, normative authority, inclining to emanate logocentric models of which are the reliable human capacities and what are the objects of knowledge.[3] Thus, a concern for philosophy, which ultimately coincides with epistemology, can not be equated with our human potential for epistemophily. We could think of epistemophily as the derivative of a profound desire for thinking, and we could think of epistemology as a response to the need, or seduction, of a reassuring, cognitive vocabulary; hence there could be a plea for a maturational coexistence between philosophy *and* epistemophily.[4]

The threat to our epistemophily enters the scene as soon as we are inclined to think of the world – persons, nature, culture – as largely made up of 'objects'[5] (and as soon as we only regard our perceptions as either true to them or somehow distorted). From this point of view, the intended concerns of the producers of knowledge are not conceived as originating from any specific place at all; the allegedly neutral place that theorists occupy renders the specifics of one's affective condition irrelevant to cognitive concerns. In Scheman's view, this feat is reserved for those theoretical agents whose contingencies are rendered inconspicuous, and whose activity in defining objects and objectives is taken to count as generically human.[6] Moreover, the different examples selected to perform in this sort of approach are such that they hardly reveal or problematise the preliminary assumptions of the whole enterprise; in this way the affective sources of knowledge are pre-emptively obscured.

As is known, on our way towards epistemic mastery of the world, we may start out thinking of objects as discrete things that can be visually identified or handled.

The Latin term *obiectum* is related to the idea of something that we can throw and that can be thrown in front of us. But the magnitude and number of 'objects', progressively extends from things that we can grasp, catch, or throw, on to ever greater and more abstract dimensions that we can control by means of intellectual prehension; an indifferent, unaffective approach to our own cognitive functions that may ultimately result in divisive objectifications of everything we deal with. The object-idea may thus even extend to the planet which we inhabit and which harbours our existence. In Quine's words: 'We persist in breaking reality down . . . into a multiplicity of identifiable objects . . . We talk so inveterately of objects that to say we do so seems almost to say nothing at all; for how else is there to talk?'[7] The correlative to the view of an independently existing domain of objects (generally equated with facts), is also the idea of an independently existing, non-contingent, non-affective subject.

By way of illustrating this deceptive outlook, we might invoke recurrent expressions such as, for instance, the titles from the front covers of prestigious journals, for example *National Geographic*[8] and *Dialogue*.[9] 'The *Geographic* asks: "Can we save this fragile earth?"'; similarly, 'Can we save the earth?' is on the front cover of *Dialogue* as a general title on the issue of energy resources. It is indeed a logocratic missymbolisation that causes us to speak of the earth as of an object, as something that we can either save or not save. Enchanted with epistemology and inhibited in our epistemophily, we may even come to ignore our primal need to save ourselves, rather than the object earth. The assertive, indifferent, non-listening quality of our language compels us to collude in talking 'so inveterately of objects' that we think that we can rescue the planet-object, the earth-thing, while it is possibly the dominating, unaffective quality of our current logic that is inexorably conducive to damaging it. As long as we indifferently adhere to the central paradigms of our linguistic games (or *jeux de massacre*) and forms of life (or ways to extinction), it will be difficult to 'save the earth' inasmuch as the symbolic expression of the project leads into the opposite direction. Our obstinate epistemic language, in fact, may infiltrate and sabotage even the most enlightened of cultural practices. The celebrated quality of the above-mentioned contributions thus comes to appear subtly constrained by premises which create the very problem that they intend to eradicate. If we speak of the earth as an 'object' that we can destroy, then we are bound to persistently ignore that, in fact, even if we irremediably damaged the planet it is the human species that might disappear, and not the earth. In spite of our cognitive powers, we are not the masters of an earth that we could save or waste, but rather so significantly dependent upon it that if we damage nature we primarily endanger the human species, while the planet's life would probably continue undisturbed. In order to 'save the earth' we should perhaps first acknowledge the constraining power of those epistemic 'subject' and 'object' conceptions which are conducive to the deterioration of our habitat and even to the possible extinction of one more species, that of the *sapiens sapiens* humans who 'master' the earth; they are, in fact, the epistemic agents who passively adhere to a logic intent upon 'breaking reality down into a multiplicity of objects'. As we are the ingenious authors of a language that produces objects of (scientific) knowledge, we erroneously use it as an inconspicuous source of authority in the deceptive equation between authorial and authoritative prerogatives; this is an illusive equivalence which begins to clearly emerge into a more extended perspective.[10] From this same perspective, we could also remark that those human beings who do not share in the benefits of our Western sense of subjectivity and objectifying logos, tendentially aspire to do so. Yet, an acknowledgement of our unprecedented achievements should obviously not exempt us from a scrutiny of limits and of pernicious implications. Of course, the old time ethic of believing that wilderness is something to be conquered is somehow being supplanted by the idea that humans are caretakers of the earth and of its creatures. But even though some images effectively depict the full life of nature, the emphasis is still on the triumph of human beings and their daring over some self-imposed risks and hardships of exploration. Nature is thus speeding by, out of focus, and the explorers' view is one of detachment.

Our fashionable language frequently resounds with worrisome terms such as 'ozone layer', 'greenhouse effect', 'acid rain', which are all sad news from nature. Yet, it is difficult to appreciate that we *hear* this news only because these phenomena have begun to affect *us*, and that in fact we actually hear *nothing* until the damage inflicted by our undeveloped epistemophily only concerns the planet which hosts us. There must be some problematic limit in our epistemologies if we only hear what nature 'tells us' when it is so seriously damaged that we cannot help but heed it, because it is damaging us.[11] In a renewed concern for the challenges of our affective life, we could perhaps explore the possibility of a partial transition from the representationalist intentions of philosophy to the interactive concerns of epistemophily.

Through discursive practices in different areas of culture, it is often suggested that rationality is not only a matter of detached theorizing, but rather a caring way of being rational or searching for rational ways of caring. Such discursive practices express curiosity and concern for human vicissitudes that are persistently eschewed in the work of reigning epistemologies.[12] Milner remarks that both the artist and the creative scientist are often aware of the inadequacies of the commonly accepted body of knowledge, and are quite sensitive to the gap between what can be talked about and the ineffable, intense particularity of experience.[13] If rationality can thus be viewed as expressing a richer way of intellectual intensity and of giving voice to vital aspects of the person, it follows that any attempt to alienate rationality from our affective sources, that is, to unwittingly submit the mind's life to any current classicity, ultimately constitutes a mutilation of our potential for thinking and relating. In the outlook of epistemophily we can increasingly strive to think of the mind's life in terms of caring interactions and projects of self creation. This presupposes a resistance to the doctrinaire seductions implicit in grand theorizing, together with a cautious confidence in the standard models of intellection.

In our initiation to theorizing we have learned to hold the world away from us, and to somehow constitute ourselves as 'superior' epistemic agents through a willed estrangement from it, almost as if the venture necessarily entailed some form of methodological detachment. It is an estrangement perhaps compensated by the comforting inhabitation of a reigning epistemology. Yet, if we are vitally concerned with the *life* of our rationality, rather than with an abstract rendition of it, and if we view our thought processes as integrated with self-creation projects, we can better perceive that the mastery of a standard epistemology primarily aims at a reassuring symbiosis with it.[14] This also entails the idealisation of an epistemic self through the identification with collective, homogeneous paradigms. As a 'juvenile' phase of our intellectual cycle this may indeed represent a necessary passage in our itinerary. 'Insider status' in a reigning general stance, however, may come at the price of obscuring conscious or unconscious desires that prompt knowledge itself and that profoundly animate our enterprises.[15] If the transient nature of the inhabitation of any epistemology is not sufficiently recognised, it may endanger our mind's affective life inasmuch as curiosity would be rendered useless. Epistemophily, in fact, manifests itself through a language that originates from passionate listening, a language that can both understand *and* carry, which is aware of limits *and* makes connections possible. The listening style especially reveals itself in enlivening confrontations with heterogeneous discourses, where its force is evidenced in metaphoric efforts to generate 'impossible' questions and connections.[16] In standing up to heterogeneous situations, one can thus appreciate its distinguishing character and its innovative potential. Above all, the language of epistemophily also leaves things in that 'elsewhere' that bears them, leaving their strangeness intact. It aims to make contacts and to cope with that something, but not to represent its structure in an alien language, or reshape it. Conversely, in the perspective of any extant classicity, the study of human understanding ultimately tends to induce a homogeneity of theoretic outlook. Hierarchy and homogenisation can be said to go hand in hand, as the first is always grounded on the assumption that differences are only differences of degree on a homogeneous scale.

Philosophy cannot be hospitable to epistemophily as long as the epistemic subject maintains cognitive authority through radical estrangements canonised by opportune lexical boundaries. Within any well circumscribed area of knowledge, the mind is supposed to be, and actually comes to 'feel', quite unitary and even well suited to the strictest logical scrutiny of events. It seems indeed the achievement of a 'proud man, most ignorant of what he is most assured, his glassy essence'.[17] A tradition of courtesy, moreover, aids in the maintenance of such privileged areas of discussion by sparing them contaminating contacts with alarming aspects of our unconscious being and with disquieting aspects of our culture that would disturb its alleged pristine wholeness. Within such a privileged frame primarily geared towards 'acceptable', canonic questions, attitudes of intellectual desire would be unthinkable, in the sense that human epistemophily reveals a concern (interest, inclination, curiosity, attraction) for disparate questions of a sufficiently different quality such as: 'What is the good of it all?', 'What joy would that bring about?', 'In which way would that be a consolation?'[18]

By way of illustration we could recall that in the 'Preface' to a now *passé* classic, the *Tractatus Logico-Philosophicus*, Wittgenstein remarks that 'Its purpose would be achieved if it gave *pleasure* to one person who read and understood it'[19] almost as if the author were 'paradoxically' proposing to offer something pleasing and satisfying, or perhaps even some form of consolation. The pleasure one could experience might be intimately bound with philosophical clarity and with clear speaking: at first glance a highly intellectual pleasure but one which, none the less, is rooted in our deep self; for clarity to be so highly prized, it must be that its contrary, namely obscurity, generates suffering, confusion, anxiety. Granted that in the *Tractatus* obscurity and clarity have an obvious 'logical' meaning, there is yet no doubt that such terms also have an 'affective' meaning: they are laden with emotion and, if this were not so, there would be no explaining that sense of 'pleasure' to which Wittgenstein makes direct reference. One has the impression that the *need* for clarity plays a central role in the genesis of the *Tractatus*, possibly even more so than the general notion of truth. In the closing phrase of the Preface '. . . it shows how little is achieved when these problems are solved'[20] he even seems to 'withdraw' the philosophical worth of what he has achieved as a logician. Rather than any abstractly theoretical satisfaction, it seems to be a sense of relief, of liberation associated with clarity, which characterises the pleasure promised by the book. Thus, paradoxically, the chance of releasing intellectual blocks and removing obstacles to communication,[21] ultimately represents an aspiration which is more significantly connected with epistemophily than with our scarcely affective 'philo'-sophies.[22]

Alternative modes of inquiry

We cannot be listening *philo*sophically – in our scarcely epistemophilic culture – as long as one keeps the role of theorist to one's elitist self, or cultural group. Theorists may even invoke so called 'marginal' experiences in order to accumulate diversified material for a more adequate theory which it would remain their prerogative to produce and authorise; one of the unfortunate outcomes of this outlook is that even curious and caring inquirers may unduly identify with such productions and gradually degenerate into ambitious impersonators of reigning theories. A minority, however, may ultimately lose interest in what comes to appear to them as an intellectual pastime that obscures their more profound affective concerns. We can perhaps attempt to remedy this ubiquitous neglect of episte-mophily by developing debates open to disparate, heterogeneous questions: the interrogatives that are typically left out of the more canonic discussions of truth, reference, and meaning.

Moreover, the idea of privileged epistemic agency is reflected in the demand that we should primarily strive for 'clarity', as though the point of discourse were to seek transparence and homogeneity. The clarity of philosophy is best attained and exhibited in argumentative contexts that are detached from embodied specificities, in a strenuous avoidance of the inconsistencies and distortions which may originate from the irreduceable diversity of speakers: the intractable problems that are usually vulnerable to obscurity. Homogeneity, clarity, and cohesiveness may thus come to function as prerequisites for an authority model whereby hierarchies are comfortably established in terms of degrees within homogeneous domains.

The resistance to abstractions (for the sake of enhancing the expressive potential and psychodiversity of those involved in the argumentative context) can be fruitfully contrasted with the claustrophilic, transparent, and homogeneous language of the more circumscribed, authoritative discourses. Conversely, the endeavours of epistemophily do not claim to be sources of authority in the sense that they primarily insist – and insist they do with precision, acumen and farsightedness – that very different speakers exist and also have something to contribute. The tentative language of epistemophily is not geared to transparent representation or unassailable argumentation. Its aims are in the direction of illuminating diversity and complexity. Berlin, for instance, is among those who remind us that we should hardly be surprised today by the suggestion that variety, in general, is preferable to uniformity. And yet, the inclination to think that diversity is 'bad' has a long, celebrated history. He also remarks that most of our diversity-tolerant beliefs are relatively novel, and draw their plausibility from a deep and radical revolt against the cultural tradition of Western thought.[23]

In comparison with the everyday practice of thinking, the process of theorisation seems to epitomise the intention to impart structure, unity and stability to our thinking: as is known, in our 'intellectual history the unification of knowledge has been a perennial theme'.[24] Some of our philosophical illusions may, in fact, originate from an inclination to overwhelm our epistemic desires with a powerful 'will-to-truth' conveyed by our socially approved overestimation of epistemology. If we consider this possibility, theoretical structures can also be viewed as forms of control over our *philo*sophical wonder and involvement – ultimately the inexhaustible sources of our desire to think. An excessive detachment from our inner sources of curiosity, for the sake of a lucid and coherent intellectual discipline, becomes close to a schizoid attitude in so far as it denies the profoundly affectual fabric of *all* of our culture.[25]

Even the norms of an exclusionary logic organising epistemic oppositions are far too simplistic to describe the relationship between affects and knowledge. And yet, affects simultaneously occupy both an external position outside of philosophy (in the sense that they are largely excluded from its scope), *and* an internal position inside philosophy by constituting its innermost source of cognitive desire. A double paradox is at work: as the precondition for research, affects are not designated as such in any theory *and*, as the matrix of research, affects cannot easily be described in the language which they contribute to generate. The theoretic relevance of our affective life remains silenced in our epistemologies, not by placing it altogether outside of the system, but rather by positioning it as a precondition, a preamble, a 'distant' precedent of the enterprise.

By way of example, we could notice that books are often dedicated to beloved creatures, without whose exalted qualities the theoretic piece would not have come to light. However, if this proleptic and systematically proclaimed gratitude were sufficiently explored, not so much in its inscrutable 'nature' but rather in its manifest expressions and logical implications, the scholarly contribution would have probably moved closer to epistemophily.

Even norms of epistemic self-constitution[26] that give rise to vast problematic residue are commonly thought of as general norms, and are thus advocated as principles to which anyone can, and indeed 'should', gain access. Of course, however, there is not much point in challenging any mainstream epistemic culture. The point is whether it may coexist with different outlooks developed in a variety of different conversations like so-called pragmatic philosophy, psychoanalytic culture or feminist epistemologies.

Although these remarks do not appear immediately focused on any specific cognitive issue or theoretical stance, they are none the less a reflection on our contemporary ways of coping with knowledge and with our minds' lives. Caring and curious humans *do* think, as they have done for time immemorial, and perhaps now especially they think about *what* they are thinking, or what they should think about, and this is the profound sense of an increasing interest in a comparative juxtaposition of discourses.[27] The choice of *what* we should think about is more affectively determined than the choice of *how* to go about doing it. The focus is on 'administration', that is, on the concern with *what* to think about – rather than on 'method', in the sense of preoccupation with the correct way of proceeding.[28] In the near or distant future, the inconspicuous thinking work of caring and curious inquirers may more visibly spring to life as if prospects were now being opened for developments to come; and yet, these inquirers may even function today with attitudes which are not in full accordance with existing epistemologies. Pristine authorship can, in fact, be an illusion: innovative modes of thinking may well be at work even before an official founder proclaims them with sufficient force and clarity to determine cultural recontextualisation of paradigms. Even though a comprehensive logic capable of accounting for both affects and deductions has not yet been expressed in human culture, it is possible that modes of relating that may generate a new rationality, are already at work. It is not impossible that in Neanderthal times some members of the human community may have 'thought Greek', that some of our contemporaries may 'think Neanderthal', and others still actually 'think Future'.[29]

Epistemology may thus come to appear as a practice that equates a self proclaimed autonomy with a latent claim to legitimise generalisations. However, any outlook that manages to 'achieve autonomy' would automatically make expansionistic claims, and the question would then be reduced to a matter of historically taking turns at the centre of the sole epistemic scene entitled to export its logic. The problem is, of course, that only a few privileged subjects have an opportunity to theorise in an unassailable language; and if the marginalised ones could sufficiently organise themselves and attain epistemic dominance, they would probably also be inclined to 'universalise' their points of view – thus marginalising others; it would become simply a matter of taking turns. The problem, then, is to pursue itineraries of epistemophily that aim to recognise, appreciate and utilise heterogeneous diversity, and to regard even the most impressive endogamous achievements as no longer 'central', no longer legitimised to determine a cultural periphery of their own making. In this sense then, paradoxically, relations *among* different attitudes seem to ultimately influence the nature of attitudes *per se*.

In Malpas' view the idea that attitudes possess a certain interdependence is an intuitively plausible thesis. The fact that this interdependence is such that attitudes are actually constituted by their relations with other attitudes may seem to accord less well with our current intuitions.[30] As a consequence of this hypothesis, any change in the relations that constitute the elements of the system will result in a qualitative change in the system overall. The interdependence of attitudes also seems to imply the lack of any independent ground from which a generic cognitive gaze and interpretation may genetically proceed. For our purposes, instead of following the thought of a theoretically boundless web of interdependencies, we try to privilege the question of the development – or the inhibition – of those intersubjective connections which are the sources of our thinking. From this perspective, the desire for life-enhancing connections acquires visibility as one of the sources of human epistemophily.[31] But perhaps a response may be due to the deceptive suggestion that if we were intent upon epistemophilic concerns, we would have to substitute subjectivity with an indefinite web of interconnections. In point of fact there is no suggestion that epistemic subjectivity should be ignored, because, on the contrary, what is advocated is precisely the attribution of cognitive agency to *more* others, even to 'lesser', 'sub-rational' others. The suggestion, in Scheman's view, is to ultimately recognise the ability of the 'lesser' others to return a theoretic gaze.[32] Epistemic agency remains intact, even though in the form of ironic, curious, caring, and inquiring attitudes. The complexive style of these attitudes can perhaps be described as constitutive of epistemophily, as a *style* of reciprocal inquiry, rather than of any monologic epistemology.

To try to say something that deviates (or surpasses) an extant epistemology, we nevertheless have to creatively use the very same vocabulary of whatever epistemology one happens to inhabit. Irony can perhaps be one of the ways of using a standard vocabulary for purposes which exceed its scope. It may be worth noting that various forms of condescending ironism are addressed to those who are marginalised by whatever classicity. But irony is also used by those who look at classicities from an induced, peripheral outside space, while the mainstream forms of thinking only respond with an indulgent, benevolent gaze because, of course, *noblesse oblige*. Thus the use of irony could also be seen as an oblique, intriguing way of actually returning the theoretic gaze. In Rorty's view, ironism implies radical and continuing doubts about anyone's 'final vocabulary', as well as an awareness that ironic expressions can neither underwrite nor dissolve these doubts.[33]

Those who are excluded from any current epistemology, or those affective aspects of our inner selves which are similarly marginalised, may be thought of as having an ardent desire to express their knowledge in one way or another. Their epistemic force is just as vigorous as that of the authorised thinkers, or of the more conscious aspects of our complex selves. Thus, speak they must. And irony is one of the mature, dynamic ways of developing such modes of impossible expression:

that is, managing to use the language of the 'establishment' for the purpose of expressing one's own alternative meanings. In Rorty's view, ironists 'do not take the point of discursive thought to be *knowing*, in any sense that can be explicated by notions like . . . the correspondence of language to reality'.[34] Indeed, ironic endeavours gravitate away from epistemology and move towards attitudes of epistemophily.

As an innovative strategy, ironism can perhaps be seen as operating not only between meanings (said and unsaid), but between persons – ironists and targets. Ironic meaning perhaps comes into being as a desire to create a relationship, or a performative conjunction of different meanings, and then to endow it with the critical force of a challenge.[35] The relational level involving the dimension of meaning-interaction also brings in other aspects of ironic meaning, such as 'both/ and' inclusiveness, or differential specificities. Both of these aspects obviously rely on the idea of ironic meaning as interactive, as the result of bringing together (even with some friction) the said and the unsaid, each of which takes on meaning only in relation to the other.[36] Probably this is not a relation between equals, for the overflowing desire of the unsaid to challenge the power of the said is one of the characterising aspects.[37] In a not dissimilar way, both our psychic creativity and pathology constantly search for ways of expression which inexorably challenge our own prevailing rationality.

We cannot reductively see ironic discourse as a straightforward semantic inversion (that is an antiphrasis: saying one thing and meaning its opposite), and thus as a static rhetorical instrument.[38] We could instead look at irony as one of the many faces of epistemophily, as a form of communicative aspiration capable of generating unexpectedly relational, differential, and inclusive meanings. The resulting edge of creative ironism is not necessarily abrasive. The emerging edge might just as well be exciting, enlivening, soothing, not only for the generators of irony, but also for the receivers of it. There is, in fact, a variegated use of irony in the many languages of intimate, affective, relations.

Ironism conveys an attitude, or perhaps a feeling, and thus it removes from the background and brings to the foreground the evaluative accent that the context confers to any expression. Both ironist and interpreter alike make affective valuations about each other's capabilities and attitudes of detachment or participation. From the point of view of both potential participants, ironism might be seen as a version of what Burke called 'the *dancing of an attitude*'.[39] In exhibiting a differential relationship between the said and the unsaid, irony ultimately seems to invite inference, not only of meaning, but also of attitudes, feelings, and emotions.

When we consider the inclusive nature of ironism, we may invoke the well-known example used by Wittgenstein in his *Philosophical Investigations*, that is, the figure that can be interpreted as either a duck or a rabbit, depending on whether you see a bird's bill or a pair of long ears in the shape extending from a central mass representing the head.[40] While some authors say that our eyes cannot experience both readings at the same time, Hutcheon[41] suggests that when it comes to the ducks and rabbits of ironism, our minds almost can. In interpreting irony, we can and do oscillate very rapidly between the said and unsaid. Although here the visual analogy needs adapting, it is not the two 'poles' themselves that are important; it is the idea of a simultaneous 'hermeneutical' *movement between* them that makes this image possibly suggestive and productive for our thinking. Ultimately, this 'vibration' is not epistemological, but rather epistemophilic. It is indeed a 'complex exercise of consciousness that accepts the simultaneity of sameness and difference'.[42] What the affective force of ironism manages to activate is a close exchange of epistemic gazes, an exchange so enlivening that it challenges the status of who is the 'agent' and who is the 'object' of whatever form of knowledge.

NOTES

1. This issue is extensively explored by Naomy Scheman in *Engenderings. Construction of Knowledge, Authority and Privilege*, London and New York: Routledge, 1993.
2. When our way of theorising a situation somehow 'transcends' the domain of available evidence, our cognitive powers become latently 'unassailable'. In Quine's view the human subject is accorded a certain input – 'certain patterns of irradiation in assorted frequencies, for instance – and in the fullness of time the subject delivers as output a description of the . . . world and its history. The relation between the meager input and the torrential output is a relation that we are prompted to study for somewhat the same reasons that always prompted epistemology; namely in order to *see how evidence relates to theory, and in what ways one's theory of nature transcends any available evidence.*' W.V.O. Quine 'Epistemology Naturalized' in *Ontological Relativity and Other Essays*, New York: Columbia University Press, 1969, pp. 82–3 (emphasis added).
3. N. Scheman, *Engenderings*, p. 7.
4. The general topic of coexistence of perspectives is variously discussed in Gemma Corradi, *Philosophy and Coexistence*, Leyden: Sijthoff, 1966.
5. Whereas the meaning of the term 'object' is relatively familiar and intuitive in the vocabulary of philosophy, in the parlance of psychoanalytic culture the term 'object' is used to indicate a person, a fellow human, a creature, the one we relate to. The custom of referring to the other as to an 'object' has diverse roots in the vast production of Sigmund Freud as well as in subsequent developments. In general we could say that in the psychoanalytic domain the idea of 'object' helps us focus on our capacity to overcome our subjective, narcissistic position and thus appreciate independent autonomous aspects of those with whom we interact.
6. See N. Scheman, *Engenderings*, p. 161. Also see Thomas Nagel, *The View from Nowhere*, New York and Oxford: Oxford University Press, 1986, p. 6.
7. W.V.O. Quine, *Ontological Relativity and Other Essays*, p. 1. Quoted with reference to the chapter entitled 'Speaking of objects' in Donald Davidson's *Inquiries into Truth and Interpretation*, Oxford: Clarendon Press, 1985, p. 191.
8. *National Geographic*, official journal of the National Geographic Society, Washington, DC: December 1988, issue 174, 6.
9. *Dialogue*, a quarterly journal of significant thought and opinion on social, political, economic and cultural issues in the United States; US Information Agency, Washington, DC: 1989, issue 3.
10. This is a point which is discussed in Gemma Corradi Fiumara, *The Symbolic Function. Psychoanalysis and the Philosophy of Language*, Oxford UK and Cambridge US: Blackwell, 1992, pp. 4–6.

11. For an extensive discussion of the many problems and paradoxes of human listening see Gemma Corradi Fiumara, *The Other Side of Language. A Philosophy of Listening*, London and New York: Routledge, 1990.

12. 'The academy thrives on theories, and rewards those who produce them, but a major problem with theories is that they flatten that complexity. However much diversity went into their construction, they are ultimately monologic. In order to construct one, you may need to listen to a lot of people, but then you retire to a quiet place and put it all together, in one anonymous voice.' N. Scheman, *Engenderings*, p. 220.

13. Marion Milner, 'The role of illusion in symbol formation', in M. Klein, P. Heimann and R.E. Money-Kyrsle (eds) *New Directions in Psycho-Analysis. The Significance of Infant Conflict in the Pattern of Adult Behaviour*, London: Tavistock Publications, 1955, pp. 107–8.

14. See 'The limits of a "lifeless" philosophy', pp. 22–6, 'Language as metabolic process', pp. 26–30 and 'Vicissitudes of self-formation', pp. 125–42 in Gemma Corradi Fiumara, *The Metaphoric Process. Connections Between Language and Life*, London and New York: Routledge, 1995.

15. It is interesting to note that Melanie Klein seems to have substantially equated the affective vicissitudes which lead to a sense of reality (and hence of its fruition) with an 'impulse for knowledge'. M. Klein, *Contributions to Psycho-Analysis 1921–1945*, London: Hogarth Press and the Institute of Psycho-Analysis, 1973, p. 34. On the topic of 'epistemophily', see also pp. 237–8.

16. A discussion of 'impossible' connections appears in G. Corradi Fiumara, *The Metaphoric Process*, chapter 3, 'The interdigitation of fields', pp. 30–41, and chapter 6, 'The relationship between digital and analogic styles', pp. 64–83.

17. William Shakespeare, *Measure for Measure*. Quoted in S.M. Harrison, 'Peirce on persons', in K.L. Ketner *et al.* (eds), *Proceedings* of the C.S. Peirce Bicentenial International Congress, Lubbock, TX: Texas Tech Press, 1981, pp. 217–21.

18. See N. Scheman's *Engenderings*, p. 97.

19. Ludwig Wittgenstein, *Tractatus Logico-Philosophicus*, London: Routledge and Kegan Paul; New York: Humanities Press, 1961, 'Author's preface', p. 3 (emphasis added).

20. Ibid., p. 3. And Wittgenstein has a precursor in William James who clearly says: 'Even divine Philosophy itself, which common mortals consider so 'sublime' an occupation . . . is but a sharpening and tightening business, a matter of points, of screwing down things, of splitting hairs . . . Very little emotion here! – except the effort of setting the attention fine, and the feeling of ease and relief (mainly in the breathing apparatus) when the inconsistencies are overcome and the thoughts run smoothly for a while', William James, *The Principles of Psychology*, vol. II, New York: Macmillan, 1901, p. 472.

21. According to Bion, when sufficiently connected inner elements are in harmony, one experiences a 'sense of truth'. Failure to integrate data, or failure to generate an affectually consistent point of view, induces a state of consciousness marked by weakness or discomfort, as if the hunger for clarity were somehow comparable to a hunger for food. Wilfred Ruprecht Bion 'A theory of thinking', *The International Journal of Psychoanalysis* vol. 4, 1962, pp. 306–10.

22. G. Corradi Fiumara, *The Symbolic Function*, chapter 9 'Epistemophily and knowledge', pp. 118–34.

23. Isaiah Berlin, 'The apotheosis of the romantic will', in *The Crooked Timber of Humanity. Studies in the History of Ideas*, London: John Murray, 1990, pp. 207–8.

24. Gerard Radnitsky (ed.), 'Introduction', in *Centripetal Forces in the Sciences*, New York: Paragon House, 1998, vol. 2., p. vii.

25. The obscuration of our profound desire for connections and relations may compromise the whole enterprise of knowledge. This is a desire which is also occasionally revealed

within extant classicities. Quine, for example, remarks that 'The method of analytical hypotheses is a way of . . . grafting exotic shoots on the old familiar bush.' *Word and Object*, Cambridge, MA: MIT Press, 1960, p. 70.

26. For a comparable discussion of this issue see Michelle Boulus-Walker, *Philosophy and the Maternal Body. Reading Silence*, London and New York: Routledge, 1998, p. 12.

27. Rosi Braidotti, *Patterns of Dissonance. A Study of Women in Contemporary Philosophy*, Cambridge: Polity Press in Association with Basil Blackwell, 1991, p. 275.

28. 'Science is both its Administration and Practice. By Administration of science, I mean . . . the art of choosing, among the infinitely many possible questions answerable by science, which questions to ask. By the Practice of science I mean the actual conduct of the research: theorizing, observing, measuring, interpreting results, and communicating results . . . Otherwise put, Administration is concerned with *what* to do, Practice is concerned with *how* to do it; or with less accuracy, Administration is, roughly strategy, practice is tactics.' A.M. Weinberg, 'Values in Science: Unity as a Value in Administration of Pure Science', in Gerard Radnitzsky (ed.) *Centripetal Forces in the Sciences*, vol. 2., p. 3.

29. This issue is discussed in G. Corradi Fiumara, *The Metaphoric Process*, p. 5.

30. J.E. Malpas, *Donald Davidson and the Mirror of Meaning: Holism, Truth, Interpretation*, Cambridge: Cambridge University Press, 1992, p. 55 (the first name of the author is omitted in the book).

31. To formulate a general theory or definition would be close to essentialising our human constructions: and thus we should appreciate the pragmatism of those who encourage us to discuss a topic of interest without the constraint of a definition.

32. N. Scheman, *Engenderings*, p. 100.

33. Richard Rorty, *Contingency, Irony, and Solidarity*, Cambridge, UK: Cambridge University Press, 1989, p. 73.

34. Ibid., p. 75.

35. Rorty refers to certain individuals as 'ironists' 'because their realisation that anything can be made to look good or bad by being redescribed, and their renunciation of the attempt to formulate criteria of choice between final vocabularies, puts them in a position which Sartre called "meta-stable": never quite able to take themselves seriously because always aware that the terms in which they describe themselves are subject to change, always aware of the contingency and fragility of their final vocabularies, and thus of their selves.' Ibid., p. 73.

36. This issue is discussed in Linda Hutcheon, *Irony's Edge. The Theory and Politics of Irony*, London: Routledge, 1994, p. 58. 'This unsaid is nevertheless said' – remarks Michel Foucault in *The Archaeology of Meaning and the Discourse on Language*, New York: Pantheon, 1972, p. 110.

37. The comparative difference between the notions of 'force' and 'power' is discussed in G. Corradi Fiumara, *The Other Side of Language. A Philosophy of Listening*; see chapter 4 'The power of discourse and the strength of listening', comprising four paragraphs entitled 'Notes on the power of discourse', 'Notes on the strength of listening', 'A differentiation between the concepts of power and strength', 'On the accepted meaning of 'strong' and 'weak' in western culture.', pp. 52–71. But there is more to irony than the creation of a dense synchronic experience implying action and interaction in the creation of a third – the actual ironic – meaning. What is not foregrounded is the sense of that critical edge or evaluative investment that Hutcheon argues to be part of the definition of irony. 'While it does not permit me to figure the fact that the unsaid is the more weighted or privileged in the mix of semantic meanings that constitute irony, this image (or, rather, the idea of the *perception* of it) does allow a way to think about ironic meaning as something in flux, and not fixed. It also implies

a kind of simultaneous perception of more than one meaning, in order to create a third composite (ironic) one . . . Irony would thus share with puns a simultaneity and a superimposition of meanings.' L. Hutcheon, *Irony's Edge*, p. 60.

38. R. Rorty, *Contingency, Irony and Solidarity*, p. 76. And also 'For the ironist, searches for a final vocabulary are not destined to converge. For her, sentences like "All men by nature desire to know" or "Truth is independent of the human mind" are simply platitudes used to inculcate the local final vocabulary, the common sense of the West. She is an ironist just insofar as her final vocabulary does not contain such notions.'

39. Kenneth Burke, *A Rhetoric of Motives*, Berkeley, CA: University of California Press, 1969, p. 9. Quoted in L. Hutcheon, *Irony's Edge*, p. 39 (original emphasis).

40. Ludwig Wittgenstein, *Philosophical Investigations*, G.E.M. Anscombe (ed.), Oxford: Basil Blackwell, 1963, part II, section 11, p. 194.

41. L. Hutcheon, *Irony's Edge*, pp. 59–60.

42. Arnold H. Modell 'The transformation of past experiences', paper presented at the Rome Institute of Psychoanalysis, (6 November 1998), p. 12. On this issue also see, chapter 5 'Solitude, passionate interests, and the generative aspects of the self' in Arnold H. Modell, *The Private Self*, Cambridge, MA and London: Harvard University Press, 1993, pp. 121–43.

Chapter 3

Thinking affects

The problem of thinking affects

A discussion of affects inevitably implies the presence of heterogeneous issues that require a multiplicity of theoretic gazes which, in turn, force us to confront the ever appearing question of epistemic agency. A clearer awareness of epistemic agency is instrumental in appreciating the composite structure of our mind's life; conversely, an insufficient consciousness of our inner synergy of knowledge and affects will silently conspire with the allegedly neutral place that the theorists occupy, and thus with the effacement of our cognitive subjectivity. We may then incline to homogenise the scope of the inquiry – and only see what we are prepared to believe. Of course, contemporary outlooks seem to allow for the study of affects, yet the mainstream theorists tend to obscure their own epistemic roles, in the sense that their contributions are made to appear as essentially neutral and impersonal, as if they were untouched by affects, emotions, and feelings. The present claim is that all 'research' does have an individual or collective subject; in its most disparate forms, inquiry does have epistemic agents, often made up of a coalition of individuals. These social subjects have a standpoint, that is a perspective, involving assumptions and values based on the kind of lives that they live.[1] Traditional research generally leaves this standpoint unexamined, and thus inconspicuously vitiates the 'objectivity' of its enterprises. If the standpoint of inquiry is not somehow examined, any ulterior outlook will silently be disparaged because it will be considered 'politically' motivated, while the original standpoint remains viewed as essentially non-sectarian and non-contingent. The thesis is that no cognitive standpoint is neutral and that each one of them needs scrutiny. As epistemic agents are the emissaries of micro- or macro-communities, we should also note that in a community the interactive patterns profoundly influence the structural quality of the group, and thus the quality of the knowledge it generates. It is another good reason for an increased awareness of epistemic agency.

What seems initially doubtful is the premise of a generic account of knowledge, one that putatively uncovers permanent justificatory standards. Not coincidentally the issues of affectivity that some inquirers try to confront, are viewed by most professional philosophers as peripheral with respect to the centre of philosophical work; this is almost a geometrical locus where the status of 'philosophy' is only accorded to thinking with a high degree of abstraction from the specifics of life, and with pretensions to a generalised consensus.

It is an unjustified claim that epistemology is free from historical and social relations that pre-emptively determine a *politics* of inquiry; it in fact produces social tools – or weapons – in the form of concepts and frameworks through which we rationalise or try to influence our forms of life.[2] The apparently permanent and pivotal problems coming across as questions, concepts and issues, which seem indifferent with respect to contingencies, are nevertheless implicitly related to, or coded by, coalitions of thinkers congregated within certain methodological outlooks. Thus, in spite of aspirations to neutral, unmotivated, and disinterested rationality, any epistemology is as susceptible to critique as any other human practice. The laborious identification of particular points of view and of specific experiences also seems to suggest the idea that the truth of certain propositions is not expressible in an altogether neutral language. In fact, any dream of neutrality could be challenged when interrogated by outsiders to any scholasticity. Along these lines one could say that human experiential knowledge is propositional in the sense that our hypotheses are only expressible in a specific idiolect.[3] This sort of argument, of course, will not make sense if we adhere to an intra-epistemic, agentless outlook, but will be quite legitimate if we opt for a freer inter-epistemic, embodied approach.

As is known, affects are differently viewed by different theorists, for they derive an understanding of our affective lives from the different basic assumptions which sustain their practice. We are thus attempting to explore the variegated continuity between prevalent affects and the epistemic reasons behind them. This, in turn, requires that we develop an awareness of cognitive agency as an alternative to granting to the unquestioned neutral theorists the 'detached' choice of examples and terrain of discussion for affects; a choice of terrain and examples that serves ultimately to legitimise the initial 'logical' or terminological assumptions. These logical assumptions, however, appear somewhat unreasonable inasmuch as they are based on the unjustifiable exclusion of all feelings and emotions. But the problem is more complicated than that. In fact, the excision of affects can be quite illusory and only apparent because the passion for power, control and mastery of cultural spaces is only formally disavowed and concealed, while probably remaining quite virulent under the disguise of detached knowledge.

With a concern for epistemic agency we could fruitfully incline to think both of cognitive efforts and of emotional vicissitudes in terms of practices, activities, or ways of doing things – which always imply an embodied subject. In Bolton's[4] synoptic view, cognition serves human action by processing information, while the ineliminable presence of affect signifies the point of the process. The goals of action have to be cognitively represented *and* its methods have to have an affective aim. From this perspective, emotion has cognitive relevance and content, while cognition will constantly involve affect inasmuch as it primarily serves to achieve aims.

The conquest of affects

Our complex and evolving rationality should perhaps be viewed as the result of a desire to think. By viewing it only as the outcome of epistemic procedures, our rationality would ultimately be rendered unreasonable through persistent and unjustifiable exclusions. Once an epistemology is thus restrictively formed – or genetically mutilated – there would be no point in suggesting alterations or integrations. Our reigning epistemologies appear inherently vitiated by preemptive exclusions of affectual components, which ultimately constrain and impede authentic development, almost as if they could not evolve but only *legitimise* their normal course of action.[5] If our research remains confined to enhancing a knowledge of human affects, or to prioritising an exploration of our affective life, the whole enterprise may remain as problematic as the truncated knowledge that it seeks to integrate. The aim of an inchoate epistemophily is thus intended as an endeavour to reorganise the profound sources of knowledge in such a way that our potential for thinking may function as the matrix of epistemic evolution.[6]

Drawing from the awesome current of affects and converting it into something consistently illuminating thus appears to be one of the main challenges of contemporary research. It is the challenge of facing intense particularities in a developing multicentred human culture. The question is what is now the place, in our celebrated Western philosophy, for other than epistemic values and for forces which animate inquiry, even though they are vulnerable to obscurity.

Propelled by a 'will-to-truth', theorists often have an inclination for global and lasting terms; 'lesser' epistemic subjects, however, view our thinking lives from more local and time-bound perspectives. Local and personal thinking is perhaps one of the best ways to do *philo*sophical research: in relying upon the particularities of inquiry, we do not transform global and permanent concepts into virtual standards and theoretical terms of comparison. Global thinking could be yet another form of ethnocentrism in disguise. In exploring local connections and developing ways to create and maintain them, we may patiently obtain what we negotiate for, and give up the illusion that we can *exact* the truth that we 'rationally' deserve. The *philo*sophical approach cannot simply remain committed to the project of 'knowing' affectual life, or of making the gradients of affects the objects of knowledge; it must also try to reorganise the 'position' of knowers as knowing subjects. If reason is a derivative of an unreasonable stance, such as the systematic denial of its affectual and corporeal origin, then even developing a modified rationality that is more hospitable to the study of affects would not be sufficient. There is no point in opening the world of inquiry to the study of our affective life if we do not also envisage a transformation of our basic ways of inquiring.

We can not, of course, think of classical rationality as essentially directed at destroying our Dionysian heritage; and even if we think that in olden times the 'enemy of reason' was rationally vanquished, our contemporary problem is that in our days it can be unwittingly disarmed and obscured. In Ferrell's view, it is not that certain scientific discourses are wrong or that they are in any way deluded; it is not that there can be no facts; on the contrary, even the production of facts is ultimately an expression of human desire.[7] Which is to say, according to Ferrell, that 'science is not recognised as worship, so real is the ontology produced' – and so pervasive. It is precisely the animation that human desire confers upon its accredited representations, while they are in fashion, that renders the preceding representations mere effigies, obsolete and desiccated; such that one could no longer imagine thinking that way. It is legitimate to wonder how much of what we affirm in the way of a justifiable belief connects and, in fact, overlaps with an expression of a desire. Rorty, for instance, notices that it is common to treat desires as if they were beliefs. This is done by regarding 'the imperative (optative) attitude towards the sentence S, "Would that it were the case that S!", as the indicative attitude: "It would be better that S should be the case than that not-S should be".'[8] Through this approach any web of beliefs can be considered not just as an attitudinal conglomeration, but also as a convergence of desires.

Thus we do not only intend to explore our mind's affective life, but also to create the appropriate setting for a novel view of the mind as rooted in affects. This outlook is concerned with developing the sort of knowledge which may emanate from our nascent epistemophily, and which perhaps originates from it. This aspiration is not only relatively free from a more traditional disposition to know and study affects, or from an outlook committed to the analysis and affirmation of desires as viable objects of knowledge. It also aims to include affects in those generative domains where they have been hitherto absent or ignored; it advocates an inchoate approach to affects that is adequate to an appreciation of their cognitive relevance. This is, of course, an outlook that exhibits varying degrees of critical distance from mainstream epistemologies.[9] But even so, this is an enterprise that requires caution: for where traditionally the putative inimical emotions were obstracised and conquered, they seem now tacitly disarmed and co-opted. A synoptic look at contemporary philosophical work on emotion ultimately presents the 'modern affects' as docile creatures, which are only prone to cause minor perturbations such as righteous indignation over children's rights, or instants of embarassment at being late. It must be said that grief and joy, terror and fascination are also sometimes listed, and their phenomenology nicely described. Yet the awesome qualities, disquieting details, and unthinkable combinations of affects are largely ignored. The affects that destroy, transform, or constrain human lives, are still avoided and left to other literary genres. Writers of literature can touch these topics with the pre-emptive stipulation that their work is, of course, fiction. The clinical production of psychoanalytic culture is the only other domain where the mind's affectual life can use, or defy, our possible forms of description. Nevertheless, the risk remains that the 'contemporary emotions' may be suitably domesticated and even prepared for inclusion into existing forms of rationality.

The amnesia of our affective lives is extensively explored by Grosz[10] and regarded as strategic in the maintenance of our traditional ways of knowing. It is illuminating that some mainstream theorists, such as Quine and Davidson, are far-sighted enough to make explicit declarations in appreciation of the essential function of attitudes like 'imagination' and 'charity'.[11] These appropriate inclusionary outlooks, however, seem to obscure the possibility of regarding human functions such as imagination and charity as actual sources of different and *ulterior* forms of rationality.

Ulterior perspectives

Some of our research attitudes could be compared to the behaviour of the proverbial drunk who looks for his keys under the lamp post, not because he has lost them there, but because that is where the light is. And yet, anyone willing to accept this image might reply that there is no way to look for something where there is no light. Perhaps the answer could come in the form of an effort to cast *any* feeble light in different areas, or to search in the dark by touching and feeling, as the blind do.

For most 'philosophers', emotions exhibit some theoretical relevance as obstacles to the progress of reason towards truth. Whatever else affects may be, the assumption that has prevailed is that they cloud the vision of the intellect and ultimately limit freedom.[12] Modern analytical philosophy, on the other hand, has perhaps dissolved the traditional opposition between reason and emotion by absorbing affective life into the domain of rationally explicable problems.[13] In this triumph over the immemorial dichotomy between our Apollonian and Dionysian dimensions, classical reason still provides the defining standard. Affective life has been somehow made to pay homage to contemporary philosophy by the semblance of its being amenable to explanation in terms of beliefs and desires. Thus conceived, it earns new rights for our standard rationality and gives a display of just how far its scope can be shown to extend in our mental life. But here again, there is perhaps too much of a compliment for such hospitable epistemologies and not enough concern for our inchoate epistemophily.

While no account is without presuppositions, the exploration of our affective lives is an attempt to step outside of some of the more restrictive assumptions that have guided theories of emotion. We also try to make a 'rational' inquiry into the nature of affects, but it is an inquiry that is ready to ignore fashionable reasons whenever necessary, and a search that remains with what is 'important' even if it becomes necessary to struggle in the dark by touching and feeling – an inquiry that meets the intractability of affective life on its own terms.[14]

This outlook seems to converge with recent perspectives originating in biological research. Longino suggests that the more complex and interactive visions of natural life encode attitudes towards nature that are different from those represented in mainstream science. The question is, of course, whether these alternative visions will survive to generate both a novel theoretical understanding and a basis for concrete interaction with natural phenomena. 'Such survival depends on whether we want to know the world under those *more complex* descriptions.'[15] That is, it depends upon whether or not we are emotionally capable of such an alternative.

At no point in this work will there be a question of trying to formulate an approach in the form of a counter-philosophical system, or of limiting our appreciation for coherence, clarity, accuracy, precision, and probity. It is more an effort to pursue itineraries which may partially differ from mainstream reflection and which may partially deviate from our customary mental habits. In fact, an inchoate epistemophily often seems indifferent to such majestic values as truth and coherence.[16] This does not mean that work in epistemophily could be described as arational or incoherent. On the contrary, much work is quite logical, rational, and true to life, but in terms of criteria and values which often begin to differ from the currently dominant ones. Moreover, the range of affective components disclosed may provide unrivalled views for exploring what is happening in our interactive lives. In our endeavours, we are sustained by a psychoanalytic account of the mind, that is, of the mind as a consequence of the demand of the organism for some enduring response to its needs. Conversely, philosophy tends to approach the human condition from the point of view of a 'developed' mind, that is from the other direction, thus envisaging the primacy of the mind with respect to our predicament as coexistential living and dying creatures. Psychoanalytic culture conceives of the living organism as coping with itself and others, and of the mind as a consequent auxiliary structure. In this perspective our rationality comes to appear as a definitely contingent process dependent upon at least two 'outside' elements: our living organism on the one hand, and the world constituted by our fellow humans on the other.

The mainstream outlook must nevertheless operate within an epistemic climate – or vocabulary – which is made to appear as preceding our genetic vicissitudes and as entitled to ignore our self-formation itineraries. Similarly, we can only use the standard language of the epoch to try to approach a topic that both escapes and challenges a current epistemology; thus, a good part of this writing should be placed within apostrophes or double inverted commas to try to convey an epistemic attitude of reluctance. Since there is no consensual language to try to approach a topic which is largely eluded by dominant views, it becomes necessary to use language in a slanted way, to twist terms somehow to try to capture what could otherwise escape, to extend terms so that they may include what a stricter rationality must leave out as indigestible elements; alternatively, the terms must be slightly forced so that they may be open to more variation. There is not much choice. Either we use language with a slight emphasis, or else we must be silent. But if the twisting is done with moderation and discretion for the sake of expanding the appreciation of our human condition, it is likely that it will be tolerated.

Calling for the signification of those affects that sustain our rationality thus transforms our most irreducible singularity into a political and epistemic challenge. The more traditional dynamics of inclusion and exclusion are apparently direct and ostensibly avoid any obliqueness on their surface. By contrast, in the present perspective a Venus' squint seems required, in the sense of attempting to conjugate affective singularity with epistemic plurality.[17] An innovative outlook is thus induced by the capacity of maintaining a tension between the most intense affectual particularity *and* the public quality of knowledge. This sort of research thus remains internally heterogeneous and irreducible to any definitive set of theses, for here the distinctions between margin and centre, or periphery and core, are much less relevant. The ordering of this book, for example, serves primarily as a writing discipline, intended as a guide through the multiple affective functions. Depending on the question asked, this gathering may be read in a different order, and no approach results as primary in every respect.

NOTES

1. As is known, this view is variously presented in numerous contributions in the domain of contemporary feminist epistemology.
2. For a discussion of this topic see Elisabeth Grosz, 'Philosophy', in S. Gunew (ed.), *Feminist Knowledge. Critique and Construct*, London and New York: Routledge, p. 148.
3. Linda Alcoff and Vrinda Dalmiya, 'Are "old wives' tales" justified?' in L. Alcoff and E. Potter (eds), *Feminist Epistemologies*, London and New York: Routledge, p. 230.
4. Derek Bolton and Jonathan Hill, *Mind, Meaning and Mental Disorder. The Nature of Causal Explanation in Psychology and Psychiatry*, Oxford and New York and Tokyo: Oxford University Press, 1996, p. 14.
5. See Elisabeth Grosz, 'Bodies and knowledges: feminism and the crisis of reason', in L. Alcoff and E. Potter (eds) *Feminist Epistemologies*, p. 207.
6. Ibid., p. 207.
7. Robyn Ferrell, *Passion in Theory: Conceptions of Freud and Lacan*, London and New York: Routledge, 1996, pp. 98–9.
8. Richard Rorty, *Objectivity, Relativism and Truth. Philosophical Papers*, vol. I, Cambridge: Cambridge University Press, 1991, p. 93.
9. See E. Grosz, 'Bodies and knowledges: feminism and the crisis of reason', p. 200.
10. Ibid., pp. 187–215.
11. W.V.O. Quine argues that 'The absence of an adequate study of imagination in our theories of meaning and rationality is symptomatic of a deep problem in our current views of cognition. The difficulty is not a matter of mere oversight. The problem is far more distressing for it concerns our entire orientation toward these issues . . .'. 'Two dogmas of empiricism', in *From a Logical Point of View*, New York: Harper Torchobooks, 1961, p. 41. In his development of the 'principle of charity' Donald Davidson argues in this way: 'Since charity is not an option but a condition of having a workable theory, it is meaningless to suggest that we might fall into massive error by endorsing it . . . Charity is forced on us; whether we like it or not, if we want to understand others, we must count them right in most matters. If we can produce a theory that reconciles charity and the formal conditions for a theory, we have done all that could be done to ensure communication. Nothing more is possible, and nothing more is needed.' *Inquiries into Truth and Interpretation*, Oxford: Clarendon Press, 1985, p. 197.
12. Claire Armon-Jones, *Varieties of Affect*, New York and London: Harvester Wheatsheaf, a division of Simon and Schuster International Group, date of publication not indicated. Oxford University thesis supervised by Kathleen Wilkes of St Hilda's College and Paul Snowdon of Exeter College, 1991.
13. Ibid., p. 1.
14. Ibid., p. 2.

15. Helen Longino, *Science as Social Knowledge. Values and Objectivity in Scientific Inquiry*, Princeton, NJ: Princeton University Press, 1990, p. 232.
16. E. Grosz, 'Bodies and knowledges: feminism and the crisis of reason', p. 209.
17. For a comparable discussion see Federica Giardini 'Public affects. Clues towards a political practice of singularity', *European Journal of Women's Studies*, vol. 6, 1999, pp. 149–59.

Chapter 4

A passion for reason

Passions in reason

One of the most inconspicuous and pervasive motives that sustains the vicissitudes of human knowledge can be described as a wish to 'annul' desire, as an inclination to 'deny' the affectual roots of our inquiring reason; it is almost a propensity to obscure the emotional components which motivate our cognitive control of the world. Paradoxically, in order to appear legitimate, rigorous, and neutral, human inquiry seems to persistently conceal its affective motivations. 'Perfect' knowledge should ultimately efface its history. And yet the affects at work in scientific ventures could derive from a desire to shape and control, predict and utilise whatever objects of inquiry. A territorial conquest of epistemic space could even be seen as an incentive for our minds to search, as though primordial affects were transposed and relived at the cognitive level in the most disparate intellectual ventures.[1] In this sense, then, we could say that desires are proper and essential to reason, including our scientific reason; so much so that perhaps the future of our knowledge may ultimately depend on the complexive quality of our mind's affective life. In our intellectual heritage, while affects are often hierarchised as inferior mental functions, at the same time they are somehow thought of as providing an indispensable motive power that needs to be appropriately integrated. As is known, Plato theorised the nature of affects as eros, Aristotle invoked the notions of *enérgeia-dynamis* to account for development, Spinoza spoke of *conatus* in the sense of effort, and Leibnitz resorted to the idea of *appetitus* as an expression of desire.

Entry into the domain of reason is often made to appear as requiring a withdrawal of affective components from all forms of knowledge. It is a denial, nevertheless, which is only superficial and misleading. Our various forms of knowledge probably stem from a drive to use and subdue, from a 'will to power' which is persistently misrecognised and often portrayed as purely cerebral or intellectual. Through an obscuration of our developmental history, knowledge may be ultimately represented as an intangible procedure, essentially made up of ideas, thoughts, and concepts. In a Nietzschean language, our different forms of knowledge could be described as deriving from a drive for mastery, or as an impulse to control, which is almost the work of 'an unsatisfied soul that feels the tamed state as a torture and finds voluptuous pleasure in a morbid unravelling of all bonds that tie it to such a state.'[2]

Even 'philosophers', as an emblematic category, would perhaps be bored with anything like the contemplation of our celebrated 'truth', for what they aspire to is the exercise of emotion and feeling within the supposedly abstract domain of reasoning. This is argued in Pascal's incisive language where he says: 'The struggle alone pleases us, not the victory. We love to see . . . fighting, not the victor infuriated over the vanquished. We would only see the victorious end; and, as soon as it comes, we are satiated. It is the same in play, and the same in the search of truth. In disputes we like to see the clash of opinions, but not at all to contemplate truth when found. To observe it with pleasure, we have to see it emerge out of strife . . . We never seek things for themselves but only for the search.'[3]

Of course, considering affects as a major vertex of observation for the appreciation of other mental phenomena can also be a disquieting theoretical option, almost as if it were a threat to our own self image and to the culture to which we belong. Emanating from still another philosophical habitat, we have a paradoxical remark of Hume 'Reason is, and ought only to be, the slave of passions, and can never pretend to any other office than to serve and obey them.'[4] This phrase is often cited, if only to be dismissed as either an empty tautology or an evident falsehood. But, perhaps, we should not interpret the remark too literally, and instead use it as a seminal, provocative suggestion. Each of us on occasion may aspire to be the slave of a passion: to be *always* otherwise would be to lack a vivid sense of self and a live engagement in the world.

With regard to our brain's knowledge, for example, it is known that in the domain of neuroscience researchers do not welcome the sort of global and ultimate questions that 'philosophers' might pose; neuroscientists are in fact specifically concerned with circumscribed, identifiable questions that are amenable to empirical testing. And yet, if they were not somehow motivated by profound questions regarding the 'basic structure' of our affectual and cognitive life, perhaps there would not be so much research and such enthusiasm in the field of neuroscience.

In the absence of desire, we could not possibly develop a connection to our world. Even reference to the external reality cannot be presented as a guarantee of its status as an independent arbiter, in the sense that the assumed objective world also participates in our constructive processes to some extent: any reference to it is somehow also filtered through human efforts and desires.[5] It is common to regard psychic reality as being merely subjective, and thus a component to be 'rightfully' marginalised in order to safeguard the validity of our 'scientific' approaches. At the basis of these outlooks, however, we increasingly recognise a personal wish to erase all desire, or a will to deny passions, even though profound, subjective longings remain at the root of our theorising. Thus, passions could be more realistically seen as simply inherent to any theoretical commitment. Ferrell remarks that the ubiquitous desire of science that there be an unpassable separation between subject and object, primarily represents a wish fulfilment; for, indeed, science 'satisfies' this desire that it constantly works on the plane of its objective facts as though they were real.[6] In Weissman's view, value is silently bestowed whenever anything is either favoured or scorned; and it is frequently these mental intentions, not the objects thereby made valuable, that energise the choice of whatever conceptual system is used to create the experience in which this passion is satisfied.[7]

At the centre of any theory, convention and observation appear increasingly interwoven. Ferrell suggests that the observed material serves to refine the concept that originally made the observation possible in such a way that any discourse, even the most literally factual, has somehow made a circular movement, by finding its premises in its conclusion: 'The only error would be the naïvety which imagines that, as a result of this, it is a "discovery".'[8] This insight is also clearly expressed by Freud, where he is compelled to recognise that 'Even at the stage of description it is not possible to avoid applying certain abstract ideas to the material in hand, ideas derived from somewhere or other but certainly not from the new observation alone.'[9] The desire of the 'scientist' may thus provoke a crisis when detected, and even then it may continue to be considered an extrinsic, contingent, remediable crisis, rather than a central problem. Psychoanalysis, on the other hand, is the typical case of a discipline in which there is no way of avoiding the question of the psychoanalyst's constitutive beliefs and desires.

Perhaps we should be more prepared to suspect pre-existing cognitive models without too many preoccupations with rectifying and supplementing existing epistemologies. Instead of taking affects and desires as the objects of analysis, we could take mainstream epistemologies as their products, *and* as their points of departure. In this sense, it is possible to begin to consider altogether different forms of knowing, or positions of epistemic enunciation, that are marked as libidically different from logocratic paradigms. In Grosz's view, there is an endeavour to rethink knowledge as a product generated by our affective lives.[10] In this respect, one can see that the elmination of affects in the enunciative positions constitutive of knowledge implies an obscured isomorphism of theory with an indifferent and unwitting attitude of domination. If epistemology has in part rationalised a control of the production of knowledge by declaring its 'interests' universal and neutral, this is because it relies upon a culturally inscribed correlation of thinking with the category of mind, and of affects with the category of the objects to be dominated by our cognitive mind.[11]

In a generically 'Freudian' outlook, we could say that the contention between the reality principle and the pleasure principle arises because the mind is the delegate of the instinctual demands directed towards the external contingencies. According to Ferrell, this makes the reality principle itself an internal phenomenon, and one which has its own desire – that of making survival possible; it is not more 'real' than pleasure which dictates a more frank wish fulfilment.[12] And she adds: 'Where secondary revision, or philosophical principle, serves to render the material of experience comprehensible, it can only be by *denying* the origin of its own impulse, the effacement of its own wish.'[13] When the work is 'perfect', all of its traces should disappear. Our rational thought is intent upon gratifying desire while at the same time repudiating it, paradoxically satisfying a desire *in* denying it; this is of course because our rationality indeed seems to include a burning wish that it should not be wishful.

From a generic anthropological perspective, we could say that *homo sapiens* has evolved within nature to fill the ecological niche of an intelligent being, and thus the demand for comprehension is one of the salient requirements of the human species. The need for information and thought orientation in our environment is as pressing a human need as that of nourishment itself: we probably develop questions because we *need* answers. Rescher notes that, as rational animals, we must feed our minds just as we must nourish our bodies, perforce settling for the best we can get at the time 'That basic demand for information and understanding presses in upon us and we try in *every* way to do what is needed for its satisfaction.'[14]

The problems of the representatives of 'pure reason' could be seen in the light of a project of self formation, even though no such project is mentioned or recognised. Scheman argues that from such obscured projects there emerges the distinct creation of an epistemically authoritative protagonist.[15] Such an inconspicuous endeavour of self-constitution leaves a vast residue of unresolved problems. The ideal of pure research and of objective knowledge could be more helpfully understood as an account of implicit projects of self-constitution, and of the incongruities that are the characteristic residue of unresolvable aspects of these problems.[16] Thus, in Wittgensteinian parlance, we could say that philosophical questions become the intellectualised version of the problems deriving from the authoritative self-constitution of epistemic knowledge. Wittgenstein claims that 'The sickness of a time' is cured by an alteration in the mode of life of human beings, and that 'it is possible for the sickness of philosophical problems to get cured only through a changed mode of thought and of life, not through a medicine invented by an individual.'[17] These problems cannot be properly resolved, but perhaps dissolved by transformations such as a possible transition from the power of discourse to the force of listening, from the identification of fields of inquiry to the creation of metaphoric links between them, and from a tradition of 'pure' epistemology to a conjugation with epistemophily.[18]

The frequently discussed 'crisis of reason' could be seen as a consequence of its claustrophilic epistemology which emanates from privileging the purely conceptual or mental factors over the affective ones. One of the consequences of this attitude is the inability of Western culture to conceive of its own processes as simultaneously relying upon *and* disavowing our pulsating passion for control. This can be especially relevant for those attempting not only to criticise, but also to creatively transform the traditional forms that knowledge has taken so far. Epistemophily implies that the regulative hegemony over knowledge, which has so far been accomplished by logocratic outlooks, may be integrated and/or transformed through approaches which are independent from the presumptions of unaffective 'purity' regulating, and ultimately constraining, our prevailing forms of knowledge.[19] This point connects with the cognate assumption that even though knowledge is generated by human creatures, it purports in no way to be personal and thus legitimately regarded as pure, impersonal knowledge. The living subject, who is the emissary of a knowledge-producing community, is illusorily exempted from the passions inherent to the knowledge claims he puts forth. Thus, knowledge would be no more than a neutral and enlightening perspective accessible to anybody who can be suitably trained. In Grosz's view, indifference, cold-bloodedness, hardness, detachment, control, which in our cultural deployments are variously described as inimitable consistency, adherence to hard facts, sword-like intelligence, and argumentative cogency, are no less 'passions' than are obsessions, fetishisms, phobias or dependencies.[20]

A collateral view might suggest that 'passion' is often publicly recognised as an attitude that signals a noble love for the topic, that connects with the marvellous implications the topic carries with it, or shows how these implications can also be used to enhance knowledge in general. However, even this benign quality is often the first characteristic to be discarded in most of the pertinent literature. And yet, scientific accuracy would not suffer because of this passion; on the contrary, it is sustained by it. The idea(l) of disinterested, dispassionate, and neutral research could thus be seen as a dream, or even as a collective dream, that still fascinates our current epistemologies. Perceived as a myth, it could also be regarded as a cluster of master symbols latently performing some relevant social function.

The pleasures of mental efficacy

The joy of intellectual efficacy and self actualisation, whether experienced by a child or by a mathematician, somehow shows the inherent pleasure that is attained by processes that reinforce the coherence and continuity of our mental functions. Modell remarks that this sort of enjoyment is different from the pleasure of 'orgastic release', and also that it cannot be simplistically explained in terms of instinctual 'sublimation'. He also believes that this capacity to find joy *within*, through the mastery of intellectual capacities, remains at the core of the self: 'When it is present, the self feels strong; when it is absent, the self feels weak and depleted.'[21] This pleasure of efficacy and competence is forcefully described by Brazelton as 'fuelling the system from *within*'.[22]

Through a growing attention to the pleasures of mental efficacy, we can almost hypothesise the presence of 'an affective logic', which implies there being a unified system with psychic polarities, in the sense, perhaps, of a cognitive and of an affectual pole. This 'system' could be thought of as an apparatus whereby we both cognitively perceive and affectively interact with persons, things, and culture. These two aspects share the same formation processes and also combine in increasingly diversified mental circuits. In this perspective, then, we should not so much speak of a parallelism, or symmetry, between affects and cognition, but rather of an enlivening polarisation whereby the maturation reached in one domain can serve as the basis for further maturation in the other.[23] In Jaggar's view, emotions are neither more basic than reason in building theory, nor are they secondary to them. Each of these human faculties reflects an aspect of human knowing that is insepa-rable from the others.[24] And yet, when addressing the pivotal question of the role of affects in the pursuit of knowledge and the development of culture, the attitude is still conspicuously apologetic and begging for any degree of legitimisation. It is as though we were constantly prefacing a discussion with preliminaries such as 'even though some plants are unedible, we do need to feed on plants', or 'even though some theories have been misleading, we still need theories'. It is thus appropriate to increasingly explore the passions at work in our allegedly neutral knowledges, together with the role of pleasurable affects in the proper functioning of our human reason. Not only is it a pleasure for humans to function intellectually, but it is also enjoyable to know that one can function, and is able to share, theorise and explore such very profound self-knowledge.

For the sake of example it is interesting to note that already Spinoza had provided illuminating paradigms showing the interwinement of affect and reason. Although speaking out from a 'metaphysical' tradition, in the chapter 'On the Origin and Nature of Affects' the philosopher remarks: 'Our mind acts at times and at times suffers: in so far as it has adequate ideas, it necessarily acts; and in so far as it has inadequate ideas, it necessarily suffers.'[25] Thus, for Spinoza, active pleasure is a concomitant of all adequate cognition, for when the mind elaborates something adequately, it is necessarily aware of this and consequently, of its own power or activity. And according to Allison's comment, it is the awareness of its activity, not the nature of the object known, that is the source of pleasure.[26] Since pain, or sorrow, reflects a diminishment of the mind's power of activity, Spinoza concludes that it can never be the result of this activity, but must always derive from the mind's inadequate knowledge, and from determination by external factors. In a Spinozistic outlook, then, primary emotions such as pleasure, pain, and desire are correlated with the transition from one state of perfection, or level of vitality, to another. Thus, pleasure or joy – *laetitia* – is defined as the emotion whereby the mind passes to a greater state of perfection, and pain or sorrow – *tristitia* – as that by which it passes to a lesser state.[27] Similarly, hope and fear are understood as pleasures and pains that arise under conditions of uncertainty, when the image of some past or future event is connected with an outcome that is in doubt.

In our contemporary culture, it is obvious enough that through the influence of such disciplines as transformational linguistics, artificial intelligence, and mathematical communication, a general trend may prevail to ignore affects and exclude them from knowledge. Syntactic strings of symbols, software, and mathematically defined signal exchangers have so far been unemotional.[28] And yet, even the cognitive theories of action have to posit goals *together* with methods of achieving them; they must provide means of determining failure and success. These goals somehow reintroduce the idea of affects. Bolton and Hill remark that the production of well-formed syntax so far has no target except itself, nor does information exchange between mathematically defined systems.[29] Computers can be made to perform tasks but they do not mind whether they achieve them or not, and in this sense the 'tasks' and the notions of success or failure are *ours* rather than *theirs*. These notions, in fact, derive from the passions which animate constructions and research. Generally speaking, the notion of goals, and of failure or success in achieving them, belongs primarily to biological systems for which success, as opposed to failure, is actually all that matters for it is essential to survival. This is the context in which the deceptively excluded notion of affect is necessarily reactivated.

Neuroscientist Damasio reports cases of patients who have undergone brain surgery and whose thinking has become computer-like, able to perform every step in the calculus of a decision, but unable to assign values to different possibilities, and consequently unable to implement them.[30] Every option remains neutral. That overly dispassionate reasoning is the core of the problem: insufficient awareness of one's own feelings about situations makes reasoning faulty. Of course, while excessively strong feelings can be detrimental to reasoning, the lack of awareness of feelings can also be ruinous, especially in evaluating decisions on which our destiny largely depends. As is well known, feelings can disrupt the processes of reasoning under circumscribed conditions, and several investigations of 'normal' reasoning reveal the potentially harmful influence of emotional biases. It is thus significant that we gradually learn to perceive the (relative) absence of emotion as no less detrimental to the rationality that makes us distinctively rational in a specifically human way – that is, as different from animals and machines.

In colloquial English we may say that we are 'gripped', 'seized', 'torn', or 'over-come' by emotion. Averill remarks that we cannot 'do' an emotion in a deliberate way.[31] In a rather classical terminology, emotions are *passions* rather than *actions*, so that a passion is something a creature suffers, that is, a condition over which a person has hardly any control. But the emphasised passivity of emotions can also be an illusion. To the extent that this myth induces us to regard emotions as alien and disruptive forces over which we have little comand, the resulting idea of 'passivity' can be detrimentally restrictive for emotional development and transformation.[32] From a neurological perspective, Damasio suggests instead that it is almost as though we were endowed with a 'passion *for* reason', or a drive that originates in the brain core, permeates other levels of the nervous system, and emerges as either feelings or as unconscious inclinations which guide decision making; from the practical to the theoretical, reason is probably constructed on this inherent drive by a process which resembles the mastering of a skill:[33] 'Remove the drive, and you will not acquire the mastery. But having the drive does not auto-matically make you a master.'[34] And for the attainment of the most disparate kinds of mastery, we embark on the acquisition of skills predisposed by our increasingly technological culture.

Abstract processes partake of affective vicissitudes inasmuch as their purpose is the potential pleasure and the challenge of prevailing upon disappointment through the development of intellectual efficacy; more precisely, the range of abstract purposes extends through the nuances between the two extremes of frustration and success – which are, indeed, intense personal experiences. Affective components also seem to characterise elementary logical processes in the sense that 'success' is unbreakably intertwined in the process. Their emotional resonance confers to each subsequent step in the immense domain of formal abstraction a specifically affective 'tone' which, in time, may be definitely attenuated, but which may also be reactivated under especially challenging circumstances. From this affectual tone, the abstract processes derive their basic motivations, which are perhaps the equivalent of their 'energies'.[35] Even though the Apollonian perspective of genetic epistemology has only rarely paid attention to the affective components of mental growth, it none the less clearly implies that the correct logical operations are also intensely pleasurable, both at their origin and whenever they are rediscovered in the subsequent stages of development. In the vast corpus of Piagetian psychology, the correct logical operations somehow appear to be pleasurable in the sense that they reduce a previous logical tension, they are more economical and harmonious of the prior condition; they eliminate a disturbance and thus create a more agreeable equilibrium, and finally they open novel opportunities for understanding and action.[36]

Even the apparently cold and neutral pleasure inherent in the solution of mathematical and theoretical problems exhibits some affective connotations which characterise the variegated domain of formal operations. Although usually concealed, the 'psychoanalytic' pleasure principle operating in the domain of formal disciplines becomes more clearly visible through its painful opposite, that is, in all cases in which a deduction does not succeed and a theorem does not prove congruent. In this sense, any formal and analytic discipline of thought may be seen as characterised by a unitary and pervasive affective quality. Ciompi suggests that in the affective domain we can envisage a polarity between pleasure and unpleasure, while in the cognitive domain we can think in terms that are adequately more abstract, that is, in terms of a polarisation between failure and success.[37] Piaget goes as far as to speak of 'euphoria' resulting from mathematical discoveries of adolescents.[38] We could thus speculate that this pleasure in creating more orderly and harmonious combinations, which also implies a reduction of tensions and a saving of energies, plays such a decisive role in our intellectual growth that we should rather speak of a synergistic rational-affectual development.

Moreover, in the experience of totally focusing on a specific task or problem, and when our state of concentration is all pervasive, we may experience what Goleman describes as a 'flow'.[39] Although the experience of 'flow' may relate to different activities, it certainly also applies to our intellectual challenges. Goleman attempts to describe it as a glorious experience, and suggests that the hallmark of flow is a feeling of spontaneous joy, or even rapture: 'It is a state in which people become utterly absorbed in what they are doing, paying undivided attention to the task, their awareness merged with their actions . . . Attention becomes so focused that people are aware only of the narrow range of perception related to the immediate task, losing track of time and space.'[40] Because flow is such a positive feeling, it is intrinsically rewarding. He adds that 'Flow is a state of self-forgetfulness, the opposite of rumination and worry: instead of being lost in nervous preoccupation, people in flow are so absorbed in the task at hand that they lose self-consciousness . . . In this sense *moments of flow are ego-less*.'[41] Therefore, paradoxically, in the moments of highest intellectual concentration, the rational functions of the ego are almost eclipsed or absorbed into a more complex and intense affectual state.

As is recognised, beginning with the perception and affective investment of objects in our tangible world, the individual moves towards increasingly abstract formal perceptions, whose interconnections become a process of logic, rather than a matter of observation. Originally actions transform objects, while subsequent mental operations transform sets of symbols. These symbol-manipulating capacities prove of the essence in higher branches of mathematics. Of course, in analytic reasoning, the symbols to be manipulated can also be words and propositions. In a sense, even the mere recognition of a regularity and of a measure of order, such as a repetition of patterns (perhaps the equivalent of an 'invariance'), is often intensely pleasurable: this is observable in both children and adults as the pleasure that we experience whenever we discern something familiar in unfamiliar contexts.[42] The component of pleasure can be regarded as highly relevant to the construction of reality and interpersonal relations, since it functions as the affective incentive for the creation of interwoven continuities; from infancy, these are conducive to the formation of rewarding and stable modes of behaviour, those habits which ultimately become so 'dear' to us that we cannot give them up.

Gardner and Ulam remind us that mathematicians who have reflected about their feelings upon solving difficult problems, regularly stress the exhilaration that accompanies the moment of breakthrough. Sometimes the intuition comes through first, then one must actually take steps to work out the details of the solution; at other times the attention to the sequence of steps suggests the solution. However accomplished, the solution of a difficult and important problem provides a thrill of a very special sort.[43] In fact, the ability not only to discover an analogy, but also to find connections between types of analogies, has been singled out as a special mathematical delight. The capacity to follow a chain of reasoning is not so elusive, but the ability to invent new mathematics is rare. Gardner reports Poincaré as stating that anyone can make new combinations with mathematical expressions but '*to create* consists precisely in not making useless combinations and in making those which are useful, and which are only a small minority: invention is discernment, choice . . . Among chosen combinations *the most fertile will often be those formed of elements drawn from domains which are far apart.*'[44] Therefore, it seems that even in the abstract domain of mathematics, creative processes depend upon our metaphoric capacity to establish fertile connections between 'domains which are far apart', or at a great conceptual distance from each other. The mathematical expressions worthy of being studied are those which, by their analogy with other areas of the discipline, are capable of leading us to the knowledge of mathematical principles. Damasio remarks that they are those which reveal to us unsuspected kinships between other heterogeneous 'facts' long known, but previously believed to be strangers to one another.[45] The creation of these kinships is certainly also rooted in our profound metaphoric potential.[46] The greatest progress is made when disparate elements are linked in such a way that a few simple rules can explain the newly observed interactions. In recalling the intuitions of his mentor, Heisenberg remarks that for Niels Bohr 'the fact that he cannot yet express them by adequate linguistic or mathematical techniques is no disaster. On the contrary, it is a great challenge'.[47] This challenge, of course, is still another example of connecting with a certain level of inner disappointment, which suitably enhances the desired attainment of intellectual pleasure.

NOTES

1. This issue is explored in Gemma Corradi Fiumara, *The Symbolic Function. Psychoanalysis and the Philosophy of Language*, chapter 11, 'From biological life to dialogic relations', Oxford, UK and Cambridge, MA: Blackwell Publishers, 1992, pp. 154–78.
2. Friedrich Nietzsche, *The Will to Power*, trans. W. Kaufman, New York: Vintage Books, 1968, p. 461.
3. Blaise Pascal, *Pascal's Pensées*, with an introduction by T.S. Eliot, New York: E.P. Dutton, 1958, paragraph 135, p. 38.
4. David Hume, *Treatise on Human Understanding*, L.A. Selby-Bigge (ed.), Oxford: Clarendon Press, 1988, part II(3), p. 415.
5. Margaret Whitford, review of Robyn Ferrell's *Passion in Theory: Conceptions of Freud and Lacan; Women's Philosophy Review* 17, 1997, p. 37.
6. Robyn Ferrell, *Passion in Theory: Conceptions of Freud and Lacan*, London and New York: Routledge, 1996, p. 100.
7. David Weissman, *Truth's Debt to Value*, New Haven and London: Yale University Press, 1993, p. 3.
8. R. Ferrell, *Passion in Theory*, p. 57.
9. Sigmund Freud, 'Papers on metapsychology' (including 'Instincts and their vicissitudes', 'Representation', 'The unconscious'), *Standard Edition*, vol. 14, 1915, p. 117.
10. Elisabeth Grosz, 'Bodies and knowledges: feminism and the crisis of reason'; in L. Alcoff and E. Potter (eds), *Feminist Epistemologies*, London and New York: Routledge, 1993, p. 208.
11. Ibid., p. 208.
12. R. Ferrell, *Passion in Theory*, p. 26.
13. Ibid., p. 26.
14. Nicholas Rescher, *Pluralism. Against the Demand for Consensus. For (though also against) Jürgen Habermas*, Oxford: Clarendon Press, 1995, p. 87.
15. Naomi Scheman, *Engenderings. Construction of Knowledge, Authority, and Privilege*, London and New York: Routledge, 1993, pp. 7–8.
16. Ibid., p. 8.
17. Ludwig Wittgenstein, *Remarks on the Foundations of Mathematics*, G.H. von Wright, R. Rhees and G.E.M. Anscombe (eds), Cambridge, MA: MIT Press, 1967, p. 57.
18. For a discussion of this topic see Gemma Corradi Fiumara, *The Metaphoric Process. Connections between Language and Life*, London and New York: Routledge, 1995.
19. E. Grosz, 'Bodies and knowledges: feminism and the crisis of reason', pp. 187–8.
20. Ibid., p. 188. Her review of the lives of great men led Virginia Wolf to the conviction that perhaps with the exception of literature, 'all the other professions according to the testimony of biography, seem to be as bloodthirsty as the profession of arms itself.' *Three Guineas*, New York: Harcourt, Brace and World, 1938, p. 63.
21. Arnold Modell, *The Private Self*, Cambridge, MA and London: Harvard University Press, 1996, p. 52.
22. T. Berry Brazelton, 'Neonatal assessment', in G. Pollock and S. Greenspan (eds), *The Course of Life*, vol. I, Washington, DC: US Department of Health and Human

Services, 1980 (emphasis added). Positive emotions indicate a pleasure in increasing organisation, with both internal and external signals providing feedback from self and others. To draw attention to this aspect of the processes of emotion in a general way, Emde invokes the idea of 'negentropy pleasure'; this notion provides a contrast with early psychoanalytic theory in which all emotions were a consequence of entropy, or drive discharge. Robert Emde, 'Moving ahead: integrating influences of affective processes for development and for psychoanalysis', *The International Journal of Psychoanalysis*, vol. 80, 1999, pp. 317–40.

23. Luc Ciompi, *Affektlogik. Über die Structur der Psyche und ihre Entwicklung. Ein Beitrag zur Schizophrenieforschung*, Stuttgart: Ernst Klett, 1982. Italian translation by F. Giancanelli and D. Maperna, *Logica affettiva. Una ricerca sulla schizofrenia*, Milan: Feltrinelli, 1994, p. 70.

24. Alison M. Jaggar, 'Love and knowledge: emotion in feminist epistemology', in A.M. Jaggar and S.R. Bordo (eds), *Gender/Body/Knowledge: Feminist Reconstructions of Being and Knowing*, New Brunswick, NJ and London: Rutgers University Press, p. 165.

25. Benedict de Spinoza, *Ethic: Demonstrated in Geometrical Order* (translated from the Latin of B. de Spinoza by W. Hale White; translation revised by A. Hutchison Stirling), London: T. Fisher Unwin, 1894, pp. 106–7.

26. Henry E. Allison, 'Spinoza, Benedict de, 1632–1677, in E. Craig (ed.), *Routledge Encyclopedia of Philosophy*, London and New York: Routledge, 1998, vol. 9, pp. 106–7.

27. Ibid., p. 101.

28. On this issue see Derek Bolton and Jonathan Hill, *Mind, Meaning and Mental Disorder. The Nature of Causal Explanation in Psychology and Psychiatry*, Oxford, New York and Tokyo: Oxford University Press, 1996, p. 13.

29. Ibid., p. 13.

30. Antonio R. Damasio, *Descartes' Error: Emotion, Reason and the Human Brain*, London: Macmillan General Books, 1996.

31. See James R. Averill and Elma P. Nunley, *Voyages of the Heart. Living an Emotionally Creative Life*, New York and Oxford: The Free Press, 1992, p. 44. Also see James R. Averill, 'In the eyes of the beholder', in P. Ekman and R.J. Davidson (eds), *The Nature of Emotion. Fundamental Questions*, New York and Oxford: Oxford University Press, 1994, p. 7–14.

32. Ibid., p. 44.

33. A. Damasio, *Descartes' Error*, p. 245.

34. Ibid., p. 245.

35. L. Ciompi, *Logica affettiva. Una ricerca sulla schizofrenia*, p. 60.

36. Ibid., p. 62.

37. Ibid., p. 71.

38. Ibid., p. 63.

39. Daniel Goleman, *Emotional Intelligence Why It Can Matter More Than IQ*, London: Bloomsbury, 1996, p. 91.

40. Ibid., p. 91.

41. Ibid., p. 91.

42. L. Ciompi, *Logica affettiva*, p. 62.

43. Stanislav S. Ulam, *Adventures of a Mathematician*, New York: Charles Scribner's, 1976, p. 120. Quoted in Howard Gardner, *Frames of Mind. The Theory of Multiple Intelligences*, London: Fontana Press, 1993, p. 141. We read in William James: 'I myself believe that all the magnificent achievements of mathematical and physical science . . . proceed from our *indomitable desire* to cast the world into a more rational shape in our minds than the shape into which it is thrown there by the crude order of

our experience.' (emphasis added). *The Will to Believe and Other Essays in Popular Philosophy*, Dover Publications, 1956, p. 115.

Henri Poincaré is quoted as saying: 'If I have the feeling, the intuition, so to speak, of an order, so as to perceive at a glance the reasoning as a whole, I need no longer fear lest I forget one of the elements, for each of them will take its allotted place in the array, and that without any effort of memory on my part.' Reported by H. Gardner in *Frames of Mind. The Theory of Multiple Intelligences*, p. 137.

44. H. Gardner, *Frames of Mind. The Theory of Multiple Intelligences*, p. 138.
45. A. Damasio, *Descartes' Error*, p. 188.
46. On this topic see G. Corradi Fiumara, *The Metaphoric Process*, pp. 33–5 and 67–71.
47. Werner Heisenberg, *Physics and Beyond*, New York: Harper and Row, 1962, p. 37.

Chapter 5

Minding the body

Mental life *and* embodied existence

In a psychoanalytic perspective, instincts, drives and impulses are generally regarded as the prototype of the somatic, in the sense of organismic energies that demand satisfaction. Yet satisfaction can only be achieved through the domain of the mental, that is, at an operative psychic level where some representation or symbolisation of instinct is made possible. The actual impulse, or the energy that supports any protomental system, however, cannot be represented as an image or symbol; the impulse, therefore, is not a proper mental element even though mental structures are an inherent part of its obtaining satisfaction. It is for purposes of psychic survival that instinctual energy is so vitally linked to representations (symbols, structures) in the character of the mental. Hence the dynamic, synergic dyads through which we constantly *attempt* to describe mental life: mind and body, image and impulse, representation and energy, sign and desire. It is indeed a complex, often paradoxical, and elusive outlook on our affective life, that is at once dependent upon social approval, *yet* autonomous in generating itself from within. Even though the complexity of our living mind is such that the 'solution' to its problems can hardly be known – probably because of our inherent limitations – we have more to gain than to lose if we consider it in relation to its biological 'receptacle'. In such a contingent perspective, it comes as no surprise that the mind exists *in* and *for* an integrated organism: our minds in fact would not be the way they are if it were not for their interplay with the body and the brain in the course of evolution, during individual development or current vicissitudes.

The distinctive quality of the celebrated Freudian outlook is the endeavour to conjugate instinct and significance, force and meaning, body and mind in an unprecedented, integrated way. Even though we cannot hope to perceive any ultimate structure of our affective life, we can appreciate the increasing fertility of theories that resist any dichotomy between 'domains' variously described as psychic and organismic, mental and corporeal, or cultural and biological. In attempting to construe mental life from within a biological perspective, instincts may be regarded not just as a bodily parallel of the mind but also as its energetic sources, and as potential intrusions into it. Thus, they are both necessary and menacing. In this outlook, even though the mind is an elaboration of its somatic substratum, the interactions of mind and body remain rather problematic. However, if we wonder how biological drives can be both beneficial and detrimental, Damasio reminds us 'that it would not be the only instance in biology in which a given factor or mechanism may be negative or positive according to the circumstances.'[1]

In Freud's *Metapsychology* we read that 'If we apply ourselves to considering mental life from a *biological* point of view, an "instinct" appears to us as a concept on the frontier between the mental and the somatic, as the psychical representative of the stimuli originating from within the organism, and reaching the mind, as a measure of the demand made upon the mind for work in consequence of its connection with the body.'[2] At times, Freud can be regarded as a naturalist and an empiricist, for the structures that govern the mind are made to appear as fundamentally biological, as if somewhere 'inside' our living organism the mind had its root. This is perhaps why he can so conveniently resort to all kinds of metaphors to speak of our conscious and unconscious psychic vicissitudes, undisturbed by his diversified metaphoric expressions; he seems confident indeed to be indirectly approaching some as yet inscrutable reality, even though he can only do so in figurative terms. At other times, Freud's outlook is more problematic. In a lecture on 'Anxiety', he struggles to define affects as a composite of thought and impulse: 'And what is affect in the dynamic sense? It is in any case something *highly composite*.'[3] The instincts of human beings of course require a mental process as part of their satisfaction. In fact, 'Since the instinct is on the threshold, belonging as much to the mind as to the body, it is not a mere echo in the mind of the body, but depends on its appearances in the mind for its satisfaction', says Ferrell.[4] In a psychoanalytic perspective, then, the body can be as demanding of the mind as the external world of persons and nature, with its many dangers and appeals; and even though it is to the body that the mind owes its existence – and the need for its existence – the mind comes to feel that it has to laboriously cope both with the inside and the outside domains. Thus, the composite nature of instincts is not only problematic, but potentially quite instructive. Freud offers this highly 'didactic' suggestion: 'Let us imagine ourselves in the situation of an almost entirely helpless living organism, as yet unoriented in the world, which is receiving stimuli in its nervous substance. This organism will very soon be in a position to make a first distinction and a first orientation. On the one hand, it will be aware of stimuli which can be avoided by muscular action (flight); these it ascribes to an external world. On the other hand, it will also be aware of stimuli against which such action is of no avail and whose character of constant pressure persists in spite of it; these stimuli are the signs of an internal world, the evidence of instinctual needs.'[5] What is interesting to note is that this very relevant distinction does not come for the individual as the result of empirical observation or intellectual reasoning, but seems rather to derive from a *feeling* of our own living condition – as if feelings could actually instruct us on these originary, corporeal experiences.

In Langer's language, the derivation of feeling from instinct is a dynamic pattern of tremendous complexity: 'Its whole relation to life, the fact that all sorts of processes may culminate in feeling . . . and that vital activity goes on at all levels continuously, make mental phenomena the most protean subject matter in the world.'[6] For, indeed, the superimposition of defining terms upon flux, and the regulation of desire by principles, produces its own discrepancy such as an obscure sense of fracture between the somatic current of drives and the mental images representing it. As is known, Lacan interprets this as a structural 'lack' of subjectivity, which amounts to an ontological distress, with the pain being only more intense in the case of mental illness, while the condition is endemic.[7] Thus, it is a 'discrepancy' which cannot be properly resolved, but can only be disguised or repeatedly confronted in the complex experiences of psychic development. An awareness of this central distress in our mental life reverberates differently in a great number of authors. William James, for instance, remarks that 'A purely disembodied human emotion is a nonentity. I do not say that it is a contradiction in the nature of things, or that pure spirits are necessarily condemned to cold intellectual lives; but I say that, for us, emotion dissociated from all bodily feeling is inconceivable.'[8] That is, although the composite nature of our affects is painfully problematic, its dissociation is almost inconceivable.

This ubiquitous problem in fact re-emerges in still different epistemic languages. In Stern's view, for example, affects are generally connected to 'momentary changes in feeling states involved in the organic process of being alive.'[9] Modell, on the other hand, regards Tomkins' contrasting the relative fixity of organismic drives with the variability of affects, as a suggestion that drives have motivational impact only when amplified by affects.[10] Person remarks that analysts of a Kleinian persuasion incline to believe that unconscious fantasies are inborn, organismic forms of psychic life, and they consequently distinguish between conscious fantasies (with an 'f'), from unconscious phantasies (with a 'ph').[11] The latter is regarded as the primary content of unconscious mental processes which tend to converge with instincts and drives. Among contemporary theorists of affects, Jones primarily believes that emotions constitute the experiential monitor of physiological conditions. By cross comparing the affective intensity of feelings that derive from different systems, the organism has a way of prioritising information, and thus reaching decisions that in turn initiate a course of action; in Jones' sense, then, we could think of emotions (from the Latin word *movere*) as forces that move us to action.[12] And feelings, according to Damasio's neurological perspective, actually enable us to '*mind the body*, attentively, as during an emotional state, or faintly, as during a background state. They enable us to mind the body "live".'[13]

More than a millenium ago, Plotinus confronted our mental-and-embodied existence in his *Enneads*, and asked: 'Pleasure and distress, fear and courage, desire and aversion, where have these affections and experiences their seat? Clearly, either in the Soul alone, or in the Soul as employing the body . . . And what applies to the affections applies to whatever acts, physical or mental, spring from them.'[14]

Knowledge as an organismic derivative

The pressures and needs which we conceptualise as instincts are experienced by human beings as inexorably requiring a response, and in this sense they come to have for us an organismic character. Instincts are felt psychically as the representatives of an organismic demand, even though they are only visible as mental images, fantasies or 'ideas'. However, the point we should emphasise is that the 'first' distinction between the psychic and the somatic level is not made on the basis of some empirical observation or intellectual hypothesis, but rather on the basis of a capacity to feel our personal condition, that is, through our diversified ways of feeling our own modes of being alive. It is from vicissitudes in self-feeling that we begin to derive a conceptual differentiation between mind and body.

In Damasio's physiological perspective, feelings have a truly privileged status. Not only are they represented at different neural levels, but because of their inextricable ties to the body they come first in development, and thus retain a primacy that subtly pervades our mental life: 'Because the brain is the body's captive audience, feelings are winners among equals' says Damasio. 'And since what comes first constitutes a frame of reference for what comes after, feelings have a say on how the rest of the brain and cognition go about their business. Their influence is immense.'[15] As argued in this work, reason cannot be as pure as we think it is or wish it were: for better or for worse, affects are profoundly interwoven in its workings. In Damasio's gaze 'The strategies of human reason probably did not develop, in their evolution or in any single individual, without the guiding force of the mechanisms of biological regulation, of which emotions and feelings are notable expressions.'[16] If we think of affects as instinctual derivatives, we can resonate with Pascal's suggestion that 'Two things instruct man about his whole nature: instinct and experience.'[17] Unless we are so judiciously instructed, we are only left with representational, 'scientific' accounts of our embodied condition. These 'accounts' will primarily exhibit physiological or natural aspects of our life while obscuring the innumerable symbolic and cultural modes of our embodied existence. Or else, in an unduly restricted outlook, anything that connects with our condition of living beings can only be monotonously marginalised with labels of biologism and naturalism. According to Grosz, in view of the 'prevailing binarised or dichotomised categories governing Western reason, and in view of the privilege accorded to one term over the other in binary pairs (mind over body, culture over nature, self over other, reason over passions, and so on), it is necessary to examine the subordinated, negative, or excluded term, *body* as the *unacknowledged condition* of the dominant term, *reason*.'[18] Thus, the view of ungenerated, independent reason produces subordination and schisms, together with a multiplicity of obscured problems. Just as the goddess of knowledge Athena sprang fully armed from the head of Zeus (Jupiter), so our 'autonomous mind' seems to claim a parthenogenic birth from the brains of a logos-father; it is a high-level, noble 'birth', unquestionably entitling it to ignore the vicissitudes of our sexuated reproduction.

To the extent that we can resist our reassuring and seductive dichotomies, we can reach for an understanding of the human mind which is inseparable from an organismic perspective. In Damasio's view, not only must the mind recede from an abstract, lifeless enclosure, and regain the level of living flesh, but it must also relate to a whole organism 'possessed of integrated body proper and brain fully interactive with a physical and social environment'.[19] In a philosophical perspective which resists the dominance of divisive paradigms as well as the dreams of representationalist reasoning, Goodman observes that 'The eye comes always ancient to its work, obsessed by its own past and by old and new insinuations of the ear, nose, tongue, fingers, heart and brain. It functions not as an instrument self-powered and alone, but as a dutiful member of a complex and capricious organism.'[20] And thus the 'eye of the mind', as the protagonist of our epistemic visual metaphors, cannot ultimately claim the status of an autonomous agent.

Grosz elaborately argues that our ways of knowledge are the expression of a drive to live and subdue, even though they misrecognise themselves as 'cerebral' activities, as the sole product of ideas, thoughts and concepts; thus ignoring their motivational origins and bodily genealogies. Our modes of knowledge 'are the products of bodily impulses and forces that have mistaken themselves as products of the mind'.[21] Experiences rooted in the presumption of pre-existent representational categories, and unambiguous concepts generated by a unified knowing subject, unburdened by the concerns of physiological and psychic survival, can be linked to man's intentional disembodiment, or willed detachment from his manliness in producing theories, paradigms and truths.[22] It is then fortunate indeed that feelings assist us by offering glimpses of what goes on in ourselves, as momentary images of our flesh reconnect with our complexive thinking.

A feeling for our inner states can modify our comprehensive notion of objects, situations and theories. Through sufficient proximity, our affective resources may confer to our mental functions a *quality* of goodness or badness, of pleasure or pain. In Modell's clinical outlook even the idea of value is 'sufficiently inclusive to extend from the organism's homeostatic systems to the domain of personal interests and personal meanings. *Value is therefore a border-crossing concept that can span the mind and the brain.*'[23]

If we regard our capacity to feel our living condition as essential to knowledge, we can appreciate that states of affairs have a 'valency' for us, positive or negative, according to whether they promote or disrupt our integrity and capacity for action. Perception of states of affairs as being positive or negative is linked closely to plans for suitable action, such as appropriate avoidance. In this sense the notions of 'correctness' or 'incorrectness' tend to lose their neutral character and acquire the vital quality of being good or bad; it is a condition that greatly helps us in making choices. But, of course, there are innumerable scenarios that may come under scrutiny in our choices, and a capacity to feel our personal functioning assists us in the process of sifting through such a wealth of detail, and in reducing the need for selection; according to Damasio, this capacity provides an automated detection of the components which are more likely to be relevant: the synergy between so-called cognitive processes and processes usually called 'emotional' should thus be apparent.[24] Adopting an evolutionary perspective, Damasio adds: 'If ensuring survival of the body proper is what the brain first evolved for, then, when minded brains appeared, they began by *minding the body*.'[25] Through a more integrated outlook we may avoid unwarranted divisions which create more problems than they can solve. An appreciation of our complex interdependecies may incline us to think of our human reason as an organismic derivative, more hospitable to integration with our diverse affects. Conversely, an autonomous reason seems hopelessly unable to regain contact with our increasingly complex living condition.

NOTES

1. Antonio R. Damasio, *Descartes' Error: Emotion, Reason, and the Human Brain*, London: Macmillan General Books, 1996, p. 194.
2. Sigmund Freud, 'Papers on metapsychology (including 'Instincts and their vicissitudes', 'Repression', 'The unconscious'), in *Standard Edition*, vol. 14, 1915, p. 121.
3. S. Freud, 'Anxiety' in 'Introductory lectures on psycho-analysis', *Standard Edition*, vols. 15 and 16, 1916, p. 395 (emphasis added).
4. Robyn Ferrell, *Passion in Theory: Conceptions of Freud and Lacan*, London and New York: Routledge, 1996, p. 9.
5. S. Freud, 'Papers on metapsychology', p. 105.
6. Susanne K. Langer, *Mind: An Essay on Human Feeling*, abridged edition by Gary van der Heuval, Baltimore and London: Johns Hopkins University Press, 1988, p. 29.
7. R. Ferrell, *Passion in Theory: Conceptions of Freud and Lacan*, p. 6.
8. William James, *The Principles of Psychology*, vol. II, New York: H. Holt, 1890, p. 452.
9. Daniel Stern, *The Interpersonal World of the Infant*, New York: Basic Books, 1985, p. 156.
10. Arnold H. Modell, *The Private Self*, Cambridge, MA and London: Harvard University Press, 1996, p. 205.
11. Ethel S. Person, *The Force of Fantasy. Its Roles, Its Benefits, and What It Reveals About Our Lives*, New York: HarperCollins, 1997, p. 226.
12. Joseph M. Jones, *Affects as Process. An Inquiry into the Centrality of Affect in Psychological Life*, Hillsdale, NJ and London: Analytic Press, 1995, p. 45.
13. A.R. Damasio, *Descartes' Error: Emotion, Reason and the Human Brain*, p. 159. And yet, with regard to this complex issue it is instructive to note that Wittgenstein throws doubt on the claim that certain sensations of feeling are to count as constituents of our emotions. He writes: 'Now granted – although it is extremely doubtful – that the muscular feeling of a smile is a constituent part of feeling glad – where are the other components? Well, in the breast and belly etc.! But do you really feel them, or do you merely conclude that they *must* be there? Are you really conscious of these localised feelings? – And if not – why are they supposed to be there at all? Why are you supposed to mean *them*, when you say you feel happy?' Ludwig Wittgenstein, *Remarks on the Philosophy of Psychology*, vol. I (translated by G.E.M. Anscombe), G.E.M. Anscombe and G.H. von Wright (eds), Oxford: Basil Blackwell, 1980, paragraphs 456 and 457.
14. Plotinus, *The Enneads*; translated by S. MacKenna, London: Faber and Faber, MCMLVI, The First Ennead, First Tractate, p. 21.
15. A.R. Damasio, *Descartes' Error: Emotion, Reason and the Human Brain*, pp. 159–60.
16. Ibid., p. xiv.

17. Blaise Pascal, *Pascal's Pensées*, with an introduction by T.S. Eliot, New York: E.P. Dutton, 1958, paragraph 396, p. 107.
18. Elisabeth Grosz, 'Bodies and knowledges: feminism and the crisis of reason', in L. Alcoff and E. Potter (eds), *Feminist Epistemologies*, London and New York: Routledge, 1993, p. 195.
19. A.R. Damasio, *Descartes' Error: Emotion, Reason and the Human Brain*, p. 252.
20. Nelson Goodman, *Languages of Art*, Brighton: Harvester Press, 1977, p. 7.
21. E. Grosz, 'Bodies and knowledges: feminism and the crisis of reason', p. 204.
22. Ibid., p. 205.
23. A.H. Modell, *The Private Self*, p. 199.
24. A.R. Damasio, *Descartes' Error: Emotion, Reason and the Human Brain*, pp. 174–5.
25. Ibid., p. 230.

Chapter 6

The terminology of affects

The question of classification and terminology

In view of the enormous variety of affective experiences, we often seek to identify some 'basic' emotions in order to attempt a temporary classification, and to attain some hierarchising terminology and working vocabulary. Perhaps we aspire to know which human affects are primary functions of our psychic life and which are derivatives. But then 'basic affects' are differently described by different inquirers who somehow reconnect affectual experiences to their own diverse basic assumptions, forming their own epistemic vocabulary. As Burrow suggests, our classificatory definitions are necessarily just as loose as the concepts for which they stand: 'The reason is that our social designations are dependent upon our personal affects, and must vary infinitely with the infinite variety of their emotional tones.'[1] Since we repeatedly confront these puzzling diversities, we are easily inclined to 'think' that a taxonomy of affects would provide a reassuring background of inquiry. Approximating the question by way of examples, we might just think of the dissimilar appreciation of affective attitudes in diverse epochs and cultures: courage and hope were respectively exalted in ancient Roman times and in the Middle Ages, while the inclination for compassion and humour are respectively loathed in totalitarian regimes and criminal organisations.

It is often asked whether being 'basic' primarily refers to a logical feature of a classification scheme, or whether it also says something about the affects classified.[2] Even though being basic is a property of our concepts and not of our emotions *per se*, our affectual vicissitudes do not remain unchanged by the different modes in which they are conceived. As a form of psychic behaviour, emotions are also constituted to some extent by the implicit theories that confer meaning upon our emotional concepts. So-called 'logical' issues are therefore inextricably interwoven with 'substantive' ones.[3] In Averill's view, simply because the concept of a particular emotion is basic within some classification scheme, it does not follow that the corresponding affect is somehow more fundamental than other emotions in the history of our affective vicissitudes.

One feature of the use of principles, such as being basic, primary, or fundamental, is that it tends to organise the whole domain of inquiry. And yet, since the many possible meanings of 'basicness' all have some claims to legitimacy, the generic notion of 'basic emotions' remains a source of problems. For one thing, the use of concepts tends to organise the domain of inquiry into paradigm cases, thus 'creating' instances that exhibit the full complement of concept-specific features, and cases that deviate to a greater or lesser degree from a conceptual focus. In this sense, concepts provide systematic principles of classification, which contrast with, say, merely practical, narrative, or piecemeal presentations.[4] These may even be literary presentations. Armon-Jones remarks that enumerative and descriptive endeavours simply exhibit similarities and differences between emotional phenomena, without organising them in such a way as to give priority as central to any particular group. It is certainly a virtue of such human products as 'concepts' that they go beyond mere enumeration in providing a more systematic scheme of classification. If used without prudence, however, the adherence to concepts invites theoretical bias concerning which cases are deemed to be primary defining instances of our affects.[5] Practical and narrative descriptions, on the other hand, are perhaps more neutral inasmuch as they do not ultimately reify any particular group of instances as central, basic, or primary. Their disadvantage, however, is that they are piecemeal, fragmentary, and contingent accounts. Therefore, we need some working discipline that may reconcile concepts and descriptions; a discipline that may function as a flexible scheme of order that does justice to the enormous variety of affects, and to our ways of talking about them. Talking about them also transforms them, by generating ever-new verbal receptacles. To meet this challenge, we could introduce the notion of a continuum, and of comparisons between different points on it. In view of the pervasive metaphoric nature of our human thinking, we should perhaps resort to the idea of a gradient, or spectrum of diversities, as a viable instrument to guide our inquiry. Instead of the stereotypical sequence of dichotomous dyads, we could strive to regard the terminology of affects as indicating continuities or intriguing differences. Contraries and oppositions imply that two binary terms are mutually exclusive and exhaustive of the field, and that one term defines the other as its negative. However, when such terms are *philo*sophically conceived as two among many others, they prove neither incompatible nor all-inclusive.[6]

In a more pragmatic outlook on continuities between different emotions, we of course cannot address ourselves to the core of the phenomena, which are too inscrutable to be directly perceived, but only to their manifestations: the domains in which they seem to share some psychic borders, acting not only as limitations but also eventually as receptacles in which they metabolise into something different. We cannot explore the essence of affects, but we can inquire into their multiple expressions, derivatives and tortuous cultural itineraries.[7]

When we ask whether any emotions are more prototypic than others, we can certainly say that in our customary categorisation of affects, anger is more 'prototypic' than chagrin, fear is more 'basic' than anxiety, pride more 'profound' than condescension – and so forth. Averill reminds us that during the Middle Ages, hope was regarded as a basic emotion while, today, it is regarded as secondary or derivative – if it is considered at all. In short, emotional constellations are not only constituted by social rules, but are sometimes made to function as the defining features of a culture and an age.[8] Thus, depending upon the epistemology that we inhabit, affects are differently hierarchised as basic or derivative, prototypes or varieties. Moreover, hierarchised affects also interdigitate with the more or less plausible attribution of affectual characteristics to different social roles: talking about imaginative servants, assertive housewives, compassionate soldiers and humble artists may generate a measure of epistemic dissonance in different cultures. This induces us to abandon the idea of an inquiry into the *intrinsic* nature of our affective life and opt for exploring the contingencies and the language of our inner vicissitudes. In the developments of our psychoanalytic view of affects we can, in fact, perceive a sequence of clinically productive metaphors, rather than an increasing understanding of the ultimate structure of our mind.

Culture often assists in developing inchoate linguistic tools for appreciating affective vicissitudes that could not have been thematised prior to the development of a particular set of descriptions, or descriptions that incipient vocabularies also help to generate. A number of theorists have explicitly or implicitly devised lists of 'primary' affects. For example's sake we could note that William James described anger, fear, love, hate, joy, grief, shame, and pride as the 'coarser emotions'[9] – perhaps in the sense of being the 'basic' ones. In elaborating upon Darwin's work, Tomkins described nine primary affects listed in the following order: interest, enjoyment, surprise, distress, fear, anger, disgust, contempt and shame.[10] As precursors of affects, Freud theorised the presence of two basic instincts ultimately classified as *eros* and *thanatos*.[11]

We constantly use the term 'affect' in scholarly psychoanalytic literature while avoiding the recognition that we hardly have a sufficient vocabulary to describe the variegated complexity of affective manifestations. We talk about 'affects-in-general' almost as we might talk in general about 'animals', that is, without problematising the comparative life styles of ants and condors, or cobras and dolphins. Of course we do use terms such as love and hatred, rage and sympathy, pride and shame, even though hardly conversant with their combinations and intricacies. In fact, we admire enormously the literary heritage of a culture, for we perceive it as an innovative and forceful generator of ways of approaching, exploring and differentiating our unfathomable affectual life. It is our symbolic potential for generating language that allows for the formulation of novel psychological features, which could not have been envisaged prior to some kind of appropriate symbolisation; our symbolic potential is not primarily geared to the 'task' of representing something which is thought to be 'out there', or inside us, but to the 'aspiration' for something new, which only springs to life by means of our novel symbolic instruments. In fact, our symbolic potential functions at its best in the service of epistemophily.[12] If there will be humans considering our times as an ancient epoch, they might, hopefully, regard our affective illiteracy in the way that we sympathetically regard the technologies of olden times.

As there are no theory-neutral definitions, we should be cautious in the contextual use of such terms as affect, emotion, feeling, passion, and mood. We should also note, with Jones, that even the apparent preference for the more scientific-sounding term 'affect' is sometimes justified on the grounds that the terms of our everyday vocabulary, words such as 'feeling' and 'emotion', are too difficult to define.[13] The problem with this propensity, however, is that for most people, the word 'affect' does not have much of an inner resonance; it can become almost a desiccated term, constantly reminding us that we are striving to speak 'scientifically'. Schafer presents a comparable position where he suggests that the terms 'affect', 'emotion' and 'feeling' cannot be differentiated: 'Such efforts have been made, but there is no general agreement as to their merit.'[14] Similarly, in the language of Rapaport: 'The term "affect" . . . will be used to stand for the terms "emotion" and "feeling" also, since there is no clear distinction in the literature of these terms.'[15]

For the sake of attaining some provisional way of exploring the mind's affective life and pursuing our endeavour, we could instrumentally refer to the 'definitions' of 'affect', 'emotion', 'feeling', 'mood', and 'passion' as provided by accredited sources of linguistic canons across our psychoanalytic culture. In recognition of our general epistemic habitat, we could for instance resort to the joint contribution of Laplanche and Pontalis[16] as well as to the 'dictionary' of Moore and Fine.[17] 'Affects indicate any affectual state, whether painful or pleasurable, vague or specific, whether in the form of a strong identifiable expression or in the form of a general tonality', as defined very comprehensively by Laplanche and Pontalis.[18] Thus, we could perhaps say that the term *affect* refers to the concept of a category of psychic phenomena that include disparate manifestations; it is therefore a rather generic term for different psychic conditions which may fluctuate between one another. With regard to *emotions*, Moore and Fine suggest that they 'refer to the manifestations of feelings which may also be outwardly observable'; they can also increase the turbulence of feelings and diminish our sense of control over what is happening.[19] When talking of *feelings* we 'refer to the central, subjectively experienced state (which may also be blocked from consciousness). Perceptions related to the immediate stimuli and their intrapsychic representations . . . determine the nature of a feeling state.'[20] *Moods* can be described as relatively enduring, complex, psychic states 'where the affective component is generally the most prominent feature. Moods are dynamic psychic constellations that regulate, contain, bind and express a complex mixture of affects.'[21] *Passions* could be viewed as intensified moods which are polarised by some specific object.[22] Surely, such minimal reference to terminological definitions should not be omitted, even though it would be tedious to further expand on it through extensive surveys.

Familiarity and continuities

The holistic conception of meaning on which hermeneutics is rooted, is expressed in the idea of the so called 'hermeneutic circle' whereby the understanding of a part is dependent upon the understanding of the whole, and vice versa. Similarly, the linguistic system with which we approach our affective life is not a domain of separate items between which certain extrinsic relations hold, but a system wherein the elements are themselves constituted by the differences and relationships between them. In Davidson's language, 'The one attribution rests on the supposition of many more – endlessly more.'[23]

In our psychic life and endeavours at self creation, we are often unable to clearly specify what it is that we want to achieve before developing the language with which we pursue a goal. Only our developing vocabularies make it possible for us to say what it is that we want to pursue. They create an opportunity to see something which could not have been envisaged prior to the inception of a new language and to those questions which the new vocabulary somehow makes possible for us.[24] The intriguing consequence of this dimension of research is that even if we could render psychic vicissitudes in 'hard' genetic or biochemical terms, this would not thereby tell the real story of our affective life, a story of which even our psychoanalytic culture offers only an allegory.[25] A 'scientific language', in fact, simply offers the familiarity and parsimony of its own figures. Ferrell suggests that 'The reader educated in the ways of the scientific genres would see the virtue of it in terms much like the advantage gained from using symbolic notation over natural grammar – it brings conceptual clarity, but it is not thereby "truer" of the relation it illustrates.'[26] In Rorty's synoptic view, the distinction between the domains of epistemology and hermeneutics is not a question of the difference between the 'sciences of nature' and the 'human sciences', or fact and value, or between objective knowledge and something more dubious: 'The difference is purely one of familiarity.'[27]

There is nothing privileged in certain accesses to reality; the claims of certain discourses rest on the basis of their being better known, and on readers having a greater facility with their narratives and metaphors. Even Freud occasionally approaches the question of the contingency of terms; that is, he wonders which of the tropes would better render the topic of psychological inquiry. The 'familiarity thesis' thus has a remarkable precursor: 'The deficiencies of our description would probably vanish if we were already in a position to replace the psychological terms by physiological or chemical ones. It is true that they too are only part of a figurative language; *but it is one with which we have long been familiar*, and which is perhaps a simpler one as well.'[28] The most powerful ideas make their presence felt holistically; thus, arguments will not be able to make their influence effective until the implications of the vocabulary permeate the system of ideas as a whole. Similarly, one must not underestimate the radical potential of an accumulation of localised efforts.[29]

Re-evaluation of our standard vocabularies forms part of irony's general frame work. It is this intentional outlook that suggests to interpreters that these attitudinal positions are, in fact, emotional, affective ones, and that they could be read as revealing some specific engagement on the part of the ironist; it is an affective but very rational response to a possible incongruity, or dissonance, that we vividly perceive.[30] The intellectual instruments provided by any extant epistemology will not allow us to dismantle – or, even better, to forget – the epistemic structures which it generates. Its language will at best allow us to beat its emissaries at *their own* game, but not to stop *those* sort of linguistic games, and opt for others. In a provocative, amplified way Burrow poses a comparable question: 'If the insane individual slogan *ego sum* is the sum of his ego, is it not equally true of our social ego with its . . . evaluations in the sphere of philosophy, politics and psychopathology, and of our broader predications generally?'[31] There seems to be something that characterises irony with even more particularity than the tension between the said and the unsaid: the 'edge of irony', in Hutcheon's language. While it may come into being through the semantic playing off of the stated and the unstated, irony is a 'weighted' mode of discourse in the sense that it is linguistically asymmetrical, unbalanced in favour of the silent and the unsaid, thus promoting incipient vocabularies and facilitating new familiarities. Hutcheon suggests that the tipping of the balance occurs in part through what is implied in the attitude of either the ironist or the interpreter: 'Irony involves the attribution of an evaluative, even judgemental attitude, and this is where the emotive or affective dimension also enters – much to the dismay of most critical discourse and most critics.'[32]

Therefore, when we speak about affects with a growing awareness of the form of life we inhabit and of the epistemic community in which we operate, we become suspicious of the idea of 'letting the data suggest'.[33] This could be a formula for replicating the inconspicuous mainstream values that some of us try to be ironic about. Longino argues that the intellectual practice of observation and reason do not exist in a purified form.[34] In an inchoate epistemic outlook we could, then, understand integrity not so much as purity but as wholeness, in that we can summon sufficient intellectual courage to tolerate the awareness of our historical condition, and do our best to reconnect the components of the enterprise. The idea of community is generally excluded by the more prestigious, non-ironic theories, which tend to be theories about some 'absolute' individual's knowledge. They address questions concerning the criteria that an individual's belief must satisfy in order to count as 'real' knowledge. The criteria are themselves perplexingly individualistic, making no reference to the subject's cultural context and vocabulary. In Longino's view the untenable assumption is that once we have settled the problem of what counts as an individual's knowing, there is no further problem of knowledge: 'Any other form of knowledge is just some form of individual knowledge or additive collections of individual knowledges.'[35]

We thus aspire to an inquiry into our affective life that is more based on continuities and transformations than on some conceptual taxonomy. We should be concerned that agreement about life worlds is primarily tactical. We could also be receptive to notions claiming that language is not essentially a device for representing the (inner) world, but an affective reality in which we live and operate. The monopoly of representational pursuits could almost be viewed as an illusion of perspective whereby one function of language usurps most of its disparate functions.[36] In a synoptic outlook we could adhere to Rescher's claim that 'the truth' is nothing but the prevalent consensus of the coalition of inquirers; once 'scientific progress' reaches a point at which 'a question is answered in a way which is thereafter maintained without change within the ongoing community of inquirers, then indeed it is the *true* answer to that question.'[37]

Vocabularies and perception of affects

As the deterioration of our affective lives is said to increase, theorists in the human sciences find themselves in search of a theory that can bring this degradation to a halt. Just as the classical hero must rescue a prototypical cherished value, person or place, so too the sought after theory should somehow demonstrate heroic qualities. It should be able, single-handedly, to rescue our ailing emotional life from the forces that have damaged it. And the inimical role, of course, can be assigned to either obnoxious theorisations *à la* Descartes, or else to benumbing, alienating conditions related to industrialisation, urbanisation or compulsive consumption. The theoretical assumptions of our psychological sciences are seen by some theorists as having the necessary intellectual power to perform this heroic feat, yet some decline to join the hunt for a salvaging theory. Perhaps we should ignore the frequent, cogent debates over what should constitute the basis for an appropriate theory of human affects and for an 'ethic' of intersubjective relations. We believe that a more contingent and pragmatic approach should be cultivated, and aim towards a preliminary exploration of the outlooks which constantly induce us to ignore and marginalise affects. Whereas some theorists concentrate on 'rescuing' our affective life, we should first endeavour to see how it has arrived at its present plight. If our view of affects has facilitated their exclusion and exploitation, then new and ulterior ways of perceiving our affectual vicissitudes should be explored. Our affective life will not be saved, or enhanced, by the power of theories, but rather through a transformed insight into our deeper self, and through transformed vocabularies with which to approach the predicament.

One dangerous virtue of our affective life is that precisely because it is so complex and elusive, it can be moulded to fit almost any theoretical framework. Thus, emotions have been variously described as visceral attitudes, pieces of knowledge, existential decisions, programmed drives, or unconscious evaluations; and of course such a list could be expanded on the basis of current literature in the field.[38] In the face of this complexity, we are understandably inclined to try to classify affects. Any attempt to hierarchise our affects is facilitated by confining our attention to single sentences and by avoiding an awareness of our vocabularies and language games. If we deal only with distinct parts of our language – such as sentences – it is easy to adhere to the 'fact' that some of our affective states make certain beliefs true by corresponding to them. The inquiry is more problematic, however, if we turn from individual sentences to vocabularies as wholes.[39] Even an approximate familiarity with psychological literature will make us alert to synchronic and diachronic differences in vocabulary; one need only think of the language games of 'orthodox' Freudians or 'militant' Kleinians, of 'teleological' Jungians or 'experimental' cognitivists. It is difficult to think of the mind's affective life as rendering one of these outlooks better than another, or as deciding between them. When the aspiration to describe the mind is not correlated to criteria-governed sentences within a single vocabulary – that is a 'firm' epistemology – but to vocabularies as wholes, then the idea of the mind 'deciding' which descriptions are the true ones becomes even more dubious. It is a healthy doubt in our view.

If we think of the general vocabulary in which our clinical hypotheses are formulated, it is easier to realise, for example, that Freud's vocabulary letting us predict behaviour more easily than Jung's does not mean that the mind is intrinsically Freudian, or that it has a Freudian structure. In the constant redescription of our affective life, we should be aware that we always make descriptions in the vocabulary of a current epistemology, and we should not take it for granted that the statements formulated in that idiom suffice to evaluate beliefs emanating from alternative epistemologies.[40] We should not automatically assume that the presence of a term in a given vocabulary ensures that it refers to something having a 'real essence'. In dealing with affects we thus come to renew our appreciation of nominalists, historicists, pragmatists – and even sophists. Our search for a vocabulary better than the one we currently use is probably inspired by the guidelines of daily making, doing and practising, rather than by the 'ideas' of finding, discovering and attaining the 'truth' of our affective life.

We should not so much focus on the inferential relations between propositions and arguments, for we should rather aim at comparing vocabularies. Perhaps very little can be achieved in this pursuit. It is a pursuit, however, which is supported by the conviction that a mono-epistemic view of our affective life and the consequent benumbment of our capacities for 'risky' listening are obscuring and blinding forces, however inconspicuous.[41] Through an awareness of terminology, and by comparing the vocabularies of different psychological cultures, we may avoid seeing theories as a simply converging series of discoveries about selfhood, that move closer and closer to the 'essential nature' of our psychic life. Rather, we aim to facilitate the possibility of gestalt switches by developing the capacity to make easier and more convincing transitions from one terminology to another.[42] This hoped-for greater mobility may not be much in itself. And yet a one-sided awareness of our affective life, together with an unwitting entrenchment in a given epistemology, are conditions increasingly to be dreaded. Potter suspects that it is the failure to pay attention to the occult distinction between a descriptive and a prescriptive analysis that allows theorists to negotiate without owning up to their discussion.[43] Ultimately, however, we could also suspect that all description is somehow a prescription inasmuch as it induces the listener, or the reader, to concentrate on one specific feature over another that automatically becomes peripheral and marginalised.

We should dread the possibility of remaining enclosed in the classificatory terminology in which we have been trained, especially when we associate only with those closer to us. Perhaps we should cherish ironists and strangers as sources of epistemic therapy.[44] The multiple presence of shocking strangers in literary genres creates a paradoxically harmonious contrast between the true and the untrue. Although we are conscious of such contradictions, we are above being frustrated by them because we are intrigued by the story itself. Conversely, in real life as in our inquiries we are not so much interested in the entertainment of the presentation as in the opening of ulterior modes of understanding.[45] The perception of ironic or puzzling juxtapositions induces us to appreciate the critical edge that is generated by the 'irony' of the situation; what is produced is an active cognition of incongruity that elicits emotional responses. A comparable outlook can be advocated with regard to our emotional life, where enlightening views can be gained by shifting our focus from distinct functions to our psychic life as a whole. Our appreciation of rationality does in fact change if we divert attention from single sentences to complexive vocabularies; it will similarly change if we shift our focus from the discrete functions of intelligence to 'intelligent' living.[46] Such transformation of perspective could be instantiated with reference to Damasio's observation of subjects with specific brain injuries. In these individuals, the faculties usually considered necessary and sufficient for rational behaviour are intact, as they have the requisite knowledge, attention, memory and flawless language, and as they can perform calculations and tackle the logic of abstract problems. However, because they display a marked alteration in the ability to experience feelings, their practical reason and decision making is so seriously impaired that it induces a constant violation of what would be considered personally advantageous.[47] If the individual is not emotionally fuelled, in spite of intact functions of intelligence, there is no integrated, intelligent living. A capacity to shift from parts to wholes seems to generate a sequence of novel perspectives which progressively reveal the affective derivation of our entire mental life.

NOTES

1. Trigant Burrow, 'The reabsorbed affect and its elimination', *The British Journal of Medical Psychology*, vol. VI(3), 1926, p. 209.
2. James R. Averill, 'In the eyes of the beholder', in P. Ekman and R.J. Davidson (eds), *The Nature of Emotion. Fundamental Questions* (series on Affective Science), New York and Oxford: Oxford University Press, 1994, pp. 7–8. Amélie Rorty's thesis is that emotions 'cannot be shepherded together under one set of classifications as active or passive; thought-generated and thought-refined or physiologically determined; voluntary or non voluntary; functional or malfunctional, corrigible or not corrigible by a change of beliefs. Nor can they be sharply distinguished from moods, motives, attitudes, character traits.' Introduction to A.O. Rorty (ed.), *Explaining Emotions*, Berkeley, CA: University of California Press, 1980, p. 1.
3. Ibid., p. 8. Trigant Burrow goes as far as to remark that 'our very highly complex mental evaluations in the sphere of philosophy and psychology . . . are built up precisely upon underlying autocratic presumptions.' 'The reabsorbed affect and its elimination', p. 211.
4. Claire Armon-Jones, *Varieties of Affect*, New York and London: Harvester Wheatsheaf, a division of Simon and Schuster International Group, date of publication not indicated. Oxford University thesis supervised by Kathleen Wilkes of St Hilda's College and Paul Snowdon of Exeter College, 1991.
5. Ibid., p. 13.

6. Elisabeth Grosz, 'Philosophy', in S. Gunew (ed.), *Feminist Knowledge: Critique and Construct*, London and New York: Routledge, 1990, p. 168. In a perspective of continuities, and as against a logic of oppositional dyads, Hume sees a continuum between 'courage' and 'pride'. 'In general we may observe, that whatever we call heroic virtue, and admire under the character of greatness and elevation of mind, is either nothing but a steady and well established pride and self-esteem, or partakes largely of that passion. Courage, intrepidity, love of glory, magnanimity, and all the other shining virtues of that kind, have plainly a strong mixture of self-esteem in them, and derive a great part of their merit from that origin.' David Hume, *Treatise on Human Nature*, L.A. Selby-Bigge (ed.), Oxford: Clarendon Press, 1988, III, paragraph 2, pp. 599–600.

7. For a discussion of this topic in the perspective of hermeneutic philosophy see Paul Ricoeur, *Oneself as Another* (translated by K. Blamey), Chicago and London, University of Chicago Press, 1992. See especially the chapters on the hermeneutics of the self, and on the paradoxes of personal identity.

8. J.R. Averill, 'In the eyes of the beholder', in P. Ekman and R.J. Davidson (eds) *The Nature of Emotion. Fundamental Questions*, p. 9.

9. William James, *Psychology. Briefer Course*, New York: Henry Holt, 1892, p. 374.

10. Silvan Tomkins, *Affect, Imagery, Consciousness*, vol. I, New York: Springer, 1988.

11. See, for instance, Sigmund Freud 'Three essays on the theory of sexuality', *Standard Edition*, vol. 7, 1905, pp. 135–243; Anna Freud, 'Comments on aggression', *International Journal of Psychoanalysis*, 1971, vol. 5, pp. 163–72; Sigmund Freud, 'The economic problem of masochism', *Standard Edition*, vol. 19, 1924, pp. 157–72.

12. The genesis of our symbolic capacity is discussed in Gemma Corradi Fiumara, *The Symbolic Function. Psychoanalysis and the Philosophy of Language*; see, for instance, the paragraphs entitled 'Generating versus using language', pp. 12–14, 'From the flow of emotion to the exchange of communications', pp. 191–4; Oxford, UK and Cambridge US: Blackwell, 1992.

13. Joseph M. Jones, *Affects as Process. An Inquiry into the Centrality of Affect in Psychological Life*, Hillsdale, NJ: Analytic Press, 1995, pp. 39–40.

14. Roy Schafer, *Retelling a Life*, New York: Basic Books, 1992, p. 275.

15. David Rapaport, 'On the psychoanalytic theory of affects', in M. Gill (ed.) *The Collected Papers of David Rapaport*, New York: Basic Books, 1967, p. 476.

16. Jean Laplanche and Jean-Bestrand Pontalis, *The Language of Psychoanalysis*, trans. D. Nicholson-Smith, New York: Norton, 1967.

17. Burness E. Moore and Bernard D. Fine (eds), *Psychoanalytic Terms and Concepts*, New Haven and London: The American Psychoanalytic Association and Yale University Press, 1990.

18. J. Laplanche and J. B. Pontalis *The Language of Psychoanalysis*, p. 9.

19. B.E. Moore and B.D. Fine, *Psychoanalytic Terms and Concepts*, p. 9.

20. Ibid., pp. 9–10.

21. Ibid., p. 121.

22. Ibid., p. 121. 'Remarkably, ongoing background emotional processes, those that occur in an everyday sense, are not much discussed by emotion theorists. The field of emotion has, instead, focused on short latency emotional reactions, longer duration moods, or the emotional predispositions referred to as temperament'. Robert Emde, 'Moving ahead: integrating influences of affective processes for development and for psychoanalysis', *The International Journal of Psychoanalysis*, vol. 80, 1999, pp. 317–40.

23. Donald Davidson, 'Paradoxes of irrationality', in R. Wollheim and J. Hopkins (eds), *The Philosophical Essays on Freud*, Cambridge, UK: Cambridge University Press, 1982, p. 302.

24. See G. Corradi Fiumara, *The Symbolic Function. Psychoanalysis and the Philosophy of Language*, p. 2.
25. This is argued by Robyn Ferrell in *Passion in Theory: Conceptions of Freud and Lacan*, London and New York: Routledge, 1996, p. 58.
26. Ibid., p. 58.
27. Richard Rorty, *Philosophy and the Mirror of Nature*, Oxford: Basil Blackwell, 1980, p. 321.
28. Sigmund Freud, 'Beyond the pleasure principle', (1920), vol. 18, *Standard Edition*, p. 60 (emphasis added). Struggling with the 'mind–body problem' Susanne Langer remarks: 'To turn "knowledge by acquaintance" into "knowledge by description" is not a simple procedure of reporting private experience, because the formal possibilities of language are not great enough to reflect the fluid structure of cerebral acts in psychical phase, by which the substructure below the threshold of sentience is suggested, guiding physical research on the highest of vital phenomena.' *Mind: An Essay on Human Feeling*, abridged edition by G. Van Der Heuval, Baltimore and London: Johns Hopkins University Press, 1988, p. 25.
29. This thesis is generally advocated by Miranda Fricker. See especially 'Knowledge as construct. Theorising the role of gender in knowledge', in K. Lennon and M. Whitford (eds), *Knowing the Difference. Feminist Perspectives in Epistemology*, London and New York: Routledge, 1994, pp. 95–109. In this connection Arnold Modell remarks that 'All sciences are autonomous, yet most share concepts that lie across their frontiers. Every discipline needs to create its own concepts and terminology in accordance with its special field of observation and theoretical requirements. In this sense every discipline is autonomous but the autonomy is only relative and not absolute.' *The Private Self*, Cambridge, MA and London: Harvard University Press, 1996, p. 198.
30. Linda Hutcheon, *Irony's Edge: The Theory and Politics of Irony*, London and New York: Routledge, 1994, p. 37.
31. Trigant Burrow, 'The reabsorbed affect and its elimination', *The British Journal of Medical Psychology*, vol. VI(3), 1926, p. 214.
32. L. Hutcheon, *Irony's Edge: The Theory and Politics of Irony*, p. 37.
33. See Helen Longino, *Science as Social Knowledge. Values and Objectivity in Scientific Inquiry*, Princeton, NJ: Princeton University Press, 1990, p. 218.
34. Ibid., p. 219.
35. Ibid., p. 231.
36. See Gemma Corradi Fiumara, *The Metaphoric Process. Connections between Language and Life*, London and New York: Routledge, 1995.
37. Nicholas Rescher, *Pluralism. Against the Demand for Consensus, For (though also against) Jürgen Habermas*, Oxford: Clarendon Press, 1995, p. 23. On this topic also see William James, *A Pluralistic Universe*, New York: Longmans-Green, 1912.
38. See Claire Armon-Jones, *Varieties of Affects*, p. 2.
39. For a discussion of these issues see Richard Rorty, *Contingency, Irony, and Solidarity*, Cambridge, UK: Cambridge University Press, 1989, p. 5.
40. Ibid., p. 6.
41. In this connection, see Gemma Corradi Fiumara, *The Other Side of Language: A Philosophy of Listening*, London and New York: Routledge, 1990.
42. R. Rorty, *Contingency, Irony, and Solidarity*, paragraph 1 of part I, 'The contingency of language', pp. 3–22. Also see G. Corradi Fiumara, *The Metaphoric Process. Connections between Language and Life*, especially the paragraph 'Problems of literality', and 'The pathology of literalness', pp. 52–60.
43. Elizabeth Potter, 'Gender and epistemic negotiation', in L. Alcoff and E. Potter (eds), *Feminist Epistemologies*, London and New York: Routledge, 1993, p. 170.

44. See G. Corradi Fiumara, *The Other Side of Language. A Philosophy of Listening*, especially the paragraphs 'Towards an awareness of benumbment', pp. 82–6, 'The listening experience as event' and 'The listening experience as transformation', pp. 90–5.
45. Ibid., 'The rebirth of thought processes', pp. 161–5.
46. See Antonio R. Damasio, *Descartes' Error: Emotion, Reason, and the Human Brain*, London: Papermac-Macmillan General Books, 1996, p. xiv.
47. Ibid., p. xiv.

Chapter 7

Affective knowledge

Affective components of reason

In psychoanalytic culture we learn that the subject is connected to its desires as much as to the world, and must therefore approach its representation of things through that double unbreakable connection between inner affects and external reality.[1] This 'special' human knowledge ultimately develops as the result of a tension between epistemic and affective capacities. The relational outlook of psychoanalytic research thus comes to engender an integrated, non-reductive, inclusionary form of knowledge. On the other hand, if we 'philosophically' regard mutual relational knowing as deriving from (or as a subcategory of) knowledge proper, we may ultimately generate a lifeless imitation, or caricature, of our human cognitive capacities.[2]

In this perspective, our sense of self could be seen as an amalgam that emerges from a combination of one's intrapersonal and external knowledge. This merger can come about in widely different ways, depending on the aspects of the person that happen to be accentuated in different cultural milieux for different forms of reciprocal knowing. A sense of self may thus refer to the balance struck by every individual between the promptings of inner affects and the pressures of the world. But the 'world', of course, begins with and includes *other* persons. Early relational knowledge is thus regarded as the basis for the development of *any* form of knowledge.[3] In this gaze, the initial, prolonged tie between infant and caretaker may be looked on as nature's 'effort' to ensure that personal intelligence is properly launched for ulterior development.[4] The mutual, relational knowing of early vicissitudes is constituted by innumerable affective adjustments to another's inner state, and by countless remedies for incomprehensible confrontations. The epistemic outcome of these affective and complex responses could be illustrated by resorting to one of James' suggestive analogies: 'The "philosophic brain" responds to an inconsistency or a gap in its knowledge, just as the "musical brain" responds to discord in what it hears.'[5]

Emotions, of course, may give rise to irrationality in some circumstances, while they are indispensable in others. It is in a 'false' and truncated 'culture' that only the former consideration is normally taken into account.[6] The human expressions that we describe as 'rhetorical strategies' may be part of mental efforts to cope culturally with our affective life, and may even be expected to underlie all thought. In relational knowledge, the difference between the many layers of our rationality could be generically thought of as the difference in degree allowed in the contest between, roughly, the 'pleasure principle' and the 'reality principle', between one's own desire and that of another. In theoretical thought, conversely, the strategy of intellectual revision is prevalent and paramount, so much so that it even tends to transform any relational knowledge into a substitute, or simulacrum, of itself. An overly intellectual way of looking at relational knowledge as a variety of knowledge proper may indicate the expression of a wish for mastery *over* the external circumstances and *over* the epistemic connections which are used in interpersonal life – not a wish to relate. The knowledge in which affects are especially relevant is of course our relational, interpersonal knowledge. In the absence of specific adverse circumstances, we are inclined to use intersubjective vicissitudes to develop this knowledge.[7] When the upsurge of affects is utilised, rather than eschewed, we can progressively rearrange our relational knowing, even when it is not explicitly stated or recognised. The newly developed knowledge may then function as an affectively suitable background for the generation of ulterior reciprocal adjustments. This knowledge does not only function in the sense that it influences the subsequent course of interactions, it is also essential to the inner reorganisation and re-evaluation of previous vicissitudes. The current exchanges that influence a conceptual reorganisation of our past also determine ways to achieve future goals. In this sense, then, both our past and our future are creatively influenced in a sort of circular dynamics. Yet when the growth of relational knowledge is opposed, the affects and cognitions will remain 'untested' and in contradiction with the motives that underpin actions.[8] It will be evident that where this mechanism applies, the task of the overarching agency of the intelligent ego – or the representer of representations – will be made particularly complex because of the conflicts between internal schemas. Thus, intelligence could not only be considered as a mechanism of survival but, paradoxically, almost as a symptom, or as the result of our difficulties in personal and interpersonal vicissitudes.

Scheman suggests that even accomplished epistemologists may occasionally feel frightened with their own children because the application of habitual tactical moves will not suffice, or may even have disastrous effects.[9] Under certain circumstances the jargon of philosophy or of any official discipline may be unnecessary, even if without it we may often feel defenceless. This is exactly the problem, however, because there is no need for an insulating mask, and we may have to 'simply' face the prospect that under our epistemology there is an insufficient epistemophily. When there are no enforceable constraints for the questions to be asked, persons in distress may express needs and expect interlocutors to speak honestly, in the sense of saying things that somehow matter to them, and are unrelated to *their* favourite generic questions. In certain circumstances, it is of course less disquieting to be epistemological than epistemophilic.

In the foreclosure of any manifestation of empathic knowledge, something potentially detrimental inevitably takes place. When the role of emotional components is sensed at a distance, but there is fear of confronting it in the relation, both our cognitive and affective functions are damaged. If the damage is not sufficiently recognised, the closure of that specific part of relational knowledge is silently stipulated, favouring the instillation of splitting habits that should then function as an ordinary procedure. This process, of course, is the prerequisite for attitudes of disaffectation and detachment. In simple terms, the contrary, of 'love', for persons, knowledge, or anything else, is not really 'hatred', but ultimately induced indifference. Conversely, empathic confrontations that are accepted carry the implication of an unknown future that can be seen as a potential impasse but also as an opportunity. Interlocutors may intuitively recognise that an occasion for some kind of innovation is being offered, even though some danger of derailment is impending. Those confrontations in which an extant epistemology does not suffice – and epistemophily becomes necessary – may initially be experienced as a disquieting, *unheimlich*, interpersonal contingency. The situation is thus open to moves that are more affective than logical. What must be decided is whether or not to use the opportunity. These confrontations somehow point to some potential, emerging feature of the intersubjective condition. The eloquently described 'moments' of the therapeutic relation articulated by the Stern group as 'present moments', 'now moments', and 'moments of meeting',[10] while exhibiting different relational features, all seem to be characterised by the potential to integrate affects, that is, by the capacity to endure affective states as an alternative to eschewing or denying them.

The culturally induced denial of affects entails a comparable lack of awareness, thus lending plausibility to the misleading myth of 'dispassionate investigation'. In this restrictive gaze, emotions are, at best, reduced to the role of inspiring hypotheses for investigation. As Jaggar suggests, 'Emotions are allowed this because the so called logic of discovery sets no limits on the idiosyncratic methods that investigators may use for generating hypotheses.'[11] The ancillary and marginalised role of affects in the pursuit of knowledge is probably due to our induced illiteracy in the realm of the mind's affective life,[12] for we often speak of 'emotions' as we do of 'animals', without really caring about whether we are referring to industrious ants, compassionate dolphins, or epistemic humans.

As is commonly known, under certain circumstances emotion does disrupt reasoning. There is, of course, wisdom in the common belief that uncontrolled emotion can be a cause of irrational behaviour: the evidence abounds in folk psychology and is probably the source of the advice, which is often directed to purported sub-rational creatures, to keep emotions at a distance and not be too influenced by them. In this cultural climate, we usually conceive of emotions as an unsolicited psychic function that accompanies our rational thinking. In this restrictive view, if emotions are a source of pleasure, we should enjoy them as a luxury, and if they are frustrating, we should suffer them as an unwelcome intrusion.[13] Most accounts of cognition, in fact, leave emotions and feelings out of their overall concept of mind; they generally resist the inclusion of emotions and feelings in their treatment of cognitive processes. Affects are considered elusive entities, unsuited to sharing in the process of the thoughts that they none the less qualify.[14] In contemporary neuroscience, however, we increasingly encounter significant suggestions such as 'Feelings are just as cognitive as any other perceptual image, and just as dependent on cerebral-cortex processing as any other image.'[15] Both the exploration and development of our rationality probably require that greater consideration be given to the 'vulnerability' of its central affective core. Damasio, moreover, is preoccupied with the acceptance of the role of feelings without there being a sufficient understanding of their complex biological and socio-cultural structure: 'The best example of this attitude can be found in the attempt to "explain" bruised feelings or irrational behaviour by appealing to surface social causes or the action of neurotransmitters, two explanations that pervade social discourse as presented in the visual and printed media; this lack of understanding is the cause of harm.'[16] As this 'lack of understanding' *pervades* our cultural life, even those situations where it could become manifest remain largely obscured. In fact, inter-personal and ethical behaviour are not primarily a matter of weighing competing values and making the proper 'rational' choices. What is crucial are the acts of empathic attention which *precede* a choice. In Murdoch's view, ethical life is not something that is switched off between occurrences of explicit moral choices; it is the quality of interpersonal life between such choices that is indeed decisive.[17] This is her argument: 'If we consider what the work of attention is like, how continuously it goes on and how imperceptibly it builds up structures of value round about us, we shall not be surprised that at crucial moments of choice most of the business of choosing is already over.'[18]

Expanding the conditions of knowledge

Instead of thinking in terms of a division between logical knowledge and affective practices, we could regard 'pure' knowledge as a form of practice involved in struggling for theoretical ascendancy where dominant and subordinate discourses compete with each other.[19] Thus, instead of opposing reason to its *others*, we might work to expand the general scope of reason. According to Grosz, this attitude would not reverse the relation between reason and its 'lesser' *others*, but instead expand reason so that its expelled elements could be included again.[20] We seek, in fact, to develop the sort of reason that is not separate from life, but rooted in its complexity. We often think of knowledge 'proper' in terms of 'knowing that' while we generally think of practices and modes of being in terms of 'knowing how'. As a precursor of these possible transformations, Ryle[21] attempted to develop an idea of 'knowing that' in terms of 'knowing how', and to conceive of 'knowing that' as a variety of 'knowing how'. Dalmiya and Alcoff suggest that the Ryleans can be happy with a reversed, but perhaps reductionist, account of 'knowing that' in terms of 'knowing how'.[22] Their own project, however, is to *expand* the scope of knowledge: unlike Ryleans they 'want to *add* to the received list of types of knowing' rather than to reverse it or substitute it with one single, abstract notion.[23] Within the domain of practical activities that can be associated with any 'doing' word such as the *verb* 'to know', we can identify relational propensities that seem to disappear altogether at the level of a more prestigious substantive word like 'knowledge', which is a 'supreme' term indeed. Abstract nouns imply a further level of linguistic achievement which claims to 'surpass' practical matters while they, indeed, lose contact with their germinal source. Laborious activities like cultivating crops, dancing, and working, for example, seem to involve a greater complexity than may be suggested by the nouns 'agriculture', 'dance' and 'work'.[24]

In trying to appreciate the cognitive status and epistemic relevance of affective knowledge, we must also confront the common paradox of definition in that instances of knowing are usually identified as whatever may satisfy the definition of knowledge.[25] Then, the very definition of knowledge may be unduly restrictive inasmuch as it reduces the scope of the definiendum by excluding instances of affective and relational knowing. If we resort to the variegated instances of relational knowing, which are especially conspicuous in the domain of clinical experience, we can appreciate that pretheoretic explorations of relational knowing often exceed conventional definitions of knowledge. The traditional conception of knowledge seems ultimately informed by what has been called the 'intellectualist legend', in the sense of cognitive or epistemic functions restricted to a domain of thinking that is said to be the detached and 'objective' apprehension of 'reality'.

The innumerable and appropriate instances of interpersonal knowing – that is, of skill in relational knowledge – suggest the need for a more pragmatic turn in epistemology. We need not look beyond attitudes to some apprehension of truth in order to characterise relational skills as epistemically significant. According to Dalmiya and Alcoff, we *know* when we non-accidentally succeed.[26] And they go on to ask whether this compromises our ability to claim that these ways of knowing are indeed genuine forms of knowledge: 'After all, replacing "truth" with "success" might appear to play right into the traditional critic's point that the "pragmatic" is not "epistemic". On the other hand, this is where the strength of the new epistemology might lie.'[27] Indeed, they strive to dislodge truth as the sole epistemological norm. Knowing is not necessarily a matter of propositionally articulating what the case is, but it can also be a sort of relational and affective involvement with the world, that is, the kind of relation that is the precursor to *all* knowledge. Of course, one could object that the knowledge status that we advocate for relational knowing differs from knowledge in the traditional sense in at least one important aspect: relational knowing can be a matter of degree, quite unlike 'knowledge proper', which is an all-or-nothing affair. Yet, if we are not pre-emptively constrained by a reductionist procedure, this asymmetry in what remain genuine cases of knowing can be ultimately irrelevant.[28]

Relational knowing

There is a tendency to refer to persons suffering from narcissistic, psychosomatic, or 'perverse' psychic structures as difficult interlocutors – or 'difficult patients'. In

McDougall's view, however, it would be more appropriate to think in terms of 'difficult encounters' between patient and therapist.[29] It is known that the inner world of the so-called 'classical' neurotic presents just as many difficulties in the course of analysis as in the more primitive systems of defence. Even though a psychic phenomenon may be relatively easy to decode, the analytic process is not rendered any easier because of this.[30] Unconscious vicissitudes that are simple enough to 'understand' are not at all simple to analyse with a therapeutic aim. Thus, we could provisionally think that the psychoanalytic function is best served in the light of a transition from understanding to 'standing-by' the patient:[31] standing by in the effort to develop mutual arrangements of affective coexistence. In McDougall's gaze, standing by involves the capacity to develop, share, and use the sort of relational knowing which may unblock the internal impasse of the suffering subject. In fact, if we assume that representation is in the service of action, we may be truly puzzled by seeing creatures continue, for instance, to seek comfort from persons who reject them. If we also assume that representations of some kind are required for these efforts to take place, then they must omit whatever information is incompatible with the enterprise.[32] We might argue that this information could simply be removed, suppressed, denied, or rendered subconscious, even though derivatives of that 'knowledge' are likely to entail some sort of oblique representation. What will be required, however, is the mental effort to ensure that this information not be used in the regulation of reciprocities. If we assume that originally, most of the time together is spent in active mutual regulation of our own and of the other's states in the service of some coexistential goal, then essential omissions present a major problem. Thus, the 'style' of forgetting disquieting information is not to be viewed as an option but rather as a necessity, as a constraint. Standing by the analysand involves a capacity to participate precisely in these constraints – however inconspicuous.

The distortion or decrease of implicit relational knowledge thus seems to require the internalisation of two 'incompatible' sets of rules: one that preserves accuracy but does not meet the survival needs of the individual, and one that sacrifices accuracy but allows for the need to create liveable reciprocities; this is a need that regards personal comfort and maintenance of the relationship with caregivers.[33] Paradoxically, no intelligible reference to individuals or to their development can take place without a prior reference to their early status as absolute 'subjects', that is, to their prenatal and original conditions of dependency. The psychoanalytic standing-by (as distinct from mere understanding) serves to attract the patient's inner incompatibilities to a more dynamic re-approachable knowledge of reciprocities.[34] However, even if our inner world were not too heavily burdened by such incompatibilities and even if our reasoning strategies were perfectly tuned, they would not cope easily with the uncertainty and complexity of personal and social problems. Our fragile instruments of rationality seem to constantly need special assistance.[35]

Of course, poignant emotions may impair the quality of relational knowledge, but failures of rationality are also due to the influence of constraints such as obedience, conformity and the desire to preserve the esteem of group leaders; these are inclinations that do not often become manifest as emotions and feelings. Indeed, we are nearly illiterate in the identification and reading of feelings, and have hardly a working terminology. For example, seeking consensus, with its related affects, is doubtlessly a good thing in various respects. The impetus to consensus unquestionably resonates with the human predicament: it reflects our inclination to adhere to epistemic standards, or our deep-rooted propensity to accept what others do, in order to achieve the comforts of easy communication and solidarity. Consensus can often provide us with the reassuring feeling of being 'on the right track'. We cannot forget, however, the potentially disastrous consequences of compensatory quests for conformity and normality. Damasio suggests that the effects of a 'sick culture' on a normal adult system of reasoning might appear to be less dramatic than the effect of a focal area of brain damage in that same normal adult system.[36] Yet he also recognises that there are various counter examples – in the totalitarian regimes closely witnessed in the twentieth century, sick cultures easily prevailed upon a presumably normal machinery of reason with devastating consequences. This connects with the fear that sizable sectors of Western society, which are almost sub-cultures, may become other tragic counter examples.[37] Imbalances in conformity and adaptation could involve detrimental outcomes for which we hardly have a vocabulary, such as the obscure and deadening pathology of indifference. Thus, the most dangerous of human perversions may be the most vulnerable to obscurity, and the more severe problems may be the inconspicuous ones.[38] In some patients with a serious mental disorder, there is no sign that they feel for others, and no sign of embarrassment or anguish in the face of a sad turn of events. The overall condition of affects is best described as 'shallow'. In less extreme cases, that are amenable to treatment, feelings are gradually restored and patients begin to manage their lives much to their own benefit. The central question, of course, concerns the prevented maturation of affects or their extinction as a result of cultural vicissitudes, and the consequent deterioration of an integrated intelligence – the mind's affective life. In other words, there are forms of psychic indifference which seem to nearly coincide with the impairment of feelings and emotions that derive from brain damage.[39]

The founding of ethics upon the twin pillars of human reason and will, may ultimately come to appear as an act of presumption. By denigrating affective and intuitive knowledge, we sever our ties with the mind's inner life. But the violence of abstraction operates in other ways as well. Wrenching an 'ethical' problem from its embedded context, detaches the problem from its roots. Not only does this detachment deny the cognitive force of affects, but it also obscures the emotional power which we unwittingly confer upon our purported adhesion to 'pure reason'. In general, what traditional knowledge tends to neglect is a notion that clearly emerges from the study of subjects with specific brain lesions, such as those described by neurophysiologists like Damasio, Sacks and Almeida: the notion that 'Reduction in emotion may constitute an equally important source of irrational behaviour.'[40] It is interesting, though, that Damasio proceeds to qualify the statement with this comment: 'The *counterintuitive* connection between absent emotion and warped behaviour may tell us something about the biological machinery of reason.'[41] But then, why should this connection be counterintuitive? The idea that reduction in emotion is as dangerous as uncontrollable emotion in producing irrational behaviour is in fact an *intuitive* connection to a great many human beings. The author, then, must have correctly assumed that some pervasive intellectualist epistemology is definitively not hospitable to intuitions regarding the indispensable synergy between thinking and feeling.

Affects and cognition

The prestigious dominance of our concerns for 'truth conditions' may perhaps serve the latent function of persistently ignoring affects so as to render them marginal, almost becoming a caricature of their function; it seems that in 'seeking truth', it is mandatory not to appreciate, evaluate, or feel. If we also consider that no 'generally acclaimed' and uncontroversial theory of truth is available, we could see that only the negative function of this dominance seems to be at work. If we also, incidentally, note that the different branches of science do not seem to openly acknowledge the proclaimed benefits of truth theories, then we could begin to think that it is the negative results that are tangible in a compelling way. To eschew this restrictive influence of the dominance of 'truth', we should better explore the cognitive function of affects, at least in the sense that (roughly speaking) affective states are cognitive in virtue of relating to objects.

In the perspective of our dominant epistemic tradition, emotions, in the 'past', were generally regarded as non-cognitive states inasmuch as they were viewed as inner conditions with which objects are only contingently connected. Emotions, moreover, were essentially identifiable as simple 'qualities' of our psychic life, being perhaps comparable to our experiences of pleasure and pain.[42] Conversely, it has recently been maintained that emotions are intentional states that involve the cognitive appraisal – or the appraising cognition – of disparate objects.[43] In fact, the adjective 'cognitive' appears in various domains of psychological inquiry, with applications ranging from stimulus processing to thinking in general, or from early vicissitudes to the construction of reality. This extended usage allows us to appreciate that even theories of affects can be legitimately thought of as somehow belonging to the cognitive tradition. The evaluation which is at the heart of each affective state is also what differentiates one emotion from another. Our agitation should be labelled anger, rather than fear, if we believe that someone has insulted us but was not about to attack us. In fact, our evaluation of the situation may have been wrong: somebody was about to attack us, and he is not the person who insulted us. Nevertheless our emotional state is still one of anger rather than fear, for our emotion is caused by what we 'cognise' about the situation and its relevance to us. Emotions are an important source of knowledge about ourselves, and of information on how we fare in our lives. We actually learn from our emotions. If we experience anger, for example, this tells us about our ways of evaluating and coping with the conditions of our lives. If we had not realised it before, we learn from anger that someone has offended us, and we even learn about the vulnerability that has led us to react in a particular way.[44] Thus, one of the inconspicuous but persistent myths for us to dispel is that emotions are irrational, or unrelated to thinking and reasoning. Contemporary literature extending from the domain of psychoanalysis to the neurosciences seems to converge in the belief that affects and intelligence may function as a synergy, which is probably why humans beings – no doubt highly intelligent beings – are such profoundly emotional creatures. In fact, whenever we experience an emotion, it indicates that something personally important is happening inside us. Far from being irrational, affects have a logic of their own that is based on meanings that we construct from the disparate situations of our lives.

If we are constrained by an unduly narrow idea of our cognitive functions, it seems to follow that emotions to which we cannot ascribe attitudes that entail a truth commitment are ultimately *non*-cognitive states. Of course, it is not to all emotions that these truth commitment features may be attributed; yet even in these cases we would not want to regard such emotions as entirely non-cognitive.[45] In calling emotions non-cognitive, we assimilate them by default to the kind of other non-cognitive phenomena such as certain pleasures and pains. In general, intentional states involve the conceptualisation of an object and not just the drive discharge. We are only now gradually discarding the immemorial habit of considering emotions irrational and as having nothing to do with what we think about. Our evaluation of what is happening in our daily occupations, their long-range existential consequences, in fact constitute primary causes of the emotions we experience. As Lazarus points out, 'appraisal' is the generally accepted word for these evalua-tions.[46] We have culturally inherited notions of reason that tend to subjugate and belittle our emotional reactions. We sometimes say that 'animals' live by emotion. In contrast, reason is said to represent the highest development of the mind and is thought to be capable of keeping in check our primitive emotions. To excel as humans beings seems to require that we exercise strong control over our affects. We say that an emotion is generated when a person with certain goals and beliefs about self and world appraises that what is happening is either harmful or beneficial.[47] Therefore, this essential appraisal *does* depend on reason, even though the reasoning may not have been propositionally cogent.

Lazarus and Smith have recently distinguished between knowledge and appraisal as playing different roles in the generation of an emotion.[48] *Knowledge* has to do with what we believe (and therefore with what we think we know) about how things work in the world. *Appraisal* is an evaluation of this knowledge, focusing on the significance of what is happening for one's personal well-being. Lazarus and Smith subsequently argue that knowledge is a necessary but not sufficient condition of emotion, while appraisal is both necessary and sufficient.[49] As appraisal is also an affective valuation, in this sense, it takes emotion to recognise other emotions. If emotions are systematically foreclosed we may hardly want to produce a knowledge which is increasingly detached from appraisal; yet once human beings gain access to knowledge, they cannot but appraise what they know. This of course transforms their knowledge and also creates ruptures along the main axis of our reigning epistemologies.

Lazarus suggests that a child who is unable to recognise an external source of thwarting, to sense that self-esteem has been lowered or to infer the basis of blame, cannot experience anger as it is appraised and experienced by an adult.[50] In his gaze, the crucial research task for appraisal theory is to explore what humans beings at different developmental stages know about how things work in the world, together with their capacity to evaluate the meaning relevant to the generation of an emotion. Emotions occur because people come to understand that they have a personal stake in confrontation with another person, the outcome of which could involve either harm or benefit. Appraisal, which is based on what one knows about the world and defined as the way this knowledge is evaluated, refers to the process through which people sense the connection between events and personal well-being. Each emotion is the result of an evaluation of the specific harm or benefit that has already taken place, or will eventuate in reciprocal adjustments. The process of appraisal results in what we could call 'relational meaning'. To understand emotional development requires that we also understand what a creature, at any stage of maturation, can sense about the way things work; we must understand the individual's knowledge of emotion-relevant variables, as well as the capacity to make a complex set of appraisal decisions that combine to produce the relational meaning. It is indeed a central task in the study of our affective development. We could even hypothesise that in the complex development of our psychic life we need an alternation of prevalently affective and prevalently cognitive moments. Perhaps a measure of emotional tension, or displeasure, is always required in order to create the 'leap' necessary to any form of integration of new cognitive elements. Further development and inclusion of cognitive schemes is only possible on the basis of tension created by some disturbance. However, if we are overwhelmed, or too desperate, to even allow for a psychic awareness of such disturbances, we cannot use them for cognitive growth. We have to be mature enough to allow for some *bearable* pain in order to enhance our capacity for intellectual growth. The 'sweet pain' of curiosity, for example, is often at work in our relational and creative knowing.

In the analysis of affect, both epistemic attitudes and objecthood are perhaps given a more central role than they deserve. There is a range of affective states that exhibit varying degrees of independence from the concept of object. Armon-Jones, for example, proposes that objectual and objectless types of affect are in general denoted by the terms 'emotion' and 'mood', respectively.[51] By means of a continuum model, we can appreciate that instances of emotion differ considerably in respects that are separate from their shared objecthood. This diversity precludes the possibility of establishing any strict or exclusive distinctions between moods, and the 'class' of all emotion instances. Generic emotional states, or moods, seem to call into question the assumption that affects are cognitive in virtue of relating to objects. Armon-Jones suggests in this connection that affective moods, in general, are *also* cognitive states because they involve construals which, though undifferentiated, are modes of conceptualising experience.[52] Her arguments point to a correlation between the distance of an emotion from the domain of compelling objects, or objects that are causally sufficient to explain it, and its susceptibility to the influence of a prior inner mood. It follows that the closer an emotion is to the blind, objectless, end of the continuum, the more vulnerable it is to the modifying or constituting forces of the subject's prevailing inner mood.

NOTES

1. See on this point Robyn Ferrell, *Passion in Theory: Conceptions of Freud and Lacan*, London and New York: Routledge, 1996, p. 75.
2. Daniel Goleman remarks that 'academic intelligence' has little to do with emotional life; 'People with high I.Q. can be stunningly poor pilots of their private lives.' He argues that 'academic intelligence' offers virtually no preparation for the turmoil – or opportunity – that life's vicissitudes bring. Emotional aptitude is a meta-ability determining how well we can use whatever other skills we have, including raw intellect. *Emotional Intelligence. Why It Can Matter More Than I.Q.*, Bloomsbury, 1996, pp. 34–6. Peirce remarks that 'the development of Reason requires as a part of its occurrence . . . all the colouring of all qualities of feeling, including pleasure in its proper place among the rest.' C.S. Peirce, C. Hartsborne and P. Weiss (eds), *Collected Papers of Charles Sanders Peirce*, Cambridge, MA: Harvard University Press, 1931–1935, vol. 1, paragraph 615.
3. This topic is discussed in Gemma Corradi Fiumara, *The Symbolic Function. Psychoanalysis and the Philosophy of Language*, Oxford, UK and Cambridge, US: Blackwell, 1992. See especially chapter 11 'From biological life to dialogic relations', and chapter 12 'The maturation of knowledge', pp. 154–94. In Kernberg's view 'The world of object representations . . . gradually changes and comes closer to "external" perceptions of the reality of significant objects throughout childhood and later life without ever becoming an actual copy of the environmental world. Intrapsychic "confirmation" is the ongoing process of reshaping the world of object representations under the influence of the reality principle, or ego maturation and development, and through cycles of projection and introjection.' Otto Kernberg, *Object Relations Theory and Clinical Psychoanalysis*, New York: Jason Aronson, 1979, p. 34.
4. This issue is discussed in Howard Gardner, *Frames of Mind. The Theory of Multiple Intelligences*, London: Fontana Press, 1993, pp. 243–5.
5. William James, *The Principles of Psychology*, vol. I, Dover Publications, 1950, chapter XXIV, 'Instinct', p. 430.
6. 'Human intelligence is not just knowing more, but reworking, recategorising, and thus generalising information in new and surprising ways'. J. Rosenfeld, *The Invention of Memory*, New York: Basic Books, 1988, p. 193.
7. This topic is widely discussed in Daniel Stern, Louis Sander, Jeremy Mahum, *et al.*, 'Non-interpretative mechanisms in psychoanalytic therapy. The "something more" than interpretation', *The International Journal of Psycho-Analysis*, vol. 79, 1998, pp. 903–21. With regard to reciprocal adjustments Goleman remarks that 'recognising a feeling as it happens is the keystone of emotional intelligence. An inability to notice our true feelings leaves us at their mercy. The art of relationship is, in large part, skill in managing emotions in others.' *Emotional Intelligence*, p. 43.
8. This hypothesis is suggested by Derek Bolton and Jonathan Hill in *Mind, Meaning and*

Mental Disorder. The Nature of Causal Explanation in Psychology and Psychiatry, Oxford, New York and Tokyo: Oxford University Press, 1996, p. 317.

9. Naomi Scheman, *Engenderings. Construction of Knowledge, Authority and Privilege*, London and New York: Routledge, 1993, p. 236.

10. 'A "present moment" is a unit of dialogic exchange that is relatively coherent in content, homogeneous in feeling and oriented in the same direction towards a goal.' The term 'now moment' – borrowed from Walter Freeman – is a special kind of 'present moment', one that gets lit up subjectively and affectively, pulling one more fully into the present.

    'A "now moment" is an announcement of a potential emergent property of a complex dynamic system. Although the history of its emergence may be untraceable, it is prepared for with fleeting or pale prior apparitions, something like a motif in music that quickly and progressively prepares for its transformation into the major theme. Still, the exact instant and form of its appearance remain unpredictable.'

    'The "moment of meeting" is the nodal event in this process because it is the point at which the intersubjective context gets altered, thus changing the *implicit relational knowing* about the patient–therapist relation.' D. Stern *et al.*, 'Non-interpretative mechanisms in psychoanalytic therapy. The "something more" than interpretation', pp. 912–13.

11. Alison M. Jaggar, 'Love and knowledge: emotion in feminist epistemology', in A.M. Jagger and S.R. Bordo (eds), *Gender/Body/Knowledge: Feminist Reconstruction of Being and Knowing*, New Brunswick, NJ and London: Rutgers University Press, p. 155.

12. Moreover, 'feeling' has acquired 'in the hearts of platonising thinkers a very opprobrious set of implications; and one of the great obstacles to mutual understanding (in philosophy) is the use of words eulogistically and disparagingly . . . ' William James, *Principles of Psychology*, p. 186.

13. This point is made by Antonio R. Damasio in *Descartes' Error: Emotion, Reason and the Human Brain*, London: Papermac-Macmillan General Books, 1996, p. 52.

14. Miranda Fricker suggests that affects cannot be adequately understood if they are sharply contrasted with reason in the sense that they are a 'discharge' of sorts as they were construed or theorised at the beginning of psychoanalytic culture. A conception of reason which is sharply contrasted with the domain of affects is misleading in the sense of being primarily a technical or formal conception of reason. We should first re-establish what we might call an integrated, fuller concept of reason and avoid remaining ensnared into an essentialistic approach to our own words. 'Knowledge as construct. Theorising the role of gender in knowledge', in K. Lennon and M. Whitford (eds), *Knowing the Difference. Feminist Perspectives in Epistemology*, London and New York: Routledge, 1994, pp. 95–109.

15. A. Damasio, *Descartes' Error*, p. 159.

16. Ibid., p. 246. Damasio further argues: 'Knowing about the relevance of feelings in the processes of reason does *not* suggest that reason is less important than feelings . . . On the contrary, taking stock of the pervasive role of feelings may give us a chance of enhancing their positive effects and reducing their potential harm. Specifically, without diminishing the orienting value of normal feelings, one would want to protect reason from the weakness that abnormal feelings or the manipulation of normal feelings can introduce in the process of planning and deciding . . . I do not believe that knowledge about feelings should make us less inclined to empirical verification. I only see that greater knowledge about the physiology of emotion and feeling should make us more aware of the pitfalls of scientific observation.'

17. Iris Murdoch, *The Sovereignty of Good*, London: Cox and Wyman, 1970, p. 37.

18. Ibid., p. 37.

19. See Elisabeth Grosz, 'Philosophy' in S. Gunew (ed.), *Feminist Knowledge: Critique and Construct*, London and New York: Routledge, 1990, p. 168.

20. Ibid., p. 169.

21. This general thesis has been advocated by Gilbert Ryle in *The Concept of Mind*, London: Hutchison, 1949.

22. Vrinda Dalmiya and Linda Alcoff, 'Are "Old wives' tales" justified?', in L. Alcoff and E. Potter (eds), *Feminist Epistemologies*, London and New York: Routledge, 1993, p. 233.

23. Ibid., p. 233.

24. A comparable argument appears in Gemma Corradi Fiumara, *The Other Side of Language: A Philosophy of Listening*, London and New York: Routledge, 1995, pp. 1–2.

25. See V. Dalmiya and L. Alcoff, 'Are "old wives' tales" justified?', p. 231. It is becoming clearer that by stipulating the definiendum of epistemology according to the schema 'S knows the p' makes it all too easy to discredit certain forms of personal experiential knowing that we commonly identify as 'knowing how'. Nearly a century of psychoanalytic culture has helped us to appreciate these processes. As Dalmiya and Alcoff indicate, what still needs to be established is that these are genuinely cognitive activities, or that the word 'know' in 'knowing how' and in affective knowing is to be taken seriously and is not a simple case of omonimity, or an accidental coincidence of signifiers. We could also insist on the adequacy of common language usage: since we do say such things as 'He knows how to care for infants', there is no reason to doubt the appropriateness of this usage. This outlook would shift the burden of proof to the sceptic who denies that cases of knowing how can be genuine cases of knowing. Dalmiya and Alcoff finally ask: 'What reasons other than the question-begging adherence to the intellectualist legend could be given for *witholding* cognitive status from knowing how?', p. 233.

26. Ibid., p. 234.

27. Ibid., p. 235.

28. Ibid., pp. 233–4.

29. Joyce McDougall, *The Many Faces of Eros. A Psychoanalytic Exploration of Human Sexuality*, London: Free Association Press, 1995, p. 238.

30. Ibid., p. 238.

31. Spezzano suggests that: 'Structural concepts gain clinical immediacy and relevance when they are understood as labels for each person's unique blend of abilities and tendencies to generate and regulate those feelings that then become the key indicators of the state of one's psyche. This key role of affect leads us to agree widely that what we feel is a more reliable clue at any given moment to what is going on "inside us" unconsciously than what we think. In fact, affects can be elaborated in ways that reduce our ability to understand and use them.' Charles Spezzano, *Affect in Psychoanalysis. A Clinical Synthesis*, Hillsdale, NJ and London: Analytic Press, 1993, p. 71.

32. See D. Bolton and J. Hill, *Mind, Meaning and Mental Disorder*, p. 317.

33. Ibid., p. 317. In this connection Butler asks 'What does it mean, then, that the subject, defended by some as a presupposition of agency, is also understood to be an effect of subjection? . . . How, then, is subjection to be thought and how can it become a site of alteration? A power *exerted on* a subject, subjection is nevertheless a power *assumed* by the subject, an assumption that constitutes the instrument of that subject's becoming.' Judith Butler, *The Psychic Life of Power. Theories in Subjection*, Stanford, CA: Stanford University Press, 1997, p. 11.

34. See D. Stern *et al.*, 'Non-interpretative mechanisms in psychoanalytic therapy', pp. 903–21.

35. This is suggested in A. Damasio's *Descartes' Error*, p. 191
36. Ibid., p. 178.
37. Ibid., p. 179.
38. A comparable argument is developed in G. Corradi Fiumara, *The Other Side of Language: A Philosophy of Listening*. See paragraphs entitled 'Toward an awareness of benumbment' and 'Toward a description of benumbment', pp. 82–90.
39. Goleman reports that in the case of damage to the prefrontal-amygdala circuit, the process of making decisions is seriously flawed while there is no evidence of deterioration in IQ or any cognitive ability. Despite intact intelligence patients can make bad choices in managing their personal lives and can even endlessly obsess over simple decisions. The theory is that decisions are so poor because they have lost access to their emotional learning. As the meeting point between thought and emotion, the prefrontal-amygdala circuit is a crucial doorway to the repository of the likes and dislikes we acquire over the course of a lifetime. Cut off from emotional memory in the amygdala, whatever the neo-cortex mulls over no longer triggers the emotional reactions that have been associated with it in the past – everything takes on a grey neutrality. D. Goleman, *Emotional Intelligence*, p. 27. We read in Damasio that 'To date we have studied twelve patients with prefrontal damage . . . and in none have we failed to encounter a combination of decision-making defect and flat emotion and feeling. The powers of reason and the experience of emotion decline together, and their impairment stands out in a neuropsychological profile within which basic attention, memory, intelligence, and language appear so intact that they could never be invoked to explain the patient's failures in judgement.' *Descartes' Error*, p. 53.
40. A. Damasio, *Descartes' Error*, p. 53.
41. Ibid., p. 53 (emphasis added).
42. The point is made by Claire Armon-Jones, *Varieties of Affect*, New York and London: Harvester Wheatsheaf, a division of Simon and Schuster International Group, date of publication not indicated. Oxford University thesis supervised by Kathleen Wilkes of St Hilda's College and Paul Snowdon of Exeter College, 1991, p. 12.
43. William Lyons suggests that the core of emotions is beliefs, including evaluative beliefs and desires, which in the 'rather inexact modern jargon come to be lumped together under the label "cognitions".' What differentiates one emotion from another, and an emotional state from a non-emotional state is a 'cognitive' something. Which sort of 'cognitive' state – belief, evaluation, or desire – is the essential one remains a matter of considerable debate. Some see the essential cognitive state, or item, to be beliefs, others argue that it is judgements, others desires, and still others appraisals or evaluations that seem to hover between pure beliefs and pure desires. 'Philosophy, the emotions and psychopathology', in W.F. Flack and J.D. Laird (eds), *Emotions in Psychopathology. Theory and Research*, Oxford and New York: Oxford University Press, 1998, pp. 10–11.
44. Richard S. and Bernice N. Lazarus, *Passion and Reason. Making Sense of our Emotions*, New York: Oxford University Press, 1996, p. 204.
45. See C. Armon-Jones, *Varieties of Affect*, p. 12.
46. See R.S. and B.N. Lazarus, *Passion and Reason*, p. 290.
47. This point is discussed in W. Lyons, 'Philosophy, the emotions and psychopathology', p. 11. He argues that evaluation is defined as 'a grading of the situation according to a wide spectrum of possible gradings or values'. The evaluation which is at the heart of each emotion is also what differentiates one emotion from another. The emotion is caused by what we 'cognise' about the situation and its relevance to us, not what some 'objective' observer guesses or even 'knows' about the situation, p. 12.
48. Richard S. Lazarus and C.A. Smith, 'Knowledge and appraisal in the cognition-emotion relationship', in P. Eckman and R.J. Davidson (eds), *The Nature of Emotions*.

Fundamental Questions, New York and Oxford: Oxford University Press, 1994, pp. 281–300.

49. Ibid., pp. 281–300.
50. R. Lazarus, 'Meaning and emotional development' in P. Eckman and R. Davidson (eds) *The Nature of Emotions. Fundamental Questions*, p. 364.
51. C. Armon-Jones, *Varieties of Affect*, p. 80.
52. Ibid., p. 104. William James a few times remarks that 'there are pathological cases in which the emotion is objectless', *Text Book of Psychology*, London: Macmillan, 1892, p. 377. Amélie Rorty remarks that 'Sometimes our emotions change straightaway when we learn that what we believed is not true . . . But often changes in emotion do not appropriately follow changes in belief. Their tenacity, their inertia, suggest that there is an *akrasia* in the emotions; it reveals the complex structure of their intentionality.' 'Explaining Emotions', in A. Rorty (ed.), *Explaining Emotions*, Berkeley, CA: University of California Press, 1980, p. 103.

Chapter 8

The price of maturity

The question of maturity

Any exposure to the media tells us with intensity how determining emotions are in the most disparate of ventures: from research to politics, from economics to literature, we invariably witness the deployment of human emotions in the most diverse combinations, or under the hegemony of a dominant affective power. In both individual and group vicissitudes, there is a constant process of prioritising some specific affective intensity regarded as the best suited to sustaining subjective persistence and social action. Lichtenberg remarks that 'Cross-sectionally, affects provide the principal means of identifying moment-to-moment shifts in motivational dominance.'[1] In other words, prevailing affects tell us in which motivational direction we are moving. Both macro- and micro-cultures can be dominated by relatively persistent motivational paradigms which are so accurately contextualised, and whose vocabulary is rendered so appealing, that they appear as totally enlightening and ultimately 'superior'. These hierarchisations, of course, can be as powerful as they are elusive and evanescent. Hierarchised priorities thus provide the affective signals not only to individual organisms, but also to the 'population', indicating which motivational paradigm is operative and inescapable. From this perspective, then, social maturity may be thought to consist, at least in part, of a sufficient awareness of reigning motivational systems. From this same perspective, the significance of psychoanalytic culture could extend well beyond the therapeutic benefits reapable by an infinitesimal fraction of humankind. Being more conversant with our complex affects in fact could generate beneficial consequences at large, in the sense that we may attain an increased possibility of envisioning their functions.

The management of affective problems probably accounts for the absorption and use of most of our world resources. Whether we seek antidotes for our fear of death or fear of loneliness, for the fear of losing physical territories or epistemic spaces, there is always the immense cost of coping with such affects; a cost which is still perplexingly ignored. This issue can at least be an indication of the irrenounceable need to somehow envisage the 'social' force of our affects, a force that is often ensnared in an endless variety of perverse mechanisms with which we can hardly deal. Our ways of coping with emotion, in fact, are too schematically abstract, and thus inapt to interdigitate with archaic or collective vicissitudes.[2] The sort of sophisticated knowledge that differentiates itself from peripheral 'weak thought' can be shown to be anything but strong; it is the sort of thinking that succumbs most easily when confronted with the slightest pressure from the vestiges of the reptilian brain that operates alongside cognitive structures in human beings.[3] Sovereign epistemologies appear inadequate to cope with the upsurge of massive, raw affects. The central 'theatres' of Western rationality are periodically shaken by horribly destructive rituals which unfold with total indifference towards the 'strong' thinking that finds itself incapable of confronting our archaic emotional vicissitudes; it is a logocratic thought that nevertheless resumes its usual performances as soon as the period of terror has come to an end.[4]

It is fashionable in our ecological culture to talk about saving the earth. But, perhaps, it is a logocentric missymbolisation that makes us speak of 'our' planet as something that we can save. In our affective illiteracy, we exhibit a propensity to ignore the fact that we need to save *ourselves* rather than the earth – a contingency we barely see. Our indifferent linguisticity causes us to believe that *we* can spare the planet, while it is possibly our collective, nonchalant narcissism that is conducive to damaging it. As long as we adhere to an abstract rationality that is silently interwoven with our linguistic games (or *jeux de massacre*), and forms of life (or ways of extinction), it may be difficult to 'save the earth' inasmuch as the linguistic expression and logic of the project lead us into the opposite direction. 'It is so convenient to be immature!' – exclaims Kant; ' . . . Thus it is difficult for the individual to work his way out of the immaturity which has become almost second nature to him. He has even grown fond of . . . formulas; those mechanical instruments for rational use (or rather misuse) of his natural endowments, are the ball and chain of his permanent immaturity.'[5] Our immature epistemic language may tranquilly infiltrate and sabotage even the most enlightened of cultural enterprises: it creates the problems that it tries to eradicate. If we speak of the earth as of an object that we can destroy, then we are bound to ignore that even if we in fact rendered the planet uninhabitable, it is the human species which might disappear, and not the earth. In spite of our logic, we are not the masters of 'our' earth – an object that we can save or waste, but, rather, we are so dependent on it that if we damage the earth, we primarily endanger the human species while the planet's life would probably continue undisturbed. In order to 'save the earth', we should perhaps recognise the benumbing power of those ways of knowledge which might be conducive to the deterioration of our habitat and possibly even to the extinction of one more species, that of the 'philosophical' humans who passively adhere to a domineering epistemology of indifference. As we are the authors of that epistemic language, we erroneously use it as a source of authority in the narcissistic, indifferent equation between authorial and authoritative prerogatives. In our affective immaturity we only begin to develop some empathic knowledge for 'our' planet when it has become so badly damaged that it becomes detrimental to us – and not before.

The mechanisms of the inclusion or exclusion of affects increasingly come to appear as a central issue. Affects are often perceived as an unbearable burden that can be avoided by dehumanising knowledge and by relegating the expression of affects to conditions that range from the situations of maximal privacy to mass situations allowing for total regression and uncontrolled clashes.[6] Affects are indeed charged with a force that can often manifest itself as an insufferable burden; our affective illiteracy, moreover, can transmute this force into a controlling power and into the perverse use of our inner resources.[7] Whenever our affective forces acquire the constraining characteristics of the mechanisms of power, they display a virulence of their own, invading all areas of subjectivity, trespassing limits of individuality in a contagious way, and even degrading the structures which they inhabit. When our affective forces deteriorate into the rigidity of power, they may even become the exclusive condition for an awareness of our existence; as such they implacably tend to perpetuate themselves and legitimise the usurped primacy of their rule. Such deterioration of emotions can ultimately sequester all cognition and blindly control it.

Through an increasing awareness of our motivational processes, it is possible to think of affects not so much as threatening forces that need to be 'mastered' by abstract forms of rationality, but as energetic sources of dynamic equilibrium, or the metabolic fuelling of our social ties. Thus affects could no longer be regarded as an unbearable burden, but may be seen as valuable psychic resources, which are somehow comparable to the *natural* resources that sustain the human species. In an issue dedicated to 'Making sense of the Millennium', *National Geographic*[8] asks specific questions regarding the economic value of soil formation, food production, climate maintenance, and other ways in which natural biodiversity currently serves the life of humans. It is estimated that the global value of 'ecosystem services' ranges annually between such puzzling figures as 10 trillion and 50 trillion dollars. If we think, by comparison, that human-produced goods and services in the world total an estimated 25 trillion dollars per year, we can easily infer that natural biodiversity and industrious humans are *equal* contributors to the sustenance of the species. However, if we think of ethological human conflicts, collapses in morale, paralysing ideological attitudes, or 'unconscious' destructiveness, we could *also* begin to seriously reflect on the costs and losses determined by the deterioration or injudicious management of our inescapable 'psychodiversity'. Conversely, we could begin envisaging enormous gains to be derived by a wiser relationship with our human affects. This is, of course, a high-toned question; and yet, in the language of Haraway, 'we are in a world of immensurable results, a world that exceeds its representations and blasts syntax';[9] a world that is perhaps ready for a new culture more hospitable to these questions.

We could indeed ask what the cost is of insufficient mathematical intelligence *and* what the cost is of insufficient affective intelligence. Questions like this, which would not make sense in a culture of years past, can now be met with adequate means for organising usable answers. We can now evaluate the costs of environmental degradation or deforestation just as we can evaluate the benefits of biodiversity or sunshine. From this point of view, affective maturity and psychic health are not 'only' positive ideals for our culture, but actually assets whose deterioration will no doubt cause serious damage. Questions such as 'What is the cost of the latest earthquake?' are now regarded as acceptable and answerable, as are questions regarding the value of a region's reception of sunshine. Similarly, we could now ask legitimate questions regarding an estimate of cost for any identifiable resurgence of chauvinism, revanchism, ethnocentrism, or racism. It is quite consequential to also ask on whom the costs will be weighing when there are prospects of affective calamities, when communities become ensnared into unstoppable sequences of perverse moods. Of course, these vital and realistic questions are paradoxically difficult to voice within theoretical spaces that are at times so deaf as to almost appear hostile to them: the paradox derives from an unprecedented conjunction between the factual possibility of asking such questions, and the persistent, inner difficulty of facing them.

While the psychoanalytic focus of attention is the cure of impaired affective capacities, in the background there is a general problem regarding the 'education' or development of these abilities. This 'general problem' is a relevant one, not because of any philosophical zeal that inclines to privilege the humanistic disciplines, but because we have reached a point of no return in globalisation and in the capacity to evaluate costs and benefits of what human beings may do. We can perhaps now begin to 'calculate' the costs of a wounded self-esteem, of a shattered cultural identity, or mistrust, which can amount to appalling costs for the human community. At one time we used such sloganised terms as 'the human community' in a somewhat pious, idealistic sense, while nowadays the term is nearly obligatory: we are in fact increasingly united, not only by the environment that we create, but also by the psychic atmosphere that we absorb. For example, we can consider that the unprecedented success of capitalism is probably due to its capacity to transform our 'natural' human greed into productive energy. For better or for worse, there are no administrative authorities capable of competing with the efficacy of the incessant search for profit propelled by capitalist economies. There seems to be no system for coordinating efforts that can reach the efficiency of systems linked to emotions as powerful as 'greed'.

We could even resort to the logic of neuroscience in order to focus on the general problem of 'educating' our affective capacities. The total emotional vacuity of certain brain-injured patients may, for example, suggest that there is a spectrum of a person's ability to use emotions. If the absence of a neural circuit leads to a deficit in emotional competence, then the relative education – strength or weakness – of that same circuit in people whose brains are intact should similarly lead to different levels of competence in affective performance.[10] It does not make too much sense to try to educate ourselves in the control of carbon emissions or polluting waste while, at the same time, we safeguard the unaffective and indifferent ways of thinking that ultimately determine an overabundance of psychotoxic waste in human relations.

The legitimacy of affects and moods

The development of a psychic legitimacy of affects, and the legitimisation of our efforts to deal with them, is perhaps the way towards a wider range of options and increasing maturity. Without a sufficient sense of its legitimacy, our inner amalgam of affects is left to itself, and nearly excluded from mental life; the person may become sadly burdened by the resentful power of marginalised affects and by their decreasing usable force. Our affective potential can in fact be reduced to silence in our subservience to the limiting vocabulary of any ruling epistemology. Affective illiteracy can only support the psychic violence associated with silenced affects. Through affective illiteracy, the victimised potential expressions cannot count on any admissible evidence, as they do not speak in the language and logic of the ruling genre of discourse. When affects can only 'speak' pathologically, it turns out to be much to the delight of rationalistic colonisers who would prefer that affects remain unheard.[11] Conversely, the articulation and differentiation of emotions, even in the non-verbal vicissitudes, may generate a sufficient state of inner harmony which in turn enhances a sense of legitimacy within oneself, a respect for one's experiences, and an opportunity to use them. This is of course not the outcome of an isolated process, but rather the result of a life-enhancing style of interactions.

In our early vicissitudes, in fact, we learn how to feel about ourselves and how others will react to our feelings; we learn how to think about these feelings and what choices we have in our dependency upon caretakers. Paradoxically, even the legitimacy of our innermost affects turns out to be relationally based. According to Foucault,[12] there is a founding subordination in the process of becoming a subject: a condition which he designates as *assujetissement*. With regard to this process, Battersby remarks that interpersonal relations do not demand equality or do not require 'selves' abstracted from the force-fields of power.[13] Perhaps power is ubiquitous, inescapable, and somehow always dangerous; this hypothesis aids us in seeing the human self as emerging together with its 'others' from intersecting force-fields of power. It is indeed a more realistic approach to understanding the use and abuse of affects. As disguised in the vernacular of the heart, all follies can be successfully advertised and rendered legitimate enough to support any equilibrium of power. In this connection, Battersby points out that there is a general inability to imaginatively grasp that the self–other relationship needs to be reconceptualised in a perspective of 'birth', and this in ways that never abstract from power inequalities; by only talking about 'individuals' with equal rights and duties, we are bound to ignore personal histories of foetal and childhood dependency.[14] These histories in fact make the 'autonomous individual' especially vulnerable. In Giardini's synoptic view, we could say that the public space precedes us, and that the access to it implies a passion for the others' presence that often does not immediately suit us; the relation to this expanding presence, entailing an intertwining of activity and passivity in the effort of exposing oneself to the collective impact of others, has a necessary affective dimension.[15] That impact, of course, greatly differs in intensity and in the way it is symbolised. To the extent that affects are the condition for sustaining the impact and becoming recognisable subjects, our affective lives can be no longer conceived as private 'habits' that we may cast off upon entering the public dimension.[16]

The Foucaultian theory of subjection, as the simultaneous subordination and formation of the individual, tends to coincide with psychoanalytic views maintaining that subjects can not develop without a passionate attachment to the caretakers on whom they depend, even if that attachment is largely ambivalent. In Butler's gaze, if there is no formation of the self without affective attachment to those by whom the inchoate person is subordinated, then submission proves essential to the development of the subject.[17] Thus, of course, the desire not only to survive, but to actually exist, is surely exploitable in divergent ways. By holding out the promise of admission into social interaction, the authority of caretakers and culture operates through the subject's desire to exist. 'I would rather exist in subordination than not exist' is one possible formulation of this crucial predicament.[18] Only when sufficiently developed and strong, the subject is able to reconsider that outlook. Of course the child's love, an attraction that is necessary for its existence, can be unduly exploited, and a passionate attachment abused; it is a condition that generates an immense, ineffable rage that takes the form of the most disparate affects. However, even this variety of transmutable affects can be lived (even if not actually felt and perceived) as sufficiently legitimate – thus they are not entirely alien and worthy only of psychic evacuation. Where parental categories offer the promise of admission into social existence, the embrace of such categories, even as they work in the service of subjection, is preferred to precipitating out of interactive life.[19] This inevitable vulnerability, however, not only makes us the exploitable kind of beings that we are, but also involves the risk that even adhesion to submission will not finally produce the desired results. An amalgam of incompatible affects that occupies our inner space, and the effort to render the affects legitimate and somehow comprehensible, seems to be a condition for the mind's survival. In a synoptic view, Kernberg remarks that the integration of loving and hating object-images is a condition for the capacity to develop stable interpersonal links.[20] Yet the insistence that subjects appear 'passionately' linked to their own subordination can be strategically invoked by those who seek to attack the emancipatory claims of the subordinated. If subjects can be 'exposed' as pursuing their subordinate status, the argument goes, then perhaps the final responsibility for that subordination resides in them. Over and against this view, Butler maintains that the attachment to subjection is produced through the workings of power, and that part of the operation of power is made clear through this psychic outcome, which is 'one of the most insidious of its productions.'[21]

Whereas the language of affective suffering often tends towards the opaqueness of narcissism, it is empathic listening that allows a subject to transform despairing and exasperated expressions into viable forms of communication. As we know, in the early vicissitudes of development, the soundness of the relation depends upon the readiness with which nascent emotions are welcomed and respected. Maieutic listening exhibits a radical difference from other forms of interaction inasmuch as it does not provide (or impose) a world view; it rather strives to let the inchoate person experience affects and even generate shareable symbolic tools that enhance communications with oneself as well as with others. Our potential inner world can only spring to life when it is sufficiently attended to, rather than there being 'something interior' that we might express to others and that they would subsequently proceed to understand. When the non-verbal expression of affects is focused upon as part of clinical inquiry, we can help to articulate what has been ineffable, thus attracting the subject into a self-observing venture, and jointly work at the construction of an increasing sense of legitimacy for all affects. Conversely, the persistence of 'non-metabolised' introjections can be the outcome of a pathological fixation of severely disturbed, early object relations.[22] From this perspective, then, it is interpersonal relations that ultimately allow us to metabolise both drive derivatives and early introjections of reciprocal adjustments.

A focus on the language of emotions helps us to identify *felt* states of the subject. A subject can feel its own affective states only to the extent that they acquire a measure of legitimacy. As feelings are of the most immediate concern to us, their legitimacy is worthy of attention. It is personal emotions that directly move us, and that involve the strongest of psychic pleasures and pains. Additionally, it is as feeling states that affects are most clearly distinguishable from other mental functions.[23] It is primarily as feelings that emotions seem to acquire their identity as distinct mental types. It is the felt aspect of affects that underpins both emotional behaviour and standing background moods. We also need to place emotions within a broader view of affects so that we can explain the continuity of emotions with other types of affective states, especially that type commonly denoted by the term 'mood'.[24] Unlike a hierarchised view, the idea of a continuum provides an opportunity to arrange phenomena at various points along some linear route, and thus offers a flexible network for the recognition and legitimisation of the greatest *variety* of affects. This outlook, at the same time, avoids the reification of one particular group of states as 'central', and enables us to perceive the equal legitimacy of our affective phenomena – which may nevertheless differ in important respects. By using a 'logic' of continua, we also counterbalance the tendency to assume that those instances of affect, to which we can ascribe the greatest complexity of elements, are in fact paradigmatic, and thus the only legitimate ones.[25] We can probably avoid regarding them as paradigms; this is not to say the contrary, that those that exhibit the least complexity are therefore the exemplars, but only to say that neither of these conceptions is a viable way of viewing affective phenomena.

The analysis of states of mind like 'moods' suggests that we have located an area of our mental life which falls outside the explanations that employ the selective network of concepts. Such a network does not yield the right apparatus with which to legitimise the complexity of an affective life that includes moods. These states call into question, moreover, the assumption that affective states are 'legitimate' in virtue of their relation to objects.[26] Mood states lack the role of motives inasmuch as they are objectless and have no goal orientation. Thus, the topic of moods as complexive states of mind becomes a puzzling one. The states of terror that we most fear, for instance, are the ones for which we have no motive, no object;

such moods are so alarming that we may feel compelled to find, forge, or invent concept-dependent motives. According to Sander, 'state' is the term for '*wholeness in the living system*', or a wholeness constructed in a continuing process through the 'complexity of unending interactions, transactions, and exchanges'.[27] Laplanche and Pontalis would agree with the view of an unending continuum, for indeed, they hold that affect 'connotes any affective state . . . whether vague or well defined, and whether it is manifested in the form of massive discharge or in the form of a general mood.'[28] In his outlook on early affective vicissitudes, Stern remarks that the newborn's experience appears to be both 'unified' and 'global';[29] these global affective patterns that accompany a state are, of course, best understood as moods. Jones suggests that 'mood' is a 'low level' concept, like the concept of state. 'The word itself certainly suggests a *general* feeling tone, rather than the specificity connected with a discrete emotion such as sadness, anger or fear.'[30] Yet, however 'low level' it may be, a sense of legitimacy for our moods is as essential as the legitimacy of affects 'proper'. The pervasive diffuseness of moods is eloquently captured by Jacobson: 'In fact, moods seem to represent, as it were, a cross-section through the entire state of the ego, lending a particular, uniform colouring to all its manifestations for a longer or shorter period of time. Since they do not relate to a specific content or object, but find expression in specific qualities attached to all feelings, thoughts and actions, they may indeed be called a barometer of the ego state.'[31]

Our instincts are part of a genetic destiny and we can only speculate about specificities at the level of biological drives. The real 'problem' is the wealth of specificity which is prevented or silenced by the insufficient vocabulary that emanates from any ruling micro- or macro-culture. The sort of affective bonds that are not represented symbolically come to be perceived as illegitimate, or as an incongruity that may predispose us to serious psychic illness, even though it may be one that hardly resembles the official pathological states. On certain creatures are often imposed the symbolic instruments with which to express emotions, and thus only the emotions envisioned by a given culture. The unexpressed, unsymbolised affects become part of an unlived, unlivable psychic condition that silently impoverishes the quality of mental development, detaching psychic life from the course of biological growth. Young individuals can feel secretly infuriated at becoming bigger and bigger without really growing. Speaking from a feminist perspective, Irigaray makes a similar point suggesting that women only borrow signifiers and cannot make their mark, or re-mark upon them, which surely keeps women 'deficient, empty, lacking in a way that could be labelled "psychotic": a *latent* but not actual psychosis, for want of a practical signifying system.'[32] Lyotard goes as far as to suggest that if there is something unable to be symbolised, then there is something which is a feeling: 'Insofar as it is unable to be phrased in the common idioms, it is already phrased, as feeling.'[33] It is a feeling that could be made legitimate.

We have an immense terminology for discrete details of observable reality, and a comparatively scarce vocabulary for what is essential to mental life. We find it so difficult to cope with our unfathomable depth all by ourselves that we constantly seek allies and support for our own psychic survival. We may, for example, be able to endure spiteful and arrogant behaviour inasmuch as we are entitled to a recognisable, legitimate reaction, while we may not endure attitudes of latent condescension that we cannot properly recognise, and for which we have no 'legitimate' emotional reaction. This is precisely why we seek help in recognising a feeling and thus rendering it thinkable. If we only consider the immense terminology of biochemistry and the comparatively few words for coping with our no less complex psychic chemistry, we can better appreciate the challenge of rendering legitimate at least a few of the innumerable vital aspects of our celebrated 'inner life'. Just having an emotion, in fact, does not prove that the subject is aware of experiencing it, is able to 'name' it, or utilise it as a signal for the self. Sometimes an experience can be conscious, yet repressed in a functional way, that is unsymbolised in order for us to somehow adjust to a dulling environment.[34] In this sort of repression, what is lacking is not consciousness or representation, but self-relatedness, ownership, responsiveness to internal feedback that would lead to our better understanding of the meaning of our own behaviour. The legitimacy of affects thus seems ultimately to depend upon an equilibrium of epistemic power. Perhaps the two main ways of describing the effectiveness of psychoanalytic therapy refer to interpretations aimed at rearranging our inner world, *and* to the 'moments' of authentic psychic encounter that influence our sense of the self. In spite of the more portentous interpretations, therapy may fail because of the insufficiency of those psychic contacts which confer legitimacy to our most disparate affective states.[35] In the psychoanalytic language of Kernberg, empathy with the patient's affect-states and the subsequent integrative formulation in the analytic process 'clarify the nature of the drive derivatives activated and defended against in the object relation predominating in the transference'.[36] Then, however, in the clarification of affective states, we often have the interaction of at least two individuals. Their subjectivity also includes the fact that both of them only have their own *version* it. Both patient and analyst have their own views of their subjectivities, however hidden or defensively expressed they may be. Schwaber remarks that 'subjectivity, by its very nature, implies the presence of aspects of ourselves about which we are not objective, and which are outside of our own awareness. Even if an analyst examines his own counter transference, that still is only his view of it.'[37] What we need is an openness on two different outlooks which may, then, not only compete but also work as a synergy. This perspective also implies that we cannot count on ourselves to be our sole discoverers – our only source of epistemic power. We need another creature to explore and reveal, in such a way that ineffable affects may reach a higher level of legitimacy. The very fact that some evanescent, but constraining feeling can be somehow symbolised renders us more capable of legitimately negotiating with our affects: if they can be shared, at least by one person, they seem to automatically begin to claim legitimacy *and* admission into the metabolism of our inner life. Conversely, when feelings cannot be symbolised they remain inexpressible, inaudible, 'unheard of' – virtually non-existent.

Silencing affects

Silencing the expression of affects is a devastating occupation which does not derive so much from special strategies or abilities, but from unacknowledged incapacities. Whenever the interlocutor, who putatively has greater responsibility within a bi-personal field, is not sufficiently aware of how challenging it is to make contact with one's own self in order to attempt to construe what the other tries to say, the relationship will be steered towards a domain of literalness – a linguistic domain hardly suited for the expression of affects. The more 'responsible' one in the dyad might only take the pathways which are already well known, and which present no threat to the epistemology he inhabits. This is the basis for the degrading automatisms of silencing.[38] The symbolic and metaphoric capacities through which we express affects, are stifled not by inflicting damage to existent structures, but rather by obtusely refusing to construe non-literal messages, and thus impeding the growth of thought. The point at issue is not the damage to something functioning, but the failure to allow something to spring to life *and* function. In this gaze, Oedipal vicissitudes connected with the desire to attain something, and the concomitant anxieties of retaliation, could be viewed as an account in fable form – a story that we can visualise – of prior, more crucial (and more difficult to grasp) experiences that have affected the early development, or inhibition, of our capacity to think.

The celebrated saying of the young Wittgenstein, 'Whereof we cannot speak, thereof one must be silent' might be taken as a not-so-surpassed and latent paradigm of sick cultures.[39] Although, of course, the early Wittgensteinian statement was aimed at the clarity of language, the suggestion might well sound like a provocation from the point of view of an inquiry into our efforts to give expression to 'inexpress-ible' thoughts and affects. It may, in fact, take years of dialogic work to bring about a good enough relationship to enable precisely those emotional vicissitudes – those that least lend themselves to utterance – to find some way of expression. For it is often very difficult, and at times practically impossible, to speak about those 'primitive' emotions that create an inner atmosphere of unworthiness, grandiosity, fragmentation, or paralysis. It is a question of expressing the unutterable suffering that one laboriously survives by trying to convey and share primal affects. We are faced with trying vicissitudes, and wallow in exasperation at precisely those times when we are not able to 'utter' emotional conflicts – when 'we must pass over in silence what we cannot speak about.'[40] A hypothetical suffering subject might make the following 'unphilosophical' comment on Wittgenstein's celebrated statement: 'But if it is precisely what I cannot manage to utter that weakens my inner life, why then is it precisely about such things that I ought not to speak?'

Affects such as aggressiveness, envy, and rage are by their very nature difficult to voice in that their explosiveness tends to elude containment by symbolic means (these being the elements which generate connection), whereas those emotions tend to split, lacerate and fragment. A far-sighted awareness of our profound vicissitudes may enable us, therefore, to better appraise the enduring difficulties attached to widening the domain of what is utterable – and thus avoid silencing; such an awareness would ultimately involve the retrieval of archaic experiences that are hardly amenable to being framed and metabolised in literal discourse. If we cannot develop a sufficient language for our inner feelings, we may have very poor contact with ourselves. 'We know ourselves so little' says Pascal 'that many think they are about to die when they are well, and many think they are well when they are near death.'[41] Conversely, we could notice that 'names', or designating terms, bring a measure of order to experience by somehow inducing a sense of familiarity. This is underscored by the sense of discomfort that we experience when we are confronted with something that we are *not* able to name: in the extreme, something of an undescribable, unpredictable nature, such as defies our rationality and available classifications. As we learn from ethnology, in certain cultural outlooks, to know a name is to possess the entity and to be able to work magic on it, so that the real name has to be kept secret and revealed only under certain conditions. Similarly, when we try to 'know' what it is that makes a person 'feel awful', or what that 'illness' is called, we may be witnessing a reliance upon 'magical' remedies. Borrowing a term may thus be regarded as a first step towards a measure of control on our way to relating more personally with inner events. In the course of especially difficult stages of life, or therapy, the individual may be struggling to communicate how much he is hounded by inner destructiveness, and will somehow ask for help with confronting a 'terror' that cannot be uttered or explained. However, resorting to some term borrowed from the jargon of psychopathology comes down to nothing more than a lame, imitative ploy involving magical expectations. It is an attempt to contain the complexity of our affective lives with terms picked from conventional language in a purely imitative fashion – that is almost tantamount to silencing. Conversely, the momentum sparked off by the experience of being able to express a mind of one's own and of having oneself understood is of enormous maturational relevance.

We are perhaps approaching an increasing 'pathology without symptoms', or an affliction deriving from a lack of development. It is the sort of malaise that the patients can hardly describe because they do not know well enough what it is that they have not achieved or what potentials have not been activated. In Lyotard's view, the French term *différend* indicates a wrong which results in silence, and more generally points to the violence of silencing, for indeed it is a 'damage accompanied by the loss of the means to prove the damage'.[42] For Lyotard there is an essential difference between a 'plaintiff' – one with the instruments to prove damage 'by means of well-formed phrases and of procedures for establishing the existence of their referent', and a 'victim' – one with no such means to prove damage. He says 'I would like to call *différend* the case where the plaintiff is divested of the means to argue and becomes for that reason a victim.'[43] A laborious perception of silencing indicates a 'negative phrase, but also calls upon phrases which are in principle possible. *This state is signalled by what one ordinarily calls a feeling* . . . A lot of searching must be done to find new rules for forming and linking phrases that are able to express the *différend* disclosed by the feeling, unless one wants this *différend* to be smothered . . . and the feeling to have been useless.'[44] The trouble with our theoretical languages is that they are imagined as preceding situations, in such a way that they tend to ignore and to silence whatever affective vicissitudes do not fit into them. When affects are excluded, we are left with a personal identity inclining to fixity, that is a condition deprived of its propelling forces. Yet, in *Against Epistemology*, Adorno seems to suggest that these forces are incoercible: 'Unconscious knowledge not entirely subject to mechanisms of control explodes in inspiration and bursts through the wall of conventionalised judgements "fitting reality".'[45]

Outright denial would bring the whole problem of silencing into clearer vistas than the obscured question of our offensive benumbment, which is only suited to making others mute. The induced invisibility of affects, however, will ultimately reveal the problem of theory itself. In order to see something, any theory or proto-theory must also entail some selective blindness; it is the blinded eye of theory that scans its non-objects and non-problems precisely so as not to look at them. Of course affects may speak, but they can hardly be listened to; they may even speak from inside philosophy and be 'heard', yet remain silenced if all they convey is finally shaped by the astute-innocent skills of the authors-and-authorities of any reigning epistemology. We also wonder what it would mean to speak from the outside; it would seem to suggest speaking in a language that is ultimately incomprehensible from the standpoint of sound reasoning.[46] So much so, that some might even opt for a gesture of indifference towards official philosophy, rather than labour for a transformation of its subjacent logic. Those who embrace the view that affects should be off-limits, as if they had no place in human intelligence, may have been seduced by the computer metaphor of the mind, forgetting that in reality, the brain is a live, pulsating part of our living self, that is subject to development, illness, and death. It is nothing like the sterilised, 'immortal' silicon that has spawned one of the guiding metaphors of the mind.

In life-enhancing language games, the early expressions of the nascent personality are met with construals that induce the belief that language is an enriching instrument and path to self-formation. In those pseudo-construals wherein personal life is sadly disconnected from linguistic life, there is no response to the efforts to express affects, but instead a steady directing away from self, towards the paradigms of adult language. A centrifugal sort of language leading away from the core of the developing self is gradually established. Through this we come to believe that life and language should ultimately be dissociated inasmuch as one's incipient affective language should be regarded as unessential to projects of 'proper' self-creation. This imposed centrifugal power seems contrary to personal growth. It is the obscure, and thus unquestioned, equivalent of intimating that there is no reasonable logic in the nascent individual and that real logic is only to be found in whatever dominant epistemology sustains a micro- or macro-culture, no matter how insane. Through constant deviation from what is personal to what is conventional, one is ultimately deprived of instruments for self-reflection and for appreciating the inner life of others. Whenever we injudiciously presume that certain interlocutors have no resources for expressing their inner worlds, we tend to make use of our own abilities to give voice to the others' experiences. As soon as such an assumption is made within a two-person interaction, one of them becomes deprived of the opportunity to exercise expressive capacities. Such an appropriation, moreover, is uniquely unnoticeable and difficult to oppose inasmuch as it comes across as an offer, or interpretative gift.[47] It is the sort of 'gift' that atrophies the symbolic and metaphoric potential of the recipient, who is overcome by the colonising attitude of the linguistically more efficient agent. Such an interaction not only implies that one person regards himself capable of vicariously speaking for the less gifted partner, but also that no expressive potential is perceived in the other – as if there was nothing worthy of being expressed. Whenever someone else voices our efforts to say something – that can only come into existence if it is sufficiently well expressed – these 'formative' offers ultimately denude and sterilise creative language. Thus, the affective language to cope with vicissitudes of hope and despair, or attachment and separation may not sufficiently develop. This language is consequently entrusted, or surrendered, to representatives of the ruling language, or to the authorial authorities of any current epistemology. Such a surrender of profound experiences to the expert managers of language could be seen as colluding in the theft of one's inner life. Indeed, the territorial and predatory heritage of our hominisation seems to have been transferred from the biological to the emotional level, and thus enacted in the symbolic domain. Indeed we now have to cope more with culture than with nature. Having relinquished contacts with the affective roots of one's own mind, one no longer faces the challenge of attempting to translate messages from the inner world into a shareable language; the subject consequently restricts language to elements borrowed from, or imposed by, the more competent, non-listening speakers. Whoever has been deprived of the task of articulating inner life will tacitly identify with 'educators', 'leaders', or 'stars', and will ultimately internalise an intrusive and predatory style that is only suited to abusing still others.[48] Such styles, of course, can be adopted both by individuals and by coalitions of persons who unconsciously share the same 'cultural' attitude.

NOTES

1. Joseph D. Lichtenberg, *Psychoanalysis and Infant Research*, Hillsdale, NJ: Analytic Press, 1983, p. 260. Also see his Foreword to Joseph M. Jones, *Affects as Process. An Inquiry into the Centrality of Affect in Psychological Life*, Hillsdale, NJ and London: Analytic Press, 1995, pp. xiii–xix.
2. On this topic see Daniel Goleman, *Emotional Intelligence. Why It Can Matter More Than IQ*, New York: Bantam, 1995, p. x. Daily news reveal the thinness of our general civility and social maturity. Such reports describe explosive manifestations of emotions out of control in our own selves and our communities. No one is immune from this erratic tide of disconnected affects which may reach into all of our lives in one way or another. These are indicators of severe emotional ineptitude, affectual immaturity, and illiteracy of our 'hearts'.
3. 'For better or for worse, our appraisal of every personal encounter and our responses to it are shaped not just by our rational judgements or our personal history, but also by

our distant ancestral past. This leaves us with sometimes tragic propensities . . . In short, we too often confront post-modern dilemmas with an emotional repertoire tailored to the urgencies of the Pleistocene.' D. Goleman, *Emotional Intelligence*, p. 5.

4. This point is also discussed in Gemma Corradi Fiumara, *The Other Side of Language. A Philosophy of Listening*, London and New York: 1990, p. 68.

5. In this gaze we could also appropriately invoke Kant's remark: 'I need not think as long as I can pay; others will soon enough take the tiresome job over for me.' Immanuel Kant, 'An answer to the question "What is Enlightenment?"', in *Political Writings*, trans. H.B. Nisbet, H. Reiss (ed.), Cambridge, UK: Cambridge University Press, 1987, p. 54.

6. A comparable point is developed in Federica Giardini, 'Public affects: towards a political practice of singularity', *European Journal of Women's Studies*, vol. 6, 1999, pp. 149–59.

7. The conceptual and practical distinction between 'force' and 'power' is discussed in G. Corradi Fiumara, *The Other Side of Language. A Philosophy of Listening*, chapter 4, 'The power of discourse and the force of listening', pp. 52–71.

8. Joel Swerdlow, 'Making sense of the Millennium', *National Geographic*, No. 1, January 1998.

9. Donna Haraway, *Modest-Witness @ Second-Millennium. Female Man Meets-Oncomouse TM: Feminism and Technoscience*, London and New York: Routledge, 1996, p. xiv.

10. See D. Goleman, *Emotional Intelligence*, p. 148.

11. This point is raised in Varena Andermatt-Conley, *Ecopolitics. The Environment in Poststructuralist Thought*, London and New York: Routledge, 1997, p. 2.

12. Michael Foucault, *Discipline and Punish: The Birth of the Prison*, New York: Pantheon, 1977, pp. 30–4. Also see 'The subject of power' and 'Two lectures' in *Power/Knowledge: Selected Interviews and Other Writings, 1972–77*, C. Gordon (ed.), New York: Pantheon, 1980.

13. Christine Battersby, *The Phenomenal Woman. Feminist Metaphysics and the Patterns of Identity*, Cambridge and Oxford: Polity Press, 1998, p. 206.

14. Ibid., p. 3.

15. F. Giardini, 'Public affects. Towards a political practice of singularity', *European Journal of Women Studies*, vol. 6, 1999, pp. 149–59.

16. Ibid. That 'The personal is political' is often sloganised in Italian feminism. Private affects have to be considered as the repressed side of the social ties that ought to be reactivated.

17. Judith Butler, *The Psychic Life of Power. Theories in Subjection*, Stanford, CA: Stanford University Press, 1997, pp. 7–8.

18. Ibid., p. 7. She also says: 'We are used to thinking of power as what presses on the subject from the outside . . . and relegates it to a lower grade. This is surely a fair description of *part* of what power does. But if, following Foucault, we understand power as *forming* the subject as well . . . then power is not simply what we oppose, but also, in a strong sense, what we depend on for our existence. The customary model for understanding this process goes as follows: power imposes itself on us, and, weakened by its force, we come to internalise or accept its terms . . . What such an account fails to note, however, is that the "we" who accept such terms are fundamentally dependent on those terms for "our" existence . . . Subjection consists precisely in this fundamental dependency on a discourse we never chose but that, paradoxically, initiates and sustains our agency.', p. 2.

19. Ibid., p. 20.

20. Otto Kernberg, *Internal World and External Reality. Object Relations Theory Applied*, New York and London: Jason Aronson, 1980, p. 295.

21. J. Butler, *The Psychic Life of Power*, p. 6. According to Ferrell 'The mind is a field of negotiation between two intransigent forces, the need for survival and an indifferent world. Psychical development, from the "helpless organism" to the philosopher king, becomes the history of the negotiation of that context. This negotiation entails increasingly sophisticated and elaborate structures at that interface, which in turn, increasingly rigid, becomes the edifice we know as character.' Robyn Ferrell, *Passion in Theory. Conceptions of Freud and Lacan*, London and New York: Routledge, 1996, p. 10.

22. Otto Kernberg, *Object Relations Theory and Clinical Psychoanalysis*, New York: Jason Aronson, 1979, p. 34.

23. Claire Armon-Jones, *Varieties of Affect*, New York and London: Harvester Wheatsheaf, a division of Simon and Schuster International Group, date of publication not indicated. Oxford University thesis supervised by Kathleen Wilkes of St. Hilda's College, and Paul Snowdon of Exeter College, 1991, p. 4.

24. Ibid., p. 2.

25. Ibid., pp. 14–15.

26. Ibid., p. 104. In any epistemic vocabulary some terms seem to prevail even though the terminology for affects is 'comparatively' scarce with respect to our so very complex emotional behaviour. In fact we commonly speak of fear, awe, delight, pity, compassion, devotion, panic, regret, remorse, grief, nostalgia, rage, disdain, condescension, admiration, gratitude, pride, indignation, contempt, disgust, resignation, shame, boredom, etc. We hardly have terms for the diversified combinations of these affects.

27. L.W. Sander, 'Thinking about the developmental process: wholeness, specificity and the organization of conscious experiencing'. Presented at the meeting of the American Psychological Association, Division 39, Santa Monica, 1995. Quoted in E.A. Schwaber 'The non-verbal dimension in psychoanalysis: "state" and its clinical vicissitudes', *The International Journal of Psychoanalysis*, vol. 79, 1998, pp. 667–79.

28. Jean Laplanche and Jean-Bertrand Pontalis, *The Language of Psychoanalysis*, translated by D. Nicholson-Smith, New York: Norton, 1967, p. 13.

29. Daniel Stern, *The Interpersonal World of the Infant*, New York: Basic Books, 1985, p. 67. It is worth noting that what something evokes in us when concentrated can be far more important than what *it* is. Indeed in emotional life, identities can function like a hologram in the sense that a single part retrieves a whole.

30. Joseph Jones, *Affects as Process. An Inquiry into the Centrality of Affect in Psychological Life*, Hillsdale, NJ: Analytic Press, 1995, p. 55 (emphasis added). For a discussion of this point see G. Corradi Fiumara, *The Metaphoric Process*, specially chapter 6 'The relationship between digital and analogic styles', paragraph 3 'Inquiries into discreteness and continuity', pp. 71–4.

31. Edith Jacobson, 'Normal and pathological moods', *The Psychoanalytic Study of the Child*, vol. 12, 1957, pp. 73–113.

32. Luce Irigaray, 'The blind spot of an old dream of symmetry', in *Speculum of the Other Woman*, trans. G.C. Gill, Ithaca, NJ: Cornell University Press, 1985, p. 71.

33. Jean-François Lyotard, *The Différend. Phrases in Dispute*, translated by Georges Van Den Abbeele, Minneapolis: University of Minnesota Press, 1988, p. 80.

34. Ruth Stein, *Psychoanalytic Theories of Affect*, New York, Westport and London: Praeger, 1991, p. 181.

35. Daniel Stern, Louis Sander, Jeremy Nahum, *et al.* 'Non-interpretative mechanisms in psychoanalytic therapy. The "something more" than interpretation.' *The International Journal of Psychoanalysis*, vol. 79, 1998, pp. 903–21.

36. O. Kernberg, *Internal World and External Reality*, p. 158.

37. Evelyne Albrecht Schwaber, 'The non-verbal dimension in psycho-analysis: "state"

and its clinical vicissitudes', *The International Journal of Psychoanalysis*, vol. 79, 1998, pp. 667–79.

38. G. Corradi Fiumara, *The Metaphoric Process*, p. 130.
39. Ludwig Wittgenstein, *Tractatus Logico-Philosophicus*, London: Routledge and Kegan Paul, 1961, paragraph 7, p. 188.
40. This is a transformation of the celebrated remark 'What we cannot speak about we must pass over in silence.' L. Wittgenstein, *Tractatus Logico-Philosophicus*, paragraph 7. We also read in the author's preface: 'What can be said at all can be said clearly, and what we cannot talk about we must pass over in silence'. Ibid., p. 3.
41. Blaise Pascal, *Pascal's Pensées*, with an introduction by T.S. Eliot, New York: E.P. Dutton, 1958, paragraph 176, p. 50.
42. J.F. Lyotard, *The Différend*, p. 5. For Lyotard this ineffable wrong involves a conflict that is impossible to resolve in any fair way because of the absence of a paradigm of judgement that is applicable to both sides of the conflictual situation. In his words 'A wrong results from the fact that the rules of the genre of discourse by which one judges are not those of the judged genre or genres of discourse.' Ibid., p. xi. Michelle Boulus-Walker suggests that we are constantly seeking new linkages that might make it possible for feelings to become audible and shareable. For Lyotard, silencing indicates a *différend*, that is the suffering of phrases that remain as yet unphrased. He reminds us that attempts to speak new phrases do not fall between the stark alternatives of sense and nonsense, but rather that they embrace feeling within the domain of knowing. *Philosophy and the Maternal Body. Reading Silence*, London and New York: Routledge, 1998, p. 71.
43. Ibid., p. 8.
44. Ibid., p. 13 (emphasis added).
45. Theodor W. Adorno, *Against Epistemology*, trans. W. Domingo, Oxford: Basil Blackwell, 1982, p. 46.
46. M. Boulus-Walker, *Philosophy and the Maternal Body*, p. 11.
47. G. Corradi Fiumara, *The Metaphoric Process*, p. 135.
48. This thesis is developed by Christopher Bollas in *The Shadow of the Object: Psychoanalysis of the Unthought Known*, London: Free Association Books, 1987, p. 19.

Chapter 9

Towards affective literacy

Naming our inner states

If we have no words for feelings, we cannot make feelings our own. We seem to relentlessly strive to attain more psychic 'goods', or more epistemic territory, in order to 'feel better'; but the question is, of course, whether we can actually *feel* the 'positive' affects that we seek and secure. We might only be reaching for them, because in fact, the positive quality of any obtained affective state seems to depend upon a personal awareness of it being good for us. The inclination to win ever more affective 'goods' may even become obsessive and overwhelming – ultimately unviable – unless we can also appreciate and use the subtle, specific kinds of good-for-us feelings. If we only yearn for something better and always more of it, or if we only seek to remedy our generic 'feeling awful' and increase our 'feeling great', the entire mechanism may become interminable; no matter how active it may be, we are never 'nourished' by it. The development of affective literacy may, on the other hand, help us to know our feelings and experience the knowledge of whatever we may have attained.[1] The sick crave for good health, but unless it can be psychically enjoyed with a minimum of affective maturity, even a condition of perfect well-being could be of scarce psychic value. If one is not sufficiently mature to *feel* a regained health, there is not much point in having been cured. Indeed, some individuals find it difficult to cope with reality when the reality involved is their own inner world. Bion remarks that people exist who are so intolerant of mental pain that they have the pain, but will not feel or suffer it, and so cannot be said to discover it.[2] Only 'negative descriptions' can be attempted of a person who is in pain and who is not quite capable of feeling it because he is unable to be aware of himself suffering, or of his suffering self. The converse of this condition, however, is even more alarming: we could reason that when a creature cannot manage to feel, or experience, pain (that is, when one can only survive it in a blunted, benumbed fashion), he cannot arrive at the discovery of the rich variety of inner states that we call 'joy'; he simply cannot feel them. To have affective pain without feeling, suffering, or realising that it is there, may be regarded as corresponding to either clashing head-on with 'reality', or avoiding any such collision, without ever developing the capacity to acquire a vocabulary for one's own relations with the objects of the outer world with which one does clash or avoids clashing.[3] In the aphorismic language of Pascal we could say that 'The greatness of man is great in that he *knows* himself to be miserable . . . It is then being miserable oneself to be miserable; but it is also being great to know that one is miserable.'[4]

It seems clear that, as a general term, 'affect' is conceptually related to 'feeling'. An ordinary emotional person is someone who *feels* emotions. Humans could not be described as 'emotional' and yet 'feelingless' or 'incapable of feeling'.[5] We commonly recognise a range of central affective types such as joy, fear, sorrow or rage which, significantly, are those often selected as basic emotions, and which are not plausibly viewed as conceptually independent of feeling. The idea of joy, for example, indicates a state that the individual, in addition to behaving in certain ways, consciously experiences as feelings of joy. Certainly, affective types vary in the extent of their conceptual dependence on feeling. As suggested by Armon-Jones, it would be easier to imagine a world in which pride is a standing emotion, but never felt as such, than one in which joy and sorrow are never really *felt* at all.[6] Even if we consider these alleged 'unfelt emotions', we can agree that to say that a person *is* angry, or jealous, or sad, does not necessarily entail that he *feels* those states. The being/feeling distinction is thus to be neither ignored or enforced, but is certainly to be considered a vital issue of concern. So, although feeling can be absent in certain instances, notably in those conditions known as 'standing emotions', in cases of self-deception, or in attention failure, what is typically absent is not the feeling as such, but the subject's recognition of the feeling. The relevance of these distinctions is in parallel to our belief that the recognition, appreciation, and awareness of a feeling is functional to the development of our entire mental life. In psychoanalytic culture, affective experience is the matrix of the mind, and thus the development of thought processes is seen as inextricably interwoven with the global process of growth. If an infant is not aided in dealing with his inchoate mind, by means of exchanges of mutual regulation, he may ultimately disown it and almost regard it as someone else's possession. Were he to 'autonomously' recognise his own primitive vicissitudes he would be terrorised. At its simplest, we could say that an inclination towards denial and the incapacity to think of one's inner life are caused by affective factors, namely a fear of mental terror and disintegration.

We should not allow the extensions of affective terms in ordinary language, facilitated by the diverse uses of the term 'to feel', to blind us to their role in describing felt, affective states. It is because we need to mark out this inner domain that we have a specifically affective use of the term 'to feel', since it has a role in appreciating states that are not only, or not at all, physical sensations, judgements, standing conditions, cultural actions, or inclinations.[7] Let us suppose that a subject describes himself as being stirred by a feeling of deep love upon seeing his beloved, or paralysed by a sudden wave of remorse upon realising that he has disappointed her. Using a reductive approach, we might suggest that the feelings involved be described as something general like happiness or sadness, which we might also call 'love' or 'remorse', or might regard as expressions of mere standing conditions of love or remorse. Yet, it is not clear whether we can remove the affective role of 'love' and 'remorse' here by this kind of approach, for we cannot ascribe to the subject any other affective term that adequately represents his feelings.[8] The person certainly feels emotions in the instances suggested above, but there is no reason to suppose that his feelings in any way simply resemble happiness or sadness. It is feelings of love, not happiness (or even mere pleasure), with which the enamoured person trembles, gasps, and sighs.[9] The feelings in these instances are of something more specific, which terms such as 'love' and 'remorse' convey *better* than others. As powerful feelings by which the person is moved, they may be regarded as *more* specific instances of affect than, for example, moderate pride in one's achievements or a feeling of slight embarassment for a delay. We thus have a constant problem of relative adequacy, accuracy, or specificness in description; or, indeed, the quality of description essentially contributes to our affective literacy and to the (consequent) indispensable legitimacy of our affective life.

In the domain of neuroscience it is sometimes suggested that 'the primitive psychological taxonomy of ordinary language', ought to be discarded in favour of a 'neurophysiological taxonomy' that would allow us to better describe, conceive and introspectively apprehend one's inner life.[10] In this gaze, we ought to replace pseudo-scientific theories about 'mental states and processes' with 'modern' neuropsychological theories, and thus have a vocabulary regarding the states of our brain and nervous system. Of course, we have an immense technical vocabulary in the domain of biochemistry and a comparatively scarce language for the 'chemistry' of our emotional life. Perhaps contributions in the area of neurophysiology could be seen not so much as reductionistic or blasphemous accounts of human affective life, but rather as a challenge for the exploration of its richness and complexity. Indeed, different methods of inquiry emanating from different outlooks may profitably resonate with incommensurable projects in other disciplines.[11]

In Gardner's synoptic view, the central function at work in the development of affective maturity is the access to our own feeling life, to one's *range* of affects and emotions: the capacity to generate instant discriminations among feelings and, eventually, to label them, to enmesh them in symbolic codes, or the instant capacity to draw upon them as a means of guiding behaviour.[12] The major accomplishment of affective maturation is the emergence of links between emotion and cognition, as well as the development of emotional regulation. If we cannot label and recognise our diversified feelings, we become constrained by an insufficient emotional vocabulary that renders us affectively illiterate in spite of the very best academic education. If we are not capable of appreciating and focusing on, for example, the range of feelings which may develop between pride and condescension, or between disappointment and humiliation, we are not so much damaged in an existing capacity but rather impeded in our affective development. The idea of a 'continuum' is invoked here to indicate some linear model that consists of a series of identifiable situations between two stipulated poles. At one conventional pole of the continuum a paradigmatic (and perhaps more familiar) example may be placed, while other instances can be placed at various points towards the 'opposite' pole of the gradient, according to the extent of their conceptual independence from the cluster of features of the paradigm case. As T.S. Eliot points out, 'in developing the language, enriching the meaning of words, the poet is making possible a much wider range of emotion and perception for other persons, because he gives them the speech in which more can be expressed.'[13] By way of example, we could note that the poetic evocation of 'Sorge' in Goethe's *Faust* is a particularly accomplished attempt; however, there are many more expressions, which may even be seen as trite, that serve to bring about the specific characteristics of our emotions; thus, at times, we even *colour* our words to describe what we feel – we say 'blue', 'grey', 'black' or 'yellow'. There are innumerable terms that may serve the same purpose,[14] while in pedantic forms of language, words about affects can be very poor or even misleading instruments. This same ongoing maturation is of course also needed to decipher and elicit the others' affects; emotional intelligence consistently 'turns outwards' towards other individuals. In relation to others, in fact, natural expressions like groaning, crying, or trembling can only be approximate indicators of what another person may feel. Schulte remarks that, in itself, weeping does not reveal the inner motives of a person's behaviour; the same is true for other 'natural' expressions like blushing or turning pale.[15] One of the ways of finding out about personal, inner motives is of course to listen attentively to utterances and expressions of any kind. It is often the *tone* of an expression that enables us to make relatively fine distinctions between types of emotions, and it is the specificness of the tone that accounts for cultural variations in the expression of feelings.[16] These are specificities that can be deadened or lost in the absence of authentic listening. But then, we are unwittingly constrained in a culture primarily capable of expression, a culture which is only slowly *beginning* to conceive of maturational listening.

For most practical purposes, according to Langer, the nature of feeling does not need to be conceptually known.[17] For the study of mind, however, such conceptual knowledge appears to be essential, in that the dynamic forms of felt experiences are major manifestations of its rhythms and integrations. Feeling is the constant but private display of what is occurring in our psychosomatic unity, or the index of much that goes on below the limen of sentience, and of the whole organic process (or life). Even in psychoanalysis, interpretation is only a (small) part of the work of understanding psychic life. The major part, perhaps, is relating to the patient's life and thus creating a suitable ambience for interpretative work. The paradox is that this essential 'something more than interpretation'[18] is an aspect of our interactive life, for which we hardly have a vocabulary. In our human condition, we have innumerable terms for our surrounding world, but only a scarce vocabulary for our inner and intersubjective vicissitudes. It is almost as though a linguistic evolution were implicitly being called for. Within psychoanalytic culture there is perhaps a parallel, submerged literature that focuses on this something more than interpretation, and makes all kinds of epistemic efforts to find names, terms, labels, concepts, or paradigms to make this vital dimension thinkable – and finally approachable.[19] One of the paradoxes of psychoanalytic culture is that affects are the closest thing we have to facts; and yet, what psychoanalytic theory says about the vicissitudes of affective states is often rather generic and obscure.[20] Of course, affects are difficult to access: the processes that produce affective states are never fully available, even to the conscious scrutiny of the patient, and possibly even less so to the analytic 'observer' who will inevitably receive the product of these processes through his own inner structures. In fact, when we speak of an inner 'world' or inner 'space', we should bear in mind that we also use these metaphors to refer to a *construction*. Before our so-called 'inner space' becomes a structure suited to hosting the internalisation of persons and intersubjective relations supporting the course of our development, this celebrated 'inner world' is perhaps indistinguishable from the internalised figures which occupy it. A scarce differentiation between the internalisation of significant others, on the one hand, and the inner personal space (place, receptacle, container, structure) which they occupy, on the other, is at the root of early affectual vicissitudes, as well as of pathological conditions. In fact, there is a fear that when an internalised significant figure disappears or moves away, it may shatter and pull away the entire inner place it occupies.[21] As the early inner world may be thought of as the container of significant others, the quality and reliability of the affective content may be experienced as a potential source of devastation. The metaphoric expressions summoned to 'describe' the origins of mentation primarily serve to indicate that, especially in our early life, affective interactions and inner structure are inextricably interwoven. In this sense, then, the linguistic expressibility of inchoate interactions is essential to psychic growth, just as its insufficiency can drastically impede inner life. In order to develop, the mind must be able to introject and retain what it has absorbed, whether it be good or bad. What we constantly need to explain, and reiterately cope with, is the passage from the predominance of attributions based on the pleasure/unpleasure principle, to the recognition of existence; this is the capacity to decide that something interior exists and is therefore nameable and thinkable independent of its pleasurable or unpleasurable quality.

As desirous of more skills in the area of emotional intelligence, the individual often seeks help in making the proper kinds of discriminations. The increasing recourse to psychic therapy in the West may certainly be seen as an effort to develop one's capacity for finer distinctions within the range of personal feelings, as well as a challenge to decipher the affective signals of those on whom we depend.[22] From this perspective, the source of pathology is not so much the existence of negative affects, but an inadequate relationship with our feelings. This is the critical factor that differentiates psychodynamics and psychopathology. Clinical literature shows us the innumerable relations that creatures have with their emotions. In a sense, psychoanalytic therapy could also be seen as emotional 'education', as the enhancement of the emotional courage to know and own what one feels, to become aware of a whole variety of nuanced, changing feelings. In a synoptic gaze, we could say with Gardner that one may develop appropriate appraisals, fine discriminations, accurate categorisations of situations, or, less happily, one can make excessively gross discriminations, generic labellings, or incorrect inferences, and thus fundamentally misinterpret confrontations with others. The less we understand the feelings of others, the more likely we are to interact inappropriately and therefore fail to secure a liveable role within whichever micro- or macro-community we inhabit.[23] Learning emotional literacy includes the capacity to increasingly recognise feelings and expand our vocabulary for them; affective literacy also takes the form of evaluating one's strengths and weaknesses. However, as personal maturation is not easy, we are often mute and dependent upon prosthetic supports: the emotional language sold to us by the emissaries of ruling epistemologies. The 'creative people' do the job for us (but with what ethics?), and we gladly pay in whatever form for their services of giving voice to 'our' affects. In the media, for example, the narratives of ordeals caused by mental fear are rather frequent.[24] They seem to be an entertaining description of the devastating impact of emotional distress upon our personal intelligence, or a vicarious witness of the power of the 'emotional brain' to overwhelm, and even paralyse, the 'thinking brain' whenever the two cannot sufficiently communicate and function as a synergy.

Our affectual illiteracy establishes a form of alienation from emotional vicissitudes that we are eager to view in the media, free from the burden of having to accept, repossess, and articulate them. This is perhaps evidenced by the endless talk shows which have promoted affective life to first rank in popular entertainment. The participants in these talk shows may come forth with exchanges of recriminations and often tell stories of pathos involving heart-rending experiences, with the present and distant audience also contributing to the enterprise. It would of course be an oversimplification to construe this pervasive custom as a sadomasochistic exercise for the viewers and participants. The fact is that we ambivalently seek access to a world of emotions that we hope to co-explore and more fruitfully inhabit.

Cultural influences

Different cultures and eras tend to privilege diverse dominant affects; and while the paradigmatic cases could be seen as the result of cultural influences, affective specificities are more linked to personal histories.[25] For the sake of example, we could remember that the romantic variety of love is the product of particular cultural expressions having their origins in the courts of eleventh-century Europe; we could also remember that in certain totalitarian regimes of *this* century, feelings such as pity, compassion and empathy were actually considered 'swinish'. Whatever is relevant in our lives arouses emotions, and thus we regularly experience a variety of affects to which we generally refer with such terms as anger, fear, shame, etc. These, however, are cultural classifications which do not necessarily coincide with the capacity to symbolically bring to life our *own* flow of personal emotions, and transform it into internal communication.[26] In this connection, we should also invoke a psychic 'condition' known as 'alexithymia', which is a notion generally attributed to Sifneos.[27] 'Alexithymia', from the Greek *a* for 'lack', *lexus* for 'word', and *thymos* for 'emotion', is a term used to describe people who seem to lack feelings; and yet, this picture might in part be due to their inability to *express* emotions, rather than to an absence of emotions altogether. In certain individuals, the symbolisation of the derivatives of somatic drives seems especially difficult. Such people greatly puzzle psychologists as they *report* no feelings or fantasies, and *recount* colourless dreams, as if they had no inner emotional life to speak of. They can blush, gasp, or weep, but they seem unable to describe their state. The central question is, however, how much of it is a psychic lack, how much is due to affective illiteracy, *and* how this can influence emotional deficits.

The reference to cultural paradigm cases also involves a conceptual point. In saying, for example, that paradigm cases of affect are felt, occurring states, one is suggesting that these features centrally define the concept of affect, and that it is on such cases that emotions depend for their cultural classification and significance as 'proper' affective states.[28] One feature of the use of paradigms is that it tends to organise the domain of cultural inquiry into paradigm cases, that is instances that exhibit the full complement of concept-specifying features, and cases that deviate to a greater or lesser degree from the paradigm.[29] In this respect, paradigms provide systematic principles of classification which contrast with, say, merely enumerative, piecemeal categorisations. These simply describe similarities and differences between phenomena, without organising them in such a way as to give priority to any particular group. It is of course a virtue of paradigms that they go beyond mere enumerations in providing a more systematic scheme of classification; however, we should also bear in mind that paradigms are cultural products, and are not quite the reflection of primal inner phenomena. For instance, the institutionalisation of morally important sentiments explains why some have argued that 'guilt' is not an emotion, and it similarly explains the difficulties surrounding such terms as 'compassion'. When we elaborate upon single terms, the danger of some variety of affective essentialism seems to re-emerge; it is the sort of essentialism that is 'wrong-in-theory-but-right-in-practice'.[30] In fact, culture is here to help our psychic survival. If, strategically, we need to talk about a certain specific, identifiable affect in order to legitimise it, then we seem to profit from a mode of conceptualising the 'essences' of psychic vicissitudes which ultimately offer us practical ways of thinking and communicating. These essentialist explorations are, of course, only instrumental whenever there is no alternative to conceiving our affective life, except in terms of the discrete, essential affects that are highlighted in culture.

NOTES

1. 'Wording determines the transformational potential of signifier in relation to the latent contents of the analysand's ideas. Choose a word and you select a direction. Choose a word and you create force. A 'colourless' word is without force, perhaps weak, but in certain moments appropriate to service considerate thought engaged with emotionally powerful issues.' Christopher Bollas, 'Wording and telling sexuality', *The International Journal of Psychoanalysis*, vol. 78, 1997, pp. 363–7.
2. Wilfred Ruprecht Bion, *Attention and Interpretation. A Scientific Approach to Insight in Psycho-Analysis and Groups*, London: Tavistock, 1978, p. 9. Levinas writes that 'enjoyment is the very pulsation of the I', and also that 'one becomes a subject of being

not by assuming being but in enjoying happiness.' Emanuel Levinas, *Totality and Infinity*, Pittsburg: Duquesne University Press, 1961, pp. 113 and 119.

3. In the acknowledged public domain, affects are always others' ones, while in the private unacknowledged side they are just one's rationality; the unwitting intertwinement of the two may only provoke blindness.

4. Blaise Pascal, *Pascal's Pensées*, with an introduction by T.S. Eliot, New York: E.P. Dutton, 1958, paragraph 397, p. 107. A moth does not suffer for not being a chimpanzee, or a computer does not rejoice for accurately performing a correct logical operation. There must be a knowledge, however unthought, of our human deadened potential that must ultimately trigger disparate forms of mute retaliation.

5. Claire Armon-Jones, *Varieties of affect*, New York and London: Harvester Wheatsheaf, a division of Simon and Schuster International Group, date of publication not indicated. Oxford University thesis supervised by Kathleen Wilkes of St. Hilda's College, and Paul Snowden of Exeter College, 1991, p. 5.

6. Ibid., p. 6.

7. This point is reiterated in C. Armon-Jones, *Varieties of Affect*. According to Goleman, for instance, learning emotional skills at the cusp of adolescence may be especially helpful, as the young seem to be better prepared at handling the routine teenage agonies of rejection. It is difficult, instead, when the greater the problem, the less the awareness of exactly what they are feeling.

8. A comparable argument is developed by C. Armon-Jones in *Varieties of Affect*, pp. 100–15.

9. Jones suggests that 'In evaluating someone as a potential spouse, we may hear a person say, "Well, I really like him a lot . . . but I don't really think that I love him" . . . It appears, then, that the difference between liking . . . and loving is not simply one of intensity; there are subtle, but very real differences in quality. What are these differences? This is the question that must be answered if the distinction is to have any real meaning.' Joseph M. Jones, *Affects as process, An Inquiry into the Centrality of Affect in Psychological Life*, Hillsdale, NJ: Analytic Press, 1995, p. 78.

10. Patricia M. Churchland, *Matter and Consciousness: A Contemporary Introduction to the Philosophy of Mind*, Cambridge, MA: MIT Press, 1988, pp. 179–80. Solomon remarks that many philosophers, like their associates in the social sciences, have turned the analysis of emotion to more public, observable criteria, that is, to the behaviour that 'expresses' emotion, the physiological disturbances that 'cause' emotion, and the social circumstances and use of emotion language in the ascription of emotions. Robert Solomon, 'Nature of emotions', in E. Craig (ed.), *Routledge Encyclopaedia of Philosophy*, vol. 3, London and New York: Routledge, 1998, pp. 281–90.

11. Our affective experience is subtly but significantly influenced by the capacity for symbolic thought. Thus, inexorably, the study of more complex affects in all of their experiential manifestations becomes virtually synonymous with the study of the human mind in its metaphoric potential. In this connection we could invoke an enlightening remark of Green: 'If the analysand makes himself known by his words, it is completely impossible to give the words equal weight because of the different states of mind in which they are spoken', André Green, 'Conceptions of affect' in *Our Private Madness*, London: Hogarth Press, 1986, pp. 174–213.

12. Howard Gardner, *Frames of Mind. The Theory of Multiple Intelligences*, London: Fontana Press, 1993, p. 240. In this same perspective we could invoke one of Nietzsche's fragments: 'I am convinced of the phenomenalism of the inner world: everything that reaches our consciousness is utterly and completely adjusted, simplified, schematised, interpreted; the actual process of inner "perception" . . . is concealed from us . . . ' Friedrich Nietzsche, *Will To Power*, vol. 15 of *Complete Works*, trans. A.M. Ludovici, Edinburgh: T.N. Fowlis, 1910, No. 477, p. 7.

13. Thomas Stern Eliot is quoted in R.W. Hebburn, 'The arts and the education of feeling and emotion', in R.F. Deardon, P. Hirst and R.S. Peters (eds), *Education and the Development of Reason*, part III, London: Routledge and Kegan Paul, 1975.
14. Joachim Schulte, 'Emotion: remarks on Wittgenstein and William James', in R. Egidi (ed.), *Wittgenstein: Mind and Language*, Dordrecht, Boston and London: Kluwer Academic Publishers, 1995, p. 261.
15. Ibid., p. 259.
16. Ibid., p. 260.
17. Susanne K. Langer, *Mind: An Essay on Human Feeling*; abridged edition by G. Van Der Heuval, Baltimore and London: Johns Hopkins University Press, 1988, p. 25.
18. The term 'something more' derives from Daniel Stern, Louis Sander, Jeremy Nahum, *et al.* 'Non-interpretative mechanisms in psychoanalytic therapy. The "something more" than interpretation', *The International Journal of Psychoanalysis*, vol. 79, 1998, pp. 903–21.
19. Ibid., p. 903.
20. Charles Spezzano, *Affect in Psychoanalysis. A Clinical Synthesis*, Hillsdale NJ and London: Analytic Press, 1993, p. ix.
21. This hypothesis is developed in Herbert Rosenfeld, *Psychotic States: A Psychoanalytical Approach*, New York: International Universities Press, 1966.
22. H. Gardner, *Frames of Mind*, p. 254.
23. Ibid., p. 255.
24. Daniel Goleman, *Emotional Intelligence. Why It Can Matter More than* IQ, New York: Bantam, 1995, pp. 78–9.
25. According to Langer, 'It may seem strange that the most immediate experiences in our lives should be the least recognised . . . We usually have no objectifying images of such experiences to recall and recognise, and we do not often try to convey them in more detail than would be likely to elicit sympathy from other people. For that general communication we have words: sad, happy, envious, nauseated, nervous, etc. But each of these words fits a large class of actual events, with practically no detail. An adjective never presents the complexities of the intraorganic processes from which overt behaviour arises, whereas feeling really begins far below the issue of such processes in visible or audible action.' S.K. Langer, *Mind: An Essay on Human Feeling*, p. 24.
26. On this point see Richard and Bernice Lazarus, *Passion and Reason. Making Sense of Our Emotions*, New York and Oxford: Oxford University Press, 1994, p. 3.
27. Peter E. Sifneos, 'Problems of psychotherapy of patients with alexithymic characteristics and physical disease', *Psychotherapy and Psychosomatics*, vol. 26, 1975, pp. 65–70. Also by Sifneos, 'Affect, emotional conflict and deficit: an overview', *Psychotherapy and Psychosomatics*, vol. 56, 1991, pp. 116–22.
28. This thesis is developed by C. Armon-Jones, *Varieties of Affect*, p. 13.
29. Stephen Hilmy suggests that Wittgenstein's remarks concerning the philosophy of psychology during the last years of his life are a sustained effort to debunk the taxonomic myth by probing the rich and diverse grammars of our psychological concepts. As he explained in a revealing note that did not find its way into the published versions of his last writings 'In order to be able to get a surview of these concepts, you must compare them with something other than what their surface grammar suggests to you . . . The concepts are disguised' (MS 134, pp. 126–9). Quoted in 'Wittgenstein on language, mind and mythology', in Rosaria Egidi (ed.), *Wittgenstein: Mind and Language*, Dordrecht, Boston and London: Kluwer Academic Press, 1995, p. 245.
30. John Searle, *Speech Acts: An Essay in the Philosophy of Language*, Cambridge: Cambridge University Press, 1969, p. 172.

Chapter 10

Affects and narratives

Joint narratives

Epistemologies that should elicit some reasonable suspicion are those based on the belief that solipsism characterises the originary cognitive scene; in spite of this silent preliminary assumption, they resist criticism for their failure to break free of their genetic one-person outlook. Their epistemic individualism seems marked by the evanescent but constraining oversight of our inescapable human bondedness: the conviction that although other people 'of course' exist, knowledge is produced by the subject through individual experience of 'the world'. Conversely, from a generic Wittgensteinian perspective, we cannot see the individual as linguistically prior to the community, and a community can hardly be imagined in terms of cognitively independent creatures. Indeed, it appears more plausibly constituted by interdependent affective agents. In this gaze, therefore, the emotional qualities, priorities, and vicissitudes that characterise any micro- or macro-community can be thought of as capable of determining our different forms of knowledge and cultural behaviour. The life of our mind is not linked to definitive modes of affective behaviour, but to ways of thinking of our inner life, as emerging from maturation and culture. According to Battersby, the self grows out of 'otherness', and sameness (or identity) is gradually patterned from experiences of difference.[1] Our early vicissitudes are in fact characterised by an ongoing process of mutual regulation of affective states; it is a process that involves a variegated sequence of adaptive moves. Thus, if sameness and difference are seen as intertwining in early dyadic adjustments, then the idea of sameness is not only useful for identifying different personal affects, but can also be instrumental to an understanding of diasporic emotions or collective feelings such as nationalism, revanchism, or ethnocentrism.

In Hankinson's view, although epistemic communities are not monolithic, they cannot dissolve into a collection of knowing individuals.[2] Because of our participation in a number of different communities, as well as by virtue of our experience as individuals, we can of course uniquely contribute to the knowledge generated by our various social identities. Yet none of us knows what no one else could. However singular an experience may be, what we know on the basis of that experience is made possible by our interactive paradigms, that is, by standards and knowledge that enable us to organise our experience into coherent personal accounts. Primal interactions are in fact meant to facilitate the engendering of these accounts. We thus need a more inclusive understanding of evidence than is allowed by an approach of solipsistic, individual derivation, and deeply related to this, we need to recognise micro- or macro-communities as the primary agents of epistemology in the sense of their being generators and repositories of our human knowledge. To reconnect these introductory philosophical considerations with a more clinical outlook, we could invoke one of Winnicott's synoptic statements: 'The autonomy of the self rests upon the paradoxical fact that its autonomy must initially be provided for by the mother. The child's creative use of solitude (aloneness) requires the presence of the caretaker in order to affirm the continuity of the self.'[3]

Although the sort of knowledge that predominates in our Western culture is truth- and world-oriented, efforts aimed at knowing more about profound interpersonal relations are given increasing recognition. Moreover, this 'secondary' but vital form of knowledge essentially integrates cognition and affects. As Stern remarks, the more intense interpersonal experiences alter the relational field, and induce the recognition that the joint experience of participants transforms the inner perception of the encounter; the encounter, in fact, epistemically expands that same psychic space in an unforeseen way. Studies of development by several authors have emphasised an ongoing process of negotiation throughout the early years of life, that involves a sequence of transformational encounters between infant and caregivers.[4] In Stern's view, each of the actors draws personal history into the interaction, thus shaping whatever adaptive manœuvres are possible for each in the lived contingency.[5] Current concepts from developmental studies suggest that what the infant internalises is not so much the person he deals with, but rather the process of mutual regulation. What is absorbed in the developing process is not 'bits' of persons, nature or culture, but rather *types* of relations with them; we internalise micro- or macro-relational paradigms. We ultimately grow through the absorption of the affective and structural links that exist between everything we experience in our inchoate vicissitudes.

One of the ways in which our affects become more conscious and intentional is the process of producing (for ourselves and for others) appropriate narrative accounts, or personally meaningful links. Whenever we tell stories of our emotional experiences to others, we allow ourselves to explore the events more consciously in the context of an enhancing relationship and in the progressive refinement of the account, almost as if reciprocal narratives were the originary medium and receptacle of all human knowledge.[6] No matter how much we study the interlocutor, or no matter how much we care for a partner, we cannot project ourselves into the other and say how it is that the world looks from in there. We can only try to understand if we are repeatedly informed by our interlocutors, and they will only inform us to the extent that we actually *care* to listen.[7] In this respect, then, the quality of the micro-community does influence the quality of the knowledge that is generated. Of course, narration to receptive others is only one way of creating meaning and safe-guarding the coherence of the self; its contrary, however, which is the impossibility

of narrating because of insufficient listening conditions, severely disrupts the formation of the self and impedes growth. Such a large proportion of human behaviour
seems precisely devoted to talking about vicissitudes of all kinds: it almost appears
to be a compelling necessity and a profound source of psychic well-being. Its
absence, in fact, often indicates a process of serious mental deterioration.

A two-person knowledge, moreover, seems to require and generate higher standards of objectivity than do those that turn away from recognising bondedness and
relatedness as the source of our knowing. The problem with a so-called 'one-person
psychology' is not that it is too biologically oriented but that it cannot evolve in a
direction that allows for intentionality and reciprocity. A collateral view is that
a person's behaviour may be best predicted by the attribution of a 'theory' (in the
sense of an interconnected set of beliefs and desires) notwithstanding the fact that
we do not, or could not, come up with any such explicit theory. This consideration,
of course, would lead to much discussion of explicit and tacit theorising.[8] My thesis
is limited to the suggestion that the attribution of a theory to persons is warranted
in so far as it facilitates the understanding of their accounts of events, almost in
view of the joint, dialogic product of *our* 'theories' and *their* accounts. These
theories exhibit different degrees of stability and fluctuation, so that throughout our
life cycle we become engaged in the constant generation of ulterior theories that
ultimately support the reciprocal regulation of our inner states.

Narrative constructions

It seems that coherence and continuity are mutually reinforcing loops: in our psychic
life, the cohesion of the self offered by a facilitating environment supports its
continuity, and vice versa. The generation of this early intersubjective synergy is
gradually internalised by the nascent personality, but never completely established.
In the older child and in the adult, however, the coherence of the self tends to become
less dependent on the valuations of others, as it is fortified through the construction
of cohesive personal narratives, moral commitments, and disparate passionate
interests. In this gaze, we could better envision interactions that may threaten the
core of the personality: these not only arise from acute or chronic traumatic experiences, but also from conflicting, confusing decrees which may come with the force
of parental authority. In these circumstances, there is an adverse and paradoxical
effect on the capacity for thought: parental narratives may assault what must
be believed if action is to continue and hence, paradoxically, they must be both
taken seriously *and* ignored.[9] It is an extreme challenge; let us remind ourselves that
we are all 'psychic survivors', in the language of McDougall.[10] The intertwinement
of cohesion and continuity thus appears to be profoundly dependent upon the joint
weaving of narrative constructions. As is known, when people are asked to recount
emotional episodes that have mobilised their true feelings, they typically describe
incidents that somehow transform or enhance their sense of self. A contingency of
intense psychic interaction can in fact create an ulterior interpersonal dimension,
and thus more scope within that previous space. In Stern's gaze, an example

provides the best illustration: if in the course of playful interaction a caretaker and infant unexpectedly achieve a new and higher level of intensity, the infant's capacity to tolerate higher levels of mutually created excitement is thus expanded for future interactions. 'Once an expansion of the range has occurred, and there is the mutual recognition that the two partners have successfully interacted together in a higher orbit of joy, their subsequent interactions will be conducted within this altered intersubjective environment.'[11] In Nozick's view, the exploration of any valuable trait, feature, or function of the self will be furthered in terms of some other trait that does not have precisely that value.[12] This cross-fertilising element is often contributed by the different-but-separate-interacting other, that is, by an empathic but sufficiently distinct person. 'A major subjective feature of a shift in implicit relational knowing is that it feels like a sudden qualitative change' says Stern.[13] This is why psychic contact with a different agent is so clearly enlivening for our thinking; the intimate contact, as a paradigmatic notion, captures the subjective experience of a sudden enhancing shift in implicit relational knowing for both persons involved in the relation. In a therapeutic perspective, all these considerations draw the experience of maturational psychic contact into a 'domain that transcends but does not abrogate the professional relationship, and becomes partially freed of transferential-countertransferential overtones'.[14] Affective knowledge, in fact, does not repel reason, but is a compoment of it. It is the development of the sort of knowledge that is *partially* free from current canons, while at the same time developing the rational core of our thinking. This sort of reason breaks free from conventional dilemmatic constraints of the either/or type. It has more to do with neither/nor experiences precisely because it grows into something ulterior, whether it be more intense, more profound, more innovative, or more far reaching. Ultimately, this is what developing humans relentlessly seek; the rest seems to be so benumbing that it nearly elicits silent rage.

As we know, emotions necessarily include personal meanings that depend on what is important to us. Each emotion, moreover, could reveal a distinctive dramatic plot that indicates what we *believe* is happening to us as well as what it signifies to our life course. According to Lazarus, there is a distinctive drama for each emotion which conveys the personal meaning that the individual has attached to the experience.[15] For each emotion, a plot seems to unfold that reveals the way we have construed a situation. If we are to understand how an emotion comes about, we must delve into the unique storyline that distinguishes it from other emotions. Why, for example, have we experienced anger and not shame or guilt? Or what level, sort, or intensity is the anger? If we know the plot, by having patiently learned it, we can develop an easier access to the emotions that the person is likely to experience.

The capacity to generate a storyline of one's emotional vicissitudes is of great importance, and so is the possibility of its failure. It is no surprise to observe that the capacity is characteristically, although not invariably, disrupted in cases of what we call major psychic disorders. According to Bolton and Hill, a person may experience a strong emotion, or find himself engaged in some course of action having no idea of the reason why; typically, the person feels ignorant, perplexed and overwhelmed.[16] Another kind of case is that in which the subject gives an account that sounds 'irrational' in the opinion of others, and perhaps even in one's own. Of course, ignorance of, or an inconsequential account of the beliefs and desires that regulate one's actions are not sufficient for so-called disorders: there are several aspects of daily action for which we have no account; we simply behave and respond in the way we do without much preoccupation with our reasons. Yet, in so far as activity or mood is relevant to us, especially if it is distressing in frequency and intensity, we generally do seek a convincing account of why it is occurring, at least so that it becomes liveable and perhaps manageable. Apart from instances of extreme severity, we are all more or less familiar with profound difficulties in making sense of disquieting, recurrent feelings. These considerations seem relevant in that if the account is impeded, or any set of reasons rendered impossible, self-coherence is ultimately threatened. If madness is to be avoided and sanity enhanced, it is clear that listened discourse should be consistently used to help individuals generate acceptable accounts of their inner worlds. Through personally generated narratives, we can construct imaginary alternatives and inner worlds that may have creative outcomes. Emde suggests that in analysis, the 'as if experiences' of transference not only provide for interpretative work, but also enhance alternative possibilities inasmuch as further configurations of affective processes are enabled.[17] In this way, the 'as if' of analysis can lead to 'what if' kinds of thinking, planning and decision making. The point of these arguments is in fact to emphasise that whenever narrative constructions are impeded, silent devastation can be inconspicuously perpetrated, almost as if no neutral itineraries could be envisioned for our mind's affective life.

For the sake of agreement and social survival we may at times disrupt our contact with our personally elaborated convictions and comply with any authoritative or fascinating account. Doing this to ourselves in our mind may have profound consequences such as preventing us from making enlivening contacts with our internal objects. Proper contact with these objects is a contact that is clear and passionate; however, this linking to our internal world, which includes ideas and values that we care about, is also an exclusive process. It sets up a barrier between one's self and others in so far as the others' internal objects, their cherished ideals, somehow differ from one's own. According to Caper, the psychoanalyst can creatively interpret to the extent that he has a mind of his own, that is, relations with his internal values that somehow exclude the patient.[18] If he can do this he is in a position to help the patient *not* to identify with the therapist who, in turn, allows the patient to identify with himself, and to have a relationship with his own internal world instead of an excessive identification with the analyst.[19] If joint constructions are to be creative and maturational, there should be constant concern for the obstinate safeguarding of the separateness of the minds.

Especially in the social sciences, certain conventionally inexplicable emotions may lead to one's making subversive observations that challenge dominant outlooks or paradigms. The expression of such feelings may indicate that what are generally considered 'facts' have been constructed in such a way as to exclude the perceptions and outlooks of the 'lesser' members of the epistemic community, or the 'lesser' parts of the self. Conversely, through appropriate and mutually respectful narrative constructions, an individual may transform the view of himself and, for example, ascertain that he is not a perverse creature but a victim of abuse, not a bandit but a revolutionist, not an inferior being but an exploited creature. Once again, the ultimate maturational outcomes will depend upon the qualitative combination of intrapsychic and intersubjective relations.

Psychoanalytic narratives

Over a century ago, Freud suggested that 'It is not the experiences themselves which act traumatically but their revival as *memory*.'[20] Reconnecting with his earliest concerns about sexual traumas, he later argued that 'they produce their effect only to a very slight degree at the time at which they occur; what is far more important is their *deferred* effect, which can only take place at a later period of growth . . . During the interval between the experiences of these impressions and their reproduction . . . the psychical apparatus . . . has undergone important development: and thus it is that the influence of these earlier . . . experiences now leads to an abnormal psychical reaction . . . '[21] Apart from the specificness of sexual offence, the general paradigm that Freud suggests is that the more conscious levels of our minds constantly retell the story according to the schemas of our more recent or current experiences. Freud had the deep insight that memory is renarrated in accordance with later experience, although he was, perhaps, not prepared to fully develop this seminal line of inquiry. Indeed, Freud's presentation of *nachträglichkeit* is hinted at in different parts of his numerous works: as early as 1896 the idea was expressed in a letter to Fliess.[22] As is known, there is an expanding literature on the topic of *nachträglichkeit*, variously referred to as 'differed effect', 'retranscription of memory', 'recategorisation of experience', and 'retrospective attribution'.

The reason why many psychoanalysts insist on having four sessions a week in an age of instant services and city traffic is perhaps more deep seated than we think. Although one of the chief arguments for defending this classic number of sessions is the effort to create a secure setting that will enhance transference phenomena, we could also think that this arrangement creates a close and demanding involvement on both parts, that is, a commitment of which we are bound to make sense; and the sense that we try to make can only take the form of a joint narrative account: the story that we try to develop – with whatever clinical instruments we have been taught to use. Thus, how one interprets and reacts to having an affect becomes an important part of one's identity through a more active use of one's emotional history.[23] As Emde suggests, clinical implications stem from a view of psycho-analysis as a developmental process, as an intense experience that relies on establishing a special kind of intimacy. Emotional communications are used in its formation, maintenance, disruptions, repairs and endings.[24] In fact, there would be no psychoanalysis without the affective intimacy of the analytic relation, and without an emotionally available psychoanalyst there would be no attempt to internally reorganise one's affective history. Stern suggests that even those analysts who adhere to a theory of mutative interpretation, usually accept the view that any transference interpretation *requires* preparatory steps, and also involves subsequent psychic resonances, ultimately constituting a structured sequence.[25] It need not be a problem that in this inclusionary view of the interpretative activity, it is not clear which part pertains to the affective encounters within the dyad, and which part pertains to insight via interpretation.[26] This insight could even be viewed as an epistemic tribute paid to the cognitive paradigms of psychoanalysis; indeed, there is no way of ascertaining whether the insights derived from optimal transference interpretations are ultimately so mutative, transformational, or curative. What we laboriously learn from psychoanalysis is not only the acumen but also the pathos of knowledge, for we cannot construct interpretations that the patient can use to know everything at once about specific origins and vicissitudes of affects. There is perhaps an interpretative circularity that we can enter at any point and around which we can creatively and indefinitely move. Of course, when Freud first discovered that knowledge of one's self brought psychic benefits, it was simply the patient's knowing which was focused upon, even though it was admittedly an elaborate process that took place with the doctor's assistance. In the subsequent maturation of our psychoanalytic culture, and with the appreciation of the transference–countertransference phenomena, the quality of the analyst's empathic knowledge comes to be regarded as co-essential to the patient's capacity to know. New psychoanalytic vocabularies, moreover, enable us to envision a narrative of our own development, of our idiosyncratic moral struggles, which are far more finely textured, far more 'tailored' to our individual cases, than the generic vocabulary which the philosophical-cultural tradition has offered us.[27]

It is possible that most experiences that contribute to representations of inter-personal relations have occurred too early to be remembered. Cognitive science, in fact, offers a key distinction between two types of memory systems, both of which have important functions in psychoanalytic treatment: a declarative or explicit memory involved with the conscious retrieval of information about the past, and a procedural or implicit memory system from which information may be drawn without the experience of remembering.[28] Procedural memory is content free, and is involved in acquiring sequences of actions, and the 'how' of behaviour. It is probably this second function of memory that is involved in the constant retranscription of our psychic histories.[29] In Edelman's view, memory is not a record in the central nervous system that corresponds to past experience, but instead, it is conceived as a *recategorisation* of experience.[30] 'The theory proposes that past experiences are not recorded in the brain in a fashion that is isomorphic with the events; rather what is stored is the potential to activate categories of experience.'[31] According to Loewald, memory as recollection manifests psychic time as *activity*; it makes the past present. The remarkable fact is that in mental life, the psychic past is not in the objective past but is active now as past, and that the psychic present manages to act on the psychic past.[32] In the light of these synergistic perspectives, we could say that those who emphasise the importance of the here and now in the analytic experience, as not only distinct, but opposed to a hermeneutic reconstruction of the past, are perhaps caught in a false dilemma or a gratuitous dichotomy. For the here and now is a repetition of the past, and the here-and-now interpretation may serve to retranscribe our memories, and thus shape a different historical paradigm, or a novel view of one's identity that can be used in the lived present. The so-called present, in turn, is utilised for shaping the future, and for envisioning further reconstructions as retrospective valuations of our past and ever-new constructions of future events.

As Emde suggests, ongoing emotional processes are continually active in relation to memory systems, although they are constructed and reshaped in different ways during the particular circumstances in which they are evoked.[33] Since emotions are linked to significant relational experiences of the past, they are likely to be activated by comparable conditions in the present. These circumstances, in analysis, are usually transformed into various psychic pressures that are addressed to the therapist. These hypotheses lead to the very useful idea that emotion schemas of self functionally relate to others.[34] The particular experiences that lead to deeply pathological ways of dealing with others may precede the development of a memory system capable of encoding and retaining the experience in a way that can be represented as a story. Therefore we must strive to create some reasonable plot that utilises the psychic pressures brought onto the analyst. These are the current vicissitudes that, unlike ancient ones, are open to encoding and reorganising. These 'pressures', however, are essentially affective requests, affective threats, or affective negotiations. Thus, once again, we confront the problem of using affectual material for the purpose of creating a convincing story. But then, what is the creation of a story if not the production of a meaningful sequence, a disciplined structure, or a 'logic' of events? Such retrospective attributions develop into insights that protect the individual from being passively lived through by forces that would otherwise be inevitable, unknown, and uncontrollable. Conversely, we are concerned with affects for the purpose of *using their force* to generate a more versatile and flexible structure. Indeed psychoanalytic narratives converge with a process of creation and re-creation of our human thinking.

Doubts about the accuracy of early memories may induce a propensity to de-emphasise the role of past experiences altogether in favour of accounts of the therapeutic action in terms of the mere integration of past accounts and the achievement of a higher level of narrative coherence.[35] Setting aside the issue of truthful correspondence, the fact that analytic material often consists of constructions of the past that are attempted in the present still implies that therapeutic action lies within the joint effort to address the nature of the patient's retrospective disclosures.[36] Although it is frequently assumed that remembering past events causes therapeutic change, Fonagy and Target maintain that the recollection of memories is an epiphenomenon, a collateral consequence of the exploration of our profound, unconscious models of dealing with others.[37] Therapeutic action lies in the transformation of preconscious representation of our ways of relating to significant others. The isolated suggestion that 'where id was there ego shall be' can be grossly misleading, even as a sloganised version of the psychoanalytic process. What is necessary is the development of harmonious interactions between whatever it is that we describe as id and ego. This is primarily attempted through attention to transference and countertransference vicissitudes. Memory of course is all important, but mainly as a mediator, instrument, or channel for communicating representations of interpersonal relations; it is not important as a more or less truthful description of events. In the analytic context, 'truth' primarily makes sense in the perspective of psychic reality, in that the target of analysis is not so much the production of an 'objective' account, but rather the development of a new narrative way of experiencing one's self with others.

'Psychoanalytic attention is appropriately mostly focused on the emotion generated in the context of particular self-other relationships' remarks Fonagy.[38] In fact, we can only use emotions to enhance psychic transformation. What determines this celebrated psychic transformation? How is it that emotions influence our ways of being with others? Here again the tremendous, fateful force of listening comes into play. For it is the quality of listening which determines the quality of the expression, and thus the maturational force of a joint live discourse that metabolises affects into new psychic models. Of course, affects are psychic realities but they probably become transformative when they are sufficiently structured into jointly produced stories and accounts. Both developmental change and continuity with affective connections benefit from personal reflectiveness, and ultimately, with repeated narrative endeavours. Bucci's thesis that 'affect attunement', which needs to occur in an acceptable range in analytic work, is worth remembering in this connection.[39] It is only when this attunement occurs that a 'referential process' linking verbal and symbolic functions to sub-symbolic processes will enable new emotional meanings and the reorganisation of emotional schemas of self in relation to others. In fact, we are often puzzled to remark that patients in treatment with therapists, who hold widely divergent theories and clinical approaches, attain important psychic change in their way of functioning. Still more significantly, we often wonder why a patient may endure an analyst, for a number of years, whose clinical behaviour could be regarded as inadequate or even insane. The reason may be that ultimately, some kind of narrative that makes a minimum of sense is indeed being generated. We are so belligerently attached to our theoretical concepts because we often believe that it is the 'rightness' of our theories that brings about psychic change or symptomatic cure. Of course, we do need *some* theory to create a measure of order in the vicissitudes of mental functioning, and to try to explain why psychic improvement should occur as a result of 'talking cures'. In the general use of clinical examples, in fact, we customarily propose material that is suitable enough to be comprehended with the theoretical instruments that we are using, or else we introduce carefully selected examples that have inspired minor modifications of our explanatory paradigms. However, a further enlightening way of using our so-called 'clinical material' would be to show the sensible joint narrative that is produced with the use of *whatever* theoretical concepts we happen to use.

From this point of view, the sense of self can be seen as the result of the evolution of intrapersonal intelligence, as aided by capacities that emerge in other aspects of our culturally enhanced intelligence. In the end, the individual can offer an account of himself that integrates in logically acceptable fashion all those properties of the self that seem more worthy of appreciation. He can also continue to edit this description of himself as events transpire over the years, and as his 'self-concept' evolves. According to Gardner, the particular account that is offered may or may not be valid, but that is not of the essence here; it is crucial, rather, that through a combination of one's own mental competences, and through the interpretative schemas provided by cultural or therapeutic aids, it is possible to produce a descriptive narrative of one's self that appears to summarise and regulate the remainder of one's existence.[40]

In McDougall's language it is suggested that analysts variously explain psychic cure on the grounds that part of 'what was unconscious has become conscious', that 'autonomous ego-functioning has increased', that the patient has 'worked through the depressive position', that the 'basic signifiers of desire have been revealed', that 'Beta elements have developed into Alpha functioning', that a 'transitional space' has been created, that the self has been liberated from its 'grandiosity and self-objects' or, she adds, that the 'internal theatre' has been reconstituted to the satisfaction of both analyst and analysand.[41] She significantly concludes, however, that 'Irrespective of the analytical explanation that is preferred, each explanation reveals that *the account of an analysis is always a narrative written by two people.*'[42]

NOTES

1. Christine Battersby, *The Phenomenal Woman. Feminist Metaphysics and Patterns of Identity*, Cambridge and Oxford: Polity Press, 1998, p. 209. What is emerging in feminist writings is the concept of a multiple, shifting and often self-contradictory identity; it is an identity made up of heterogeneous and heteronomous representations of gender, race and class. See Teresa De Lauretis (ed.), *Feminist Studies/Critical Studies*, Bloomington, IN: Indiana University Press, 1986, p. 9. Nancy Holland remarks that 'It is only those who need not take the reality of others seriously, whose lives do not depend on understanding how others see the world, who can assume that all lives . . . are basically the same – and that very assumption perpetuates their power.' *Is Women's Philosophy Possible?*, Savage, MD: Rowman and Littlefield, 1990, p. 90.
2. Lynn Hankinson Nelson, 'Epistemogical Communities', in L. Alcoff and E. Potter (eds), *Feminist Epistemologies*, London and New York: Routledge, 1993, p. 150. She also remarks that epistemological communities are dynamic and unstable: they revolve, disband, realign and cohere as interests and undertakings evolve. Of course there are sub-communities that develop categories, methods and standards in addition to those that they share with larger communities; p. 148.
3. Donald Winnicott, 'Communicating and not communicating leading to a study of certain opposites', in *The Maturational Process and the Facilitating Environment*, New York: International Universities Press, 1965, p. 77.
4. Daniel Stern, Louis Sander, Jeremy Nahum, *et al.*, 'Non-interpretative mechanisms in

psychoanalytic therapy. The "something more" than interpretation', *The International Journal of Psycho-Analysis*, vol. 79, 1998, pp. 903–21.

5. Ibid., p. 905.
6. Oatley and Jenkins remark that we human beings are born not just into the world, but into society, where a history is constantly forming about what we people are negotiating with each other. 'In such historical constructions, emotions and our understanding of them are the pivotal points. From ancient times to the present, written or oral narrative literature concentrates an our emotional lives and their problematics – as if story telling and story listening had always been attempts to understand these matters. The activity is in many ways edifying because stories provide opportunities for vicarious action and possible solutions to the problem of how to be a person in the society that is depicted.' Keith Oatley and Jennifer M. Jenkins, *Understanding Emotions*, Oxford, UK and Cambridge, US: Blackwell, 1996, p. 366.
7. This thesis is extensively presented in Gemma Corradi Fiumara, *The Other Side of Language. A Philosophy of Listening*, London and New York: Routledge, 1990.
8. This view is presented by Derek Bolton and Jonathan Hill in *Mind, Meaning and Mental Disorder. The Nature of Causal Explanation in Psychology and Psychiatry*, Oxford, New York and Tokyo: Oxford University Press, 1996, p. 39.
9. Ibid., p. 308.
10. Joyce McDougall, *The Many Faces of Eros. A Psychoanalytic Exploration of Human Sexuality*, London: Free Association Books, 1995, p. 245. Thus, the vicissitudes of our affective life can be seen as processes of survival as well as styles of thinking and relating to others.
11. D. Stern, 'Non-interpretative mechanisms in psychoanalytic therapy', p. 909.
12. Robert Nozick, *Philosophical Explanations*, Cambridge, MA: Harvard University Press, 1981, p. 633.
13. D. Stern, 'Non-interpretative mechanisms in psychoanalytic therapy', p. 906.
14. Ibid., p. 917.
15. See on this topic Richard and Bernice Lazarus, *Passion and Reason. Making Sense of Our Emotions*, New York: Oxford University Press, 1996, p. 6.
16. This view is presented and discussed by D. Bolton and J. Hill in *Mind, Meaning and Mental Disorder*, pp. 42–3.
17. Robert Emde, 'Moving ahead: integrating influences of affective processes for development and psychoanalysis', *The International Journal of Psychoanalysis*, vol. 80, 1999, pp. 317–40.
18. Robert Caper, 'A mind of one's own', *The International Journal of Psychoanalysis*, vol. 78, 1997, part 2, pp. 265–78.
19. Ibid., p. 272.
20. Sigmund Freud, 'The neuro-psychoses of defence', *Standard Edition*, 1896, p. 164.
21. Sigmund Freud, 'Sexuality and the Aetiology of the Neuroses', *Standard Edition*, 1898, p. 281.
22. 'I should like to emphasise the fact that the successive registrations represent the psychic achievement of successive epochs of life. At the boundary between two such epochs a translation of the psychic material must take place.' Letter dated 6 December 1986. J. Masson (ed. and trans.) *The Complete Letters of Sigmund Freud to Wilhelm Fliess*, Cambridge, MA: Harvard University Press, 1985, p. 207.
23. As contrasted with the active use of one's emotional history, a 'passive' use of one's inner life can be a source pathology. 'The actions of the mind arise from adequate ideas alone, but the passions depend upon those alone which are inadequate.' Benedict de Spinoza, *Ethic: Demonstrated in a Geometrical Order*, 'On the origin and nature of affects', Proposition III (translated from the Latin by W. Hale White), London: T. Fisher Unwin, 1894, p. 12.

24. R. Emde, 'Moving ahead', pp. 317–40.
25. D. Stern, 'Non-interpretative mechanisms in psychoanalytic therapy', p. 904.
26. 'The removal of repression is no longer to be considered a key to therapeutic action. Psychic change is a function of a shift of emphasis between different mental models of object relationships.' Peter Fonagy, 'Guest editorial. Memory and therapeutic action', *The International Journal of Psychoanalysis*, vol. 80, 1999, pp. 215–23.
27. This point is discussed in Richard Rorty, *Contingency, Irony, and Solidarity*, Cambridge, UK: Cambridge University Press, 1989, p. 32.
28. P. Fonagy, 'Guest editorial', pp. 215–23.
29. Ibid., pp. 215–23.
30. Gerald Edelman, *Neural Darwinism. The Theory of Neuronal Group Selection*, New York: Basic Books, 1987; *The Remembered Present. A Biological Theory of Consciousness*, New York: Basic Books, 1989; *Bright Air, Brilliant Fire*, New York: Basic Books, 1992.
31. Arnold H. Modell, *Other Times, Other Realities. Toward a Theory of Psychoanalytic Treatment*, Cambridge, MA and London: Harvard University Press, 1995, p. 3.
32. Hans Loewald, 'Psychoanalysis as an art and the fantasy character of the psycho-analytic situation', in *Papers on Psychoanalysis*, New Haven: Yale University Press, 1988, pp. 44–5. Also see 'The symbolic function and the development of inner time' (chapter 6) in Gemma Corradi Fiumara, *The Symbolic Function. Psychoanalysis and the Philosophy of Language*, Oxford, UK and Cambridge, US: Blackwell, 1992, pp. 63–79.
33. R. Emde, 'Moving ahead', pp. 317–40. Russo points out that an alternation exists in our psychic apparatus between the primacy of representations over affects and the primacy of affects over representations. This bipolar and bifocal outlook can be recognised in several of Freud's papers and especially in 'The question of lay analysis' *Standard Edition*, 1930, vol. 20, Lucio Russo, *L'indifferenza dell'anima*, Rome: Edizioni Borla, 1998, p. 87.
34. Wilma Bucci, *Psychoanalysis and Cognitive Science. A Multiple Code Theory*, New York: Guilford Press, 1997.
35. Roy Schafer, 'Narration in the psychoanalytic dialogue', *Critical Inquiry*, vol. 7, 1980, pp. 29–53; *Narrative Actions in Psychoanalysis*, Worcester, MA: Clark University Press, 1981; *Retelling a Life*, New York: Basic Books, 1992.
36. P. Fonagy, 'Guest editorial', pp. 215–23.
37. Ibid., pp. 215–23.
38. Ibid., pp. 215–23.
39. W. Bucci, *Psychoanalysis and Cognitive Science*.
40. Howard Gardner, *Frames of Mind. The Theory of Multiple Intelligences*, London: Fontana Press, 1993, p. 297.
41. J. McDougall, *The Many Faces of Eros*, p. 236.
42. Ibid., p. 236.

Chapter 11

Affects and identity

Identity and affects in the psychoanalytic relation

Our propensity to seek familiar affective experiences often seems to prevail upon a desire for pleasure and well-being, almost as if creatures were constantly scanning their human environment in order to attain comparable types of affects. As is known, this quest may not only result in securing emotional experiences similar to the ones that have been internalised, but may also induce the replication of events in the sense that the projection of affects, whether in analysis or daily life, may elicit a complementary response – thus a confirmation of archaic affective paradigms. In a psychoanalytic setting, however, the induction of countertransference affects can be utilised not only to perceive and evoke certain familiar affect categories but also, hopefully, to disconfirm them by means of interpretation – as distinct from (re)action. Instead of reinforcing them through collusion or retaliation, affects can in fact be used in the metabolism of psychic maturation.[1] Transference brings affective events from the past into the relational present where the therapist may offer a novel interpersonal relation so that repetition of attitudes can be used to experiment with new configurations, different versions, or ulterior transcriptions, of past affective experiences.

Since psychoanalysis cannot influence our genetic code, and since it cannot change the historical and maturational 'events' of our early life, one should constantly wonder in which way it endeavours to function therapeutically. One consequently delves into the reasons why the projection of inner mental states is so vital and necessary. As transference 'love' can be described as a construct which is both 'real' and unreal, the analytic relation can also be viewed as essentially paradoxical: it can be regarded as an actual relationship occurring in the here and now, as well as a symbolic reproduction of the early aspects of the parent–infant interaction. If the analyst 'internalises' a patient's projection, the latter may find someone sufficiently 'similar', and finds thus an opportunity for metabolic exchanges, or cross-fertilisations, which would be impossible with an excessively alien interlocutor. Acceptance of projections is a necessary condition for any further development, be it psychoanalytic or not. The thesis is that the capacity to accept and utilise the force of the patient's affects is directly proportional to the capacity to be in (clear and passionate) contact with one's *own* profound self and also, paradoxically, to the courage of excluding others. Insufficient contact with one's own self renders the other's affect potentially too threatening and thus unacceptable. For some developing subjects the forced acceptance of parental views of reality may be experienced as a threat to their affective life, producing a state of unrelatedness with oneself and uncertainty about one's emotions. One of the paradoxes of the analytic situation is that a comparable state of unrelatedness and uncertainty, inasmuch as it is experienced with and in the devoted presence of the analyst, can be gradually used for purposes of self integration. The experience of feeling safe in one's affective states seems to require the presence of another person who is relatively unafraid of psychic intrusion and is not obsessed with 'converting' others. Thus, the mind's affective life can also be viewed as a paradoxical phenomenon in the sense that the quality of the contacts with one's affects is essentially a private experience, while at the same time it is also dependent upon the inner lives of others.

The analyst's identification with the patient's projections can be seen as a 'pathological' expression of his receptivity; this condition can be exacerbated by the patient's vehemence and skill in producing states of mind that the analyst is supposed to identify with. The analysand exercises this strategy by means of psychic pressures, by trying to manipulate the analyst's relationship with his internal values. In fact, there is a general, if not total, neglect in the literature of the difference between the affective involvement of the analyst and that of the analysand; of course, the patient has abundant inner forces to utilise inasmuch as he only has one analyst, while the therapist may well have ten patients. But patients are not inimical, they are just trying to make themselves understood, listened to, and taken seriously. If these pressures and manipulations are perceived as sheer violence, the ultimate result is rejection, retaliation and indifference rather than analysis. The phobic avoidance of 'concordance' may result in silently refusing the projection and thus impeding or deferring a lively analytic work.

As is known, the use of affects is essential in analysis because 'information' is simply not sufficient. The 'suffering other' is in fact a precious source of maturational knowledge because it marks a point of dispute wherein language itself becomes a problem, wherein one person's painful 'injustice' cannot be registered in the language of the other; the ones whose development has been impeded are often unable to symbolise the wrong that is in them. As the effort to find a level of discourse for the affects is so difficult and multi-faceted we should perhaps develop a metaclinical 'theory' to account for 'gaps in personhood', that is, for vicissitudes that are hardly amenable to symbolisation, that do not belong, and may never come to belong, to the self experience of a person.[2] These 'black holes', however, have a force of their own. Any linguistic struggle bears witness to the illuminating experience of the effort to give voice to something that could not come to exist if it was not adequately symbolised. The life of victims cannot be easily expressed in ordinary language. Their inner life is thus best expressed through psychic action addressed to another – the therapeutic other. To only work with memory associations involves the more adult aspects of the personality, while the part that is really in need of being understood is best communicated through the pressures brought onto the analyst. From this perspective the investing force of affects almost equals an attack in the sense of an extreme form of contact and impact.[3] The idea of force is essential to an understanding of affects; it is their constantly changing force that accounts for their potentially disruptive function, ranging from a capacity to transform to a devastating power. Affects can in fact occupy and take hold of any area of psychic life. In their ability to transform whatever they permeate, affects may even bend the psychic structures which they invest. And here a further disanalogy appears between the analysand's and the analyst's participation: even for the most dedicated therapist the relationship is a matter of professional *work*, while for the patient it is a matter of psychic *survival*. There is no comparison between the two involvements.

In Green's view, the addressee of communications, who is originally regarded as a witness or an object of demand, may even undergo a transformation at different levels of consciousness and become, for the patient, the 'cause' of his expressions. Although the therapist is initially and consciously defined as the person to whom communication is addressed 'unconsciously this condition of receiver of the message is changed into that of the inductor.'[4] The analyst seems to become the provoker in force of the affects emanating from what the analysand projects onto him. For better or for worse, the affects invest the analyst and then almost seem to exercise a force which appears to be emanating from the invested person. In analysis patients can activate narcissistic, intrusive aspects of the self which, hopefully, fail to disrupt the creative contact of the analyst with his own basic innerness, that is, fail to undo the therapeutic dyad, so that the patient can only illusively homogenise himself with the other.[5] When patients gradually recognise how destructive homogenisation can be to contacts with oneself, they may even arrive to overcome occult forms of guilt, that is, a sense of persecution for being sane and separate. And of course, intrusive homogenising attitudes can also be active on the part of the 'therapist'. 'The capacity to enter into the other's experience and yet remain separate enhances the agency of the self' suggests Modell 'and provides the individual with an additional degree of freedom.'[6] The sort of creative freedom that is essential to the analytic process. A common human propensity – the urge to 'convert' others – may become especially evident in the analytic process. With different degrees of virulence and visibility we often try to homogenise others to our views. This is revealed in the most disparate cultural areas ranging from the scientific to the religious: epistemic seduction of others is as pervasive as it is inconspicuous in our cultural practices. In the analytic relation, as well as in the analytic milieux, this is often more clearly appreciable – and puzzling.

According to Caper, the analyst's receptivity to the patient's unconscious states of mind, and the consequent pressures placed on him, depend in part on his capacity to be affected by these projections.[7] But this receptivity is complicated by the tendency of these projected states of mind to produce in the receptive analyst what Bion calls a 'numbing feeling of reality'[8] about themselves, a feeling that the projected elements are 'real'. That is, the analyst may end up feeling not simply *as if* he were the patient's external fantasy object; he may end up feeling that he is that object, and begin to act accordingly.[9] The danger is that the therapist may fail to maintain lively contacts with his own profound self. And, in fact, if contacts with oneself are not passionate, they would not be sufficiently clear, for they would be opaque and colourless as are myriads of other mental contents – the billions of thoughts that neuroscientists say occupy our minds.

Empathy and identity

In so called post-modern literature the topic of empathy is experiencing an inflationary success, and empathy comes to appear as potentially capable of resolving relational difficulties and profoundly influencing the course of interactive events. Yet empathy should be patiently explored if we are not to create a 'myth' of it, and if we want to look for its 'stronger' character both as a goal and as a method.[10] Human attitudes tending to collude, conflate, concord and homogenise are clearly not empathic in a 'strong' sense. By an excess of intentionality and adherence to sloganised paradigms one may become 'empathic' beyond the level of one's personal involvement and thus produce some fictional, imitative attitude. It is worth noting that naturalistic accounts of the affects which sustain 'empathic' listening may undermine the arguments illustrating the cognitive and cultural basis of its practice. For if empathy is simply 'natural', a manifestation of the biological qualities of certain individuals, then it is impossible to see it as the laborious maturational achievement that it often is. So long as the idea of natural empathic attitudes remains essentially attached to stereotypes – such as those of gentle ladies, warm Italians, or good 'savages' – there is no question of extending its scope beyond marginal, local domains and into the development of knowledge and culture; there would be no point in suggesting that listening, compassion and empathy are highly self-reflexive and knowledge-saturated practices, that they are the result of great maturity and that any human being could fruitfully work at them. The idea of affective knowledge may in fact lose its meaning when empathy comes to be regarded as a merely instinctual phenomenon.

In a psychoanalytic outlook, if the communications from the patient are manipulative attempts to transform us into narcissistic 'good objects', we may ignore them or even respond with a stony silence. But analysis can probably only work if we are capable of letting ourselves be invaded by manipulative pressures and then, subsequently, offer interpretations by virtue of the resilience due to the quality of the links with our inner resources. When we are apparently submerged, but still capable of lively thinking and creative interpretation, then the therapeutic contact can be truly beneficial.[11] If contact with one's internal values is passionate and clear, one can be easily receptive without the fear that these links may be disrupted by the intrusive projections of the patient. When there is an excessive risk of disruption one can opt for a view of transference as sheer repetition, rather than for a view of transference as construction. Viewing transference as mere repetition is perhaps safer, in the sense that transferential phenomena are simply regarded as having nothing to do with the analyst. This is a pre-emptive manœuvre which putatively guarantees that therapists will not be flooded, manipulated or upset by patients. Most analysts do not view empathy as a 'mystical' or intangible experience, for indeed the patient's verbal and non-verbal expressions influence the analyst at work, generating profound resonances and parallel states. As is known, the analyst's self-perceptions or introspections often become a source of 'information' about the analysand. Yet immediate, first-hand empathic data need to be reviewed and integrated with other information to yield full therapeutic insight. Thus empathy seems to involve diverse factors such as cognitive, inferential and synthetic capacities. Empathy is in fact relatively neutral and non-judgemental, unlike the related phenomena of pity and sympathy from which it should be distinguished. According to Moore and Fine, pity and sympathy lack objectivity, encourage overidentification, and sometimes lead to enactment of rescue fantasies.[12]

Paradoxically, a significant part of the effort required to do and conclude analysis might be said to consist in trying *not* to identify with the patient, and striving to bring the patient to cease identifying with us.[13] The tendency towards identification is often spontaneous, requiring no conscious effort on the part of either participant. The analysand identifies with what he has projected into the analyst, and the analyst is inclined to identify with these same projections. Caper suggests that 'Under favourable conditions, however, the analyst is able to carry out the analysis further by bringing into play a second capacity . . . his ability to establish enough distance from the patient's projections to permit him to recognise that they *are* projections and that the state of mind he is experiencing has arisen from outside himself. To summarise, in this process the analyst tends to fall spontaneously into a counter transference illness as part of his receptivity to the patient's projections, and he must cure himself of it if the analysis is to progress.'[14] Indeed, empathy can be the end result rather than a prefabricated instrument of analytic work. This is especially relevant today. As women, for instance, are 'generally' thought to be naturally capable of an empathic attitude, and since feminist epistemologies can be misrepresented in our culture, a caricature of empathy may be offered which ultimately replaces the complex, laborious itineraries of achieving life-enhancing empathy. The pervasive effects of this parody may even induce women to stereotypically empathise, as if compelled by the latest fashion.

Conducting analysis while resisting the temptation to 'cure' the patient by transforming his inner structures, homogenising him with our 'healthy' minds, and converting him to the epistemic models of our interpretations, the analyst comes to fully recognise and appreciate the patient's own mind.[15] The situation may instead be subtly and ubiquitously governed by a paradigm in which the patient feels that he can invade and control the mind of the therapist, and that the latter can only do the same in return. This is a paralysing attitude that may, of course, also unconsciously originate from the 'therapist'. This dreadful condition is a very real risk because the patient concentrates all of his inner forces on one single analyst while the analyst has different patients and has to share his forces; in being able to regain this awareness whenever it vanishes, the therapist will create a vital respect for the suffering other. This quality of respect tends to enhance in the patient a sense of freedom and separateness as well as a sense of responsibility for himself. The patient's fear that the therapist will prove to be an inadequate container of invasive affects – and turn into a proselytising agent – remains a serious limiting factor which contributes to the inability of such patients to trust the safety of the therapeutic setting. Creatures often seem to curtail and restrict their lives within narrowing epistemic and affective perimeters because of the fear of being homogenised, converted or absorbed. A diffuse illness of our times seems to include the consequences of unbearable anxiety arising from vicissitudes of separation and fusion, independence and concordance. This pathology, which is also subtly expressed in epistemic anxiety and neophobia, is as pervasive as it is inconspicuous. If the analyst is aware of the fear of these 'threats', patients can feel better validated whenever they come to laboriously exhibit a mind of their own.

In the analytic setting, as well as in the analytic milieu, a tendency may prevail to eliminate important differences between patients and therapists, disciples and teachers because, of course, there is much to be admired in what 'nurturers' have to say. Yet, concordance, homogeneity, and commensurability may even induce a climate of madness. Individuals may be inconspicuously forced to ignore the attachment to their own patiently elaborated vistas and values in order to create a liveable 'harmony' with the figures they admire. With clinical acumen, Caper describes the case of a patient who often identified with his interpretations in ways that were not easy to detect.[16] While appearing to agree with the interpretations the analysand would bend their meaning slightly so that they became hard to distinguish from what she was already conscious of; at the same time, she appeared to make an effort to accommodate herself to some part of the interpretation – to make herself 'fit' it. The crux of the problem, however, was that the specific point which actually differed from what she consciously thought inevitably became lost. These manœuvres created a spurious sort of like-mindedness between the dyad members. The analyst was left with the feeling that this might be true in a way, but that there was a way in which it was not true, that there was something in what she was saying that she did not know, but which had been lost, and he was unable to pin point it. This was also the patient's problem with an admired figure of her professional life. Indeed, if the two cannot tranquilly count on a mind of their own, specific, precise and exact features are constantly and inconspicuously being lost, producing, eventually, the end of empathy.[17]

In a Nietzschean perspective, the achievement of self-knowledge is not a process of coming to know a truth which was either out there or inside here all the time. Nietzsche sees self knowledge as an itinerary of self creation. In this same view, according to Rorty, 'any *literal* depiction of one's own individuality, which is to say any use of an inherited language-game for this purpose, will necessarily fail. One will not have traced that idiosyncrasy home, but will merely have managed to see it as not idiosyncratic after all, as a specimen reiterating a type, a copy or replica of something which has already been identified.'[18] Indeed, an imitative deterioration of self knowledge. In the impairment of knowledge, according to Bion, we encounter a super-ego 'that has hardly any of the characteristics of the super-ego as understood in psychoanalysis; it is a "super" ego. It is an envious assertion of moral superiority without any morals.'[19] It seems indeed that 'withoutness' is a main characteristic of what Bion tries to indicate by the expression 'Minus-k'; it indicates an anti-cognitive mode of operation that makes a distinct domain of bizarre objects.[20] As a result, this opens a major problem for us. If knowledge (and its connection with the 'reality principle) is one of the key functions of psychoanalysis, as well as the uncontroversial axis of western culture, we should be especially attentive to those subtracting conditions that render it prone to deterioration. It is the sort of degradation which is most difficult to monitor inasmuch as it affects the cognitive instruments for detecting it; this is an attitude which is as dangerous as it is inconspicuous and unapproachable. The opposite of knowledge, in fact, not only indicates ignorance, but also a fearsome propensity to safeguard ignorance, adopting attitudes in which there is an alleged gain in avoiding awareness and a clear danger in pursuing truth.

Jaggar suggests that human beings develop in emotionality as well as in other dimensions; they increase the range, variety and subtlety of their emotional responses in accordance with their life experiences and their reflections on these.[21] Yet it seems that developing subjects require the confirming support of others in order to feel the legitimate possession of their *unique* affects and intuitions. When the human environment has not been sufficiently enhancing, there may be adults who demand that, for instance, their analysts identify with what they are feeling, because they are personally incapable of being in contact with their own affects. But how can a suffering person gain some assurance that an analyst is indeed capable of perceiving and sharing feelings that he cannot accept or recognise? Here again, the patient needs no profuse discourse, but just enough to signify that the listener has absorbed the essential affective *quality* of whatever has been communicated. Because, of course, even though patients are not conversant with their affects, they do communicate them to the therapist; they do so cryptically despite the conventional language that they use. Psychoanalytic listening is, in fact, expected to capture ulterior meanings presented under cover of literal discourse. In Caper's view, despite the desire to homogenise their ideas with those of the analyst, in order to feel that they are really just extensions of each other, patients can also be very grateful when they feel that the analyst has been able to make an interpretation with enough clarity and conviction to make it obvious that it is not something that they had already known.[22] This is certainly not the same as like-minded contact, and this is the critical point. It is not a matter of concordance, but of empathy. According to Caper, it is contact with aspects of his own self – his commitment to the value of psychoanalysis – that enables the therapist to make proper analytic contact with patients. The confusion that analysands try to draw him into interrupts the vital connection with his internal objects, the linkage required to make proper analytic work; they can be aware, at different levels of consciousness, that his ability to analyse them depends on his being in contact with something inside himself – and that this contact excludes them.[23]

What is necessary in empathy, of course, is contact with the parts of the inter-locutor's psyche that have been separated from consciousness. Interest in these segregated parts can only come to the fore after the acceptance of the ego-syntonic aspects, even if these constitute a false self or any form of character pathology.[24] There is always the danger that in an 'effort' to empathise, the analyst may adapt to the other's style of functioning and thus move in the direction of colluding and becoming a good narcissistic object. But perhaps there is no way of avoiding this risk: if the false self is not thoroughly accepted (and why should it not, if it is one's best construction for psychic survival?), there is no way of creating space for the embryonic real self to appear. When segregated aspects of the personality, or an encapsulated real self, are not reached, the analyst may be left with the feeling that he has been unable to establish proper communication with the patient, and also that he is no longer in contact with his own self. In Caper's clinical material this is also the symptom that plagues his patient, that he describes as a 'spaced-out' feeling. The therapist may have succumbed to the transference role of a like-minded, narcissistic object, but this is of course his problem and not the patient's, that he can be drawn into this role.[25] Underestimation of these difficulties of transference vicissitudes may easily induce the analyst to attempt to achieve empathic contact by force, turning it into a stereotyped task.[26] Patients readily perceive the rigidity of such a posture which silently forces them into a condition of conscious gratitude and unconscious rage; a condition they strive to indirectly represent, as if they were afraid of thereby wounding the analyst. In Pao's view empathy may sometimes arise after a long time and not as the result of an 'empathic', concordant, or homo-genising attitude, but rather as the outcome of a laborious process of sufficiently continuous two-way exchanges and reconnection of details in an expanding interactive field.[27]

Therapeutic action results from the juxtaposition of different levels of psychic reality inasmuch as the contrast between present interactions and archaic relations enhances the transformation of affect categories. The analytic setting, in fact, brings the dangers of the past and the opportunities of the present very close together. Patients, or interlocutors, constantly test us for our ability to hold together heterogeneous elements and contrasting challenges, so that they can only venture within safety limits, not wishing to exceed personal capacities. We could say that the way the therapist and the patient know that they have entered real empathy, and that it is distinct from the more usual exchanges, is that these moments, para-doxically, may even appear unfamiliar, unexpected in their exact form and timing, or even strange; they may even be 'confusing' as to what is happening or what they should do. And yet the contact becomes very dense subjectively, as in the more transformational 'moments of truth'.

From the beginning of life, we may perhaps want to be exposed to an attenuated, personalised empathy, rather than to a total and overwhelming pseudo-empathic attitude. A reconciliation within the subject, in fact, moves from the inside out, not from the objects of an external world. When the latter is imposed, in therapy or in culture, the result can be disastrous. 'The captation of the subject by the situation gives us the most general formula for madness' says Lacan 'not only the madness that lies behind the walls of asylums, but also the madness that deafens the world with its sound and fury.'[28] Deep humanity is being a witness and not a teacher, according to Kierkegaard; and this is worth a good deal more than the 'silly participation in others', which is falsely honoured by the name of sympathy, whereas it is in fact nothing but vanity.[29]

Reprocessing our inner past

Of course we are quite powerless with regard to what has happened in the past as there is nothing we can do about it now. And yet we are also reasonably free and powerful in the processes of re-evaluation, reconsideration, and retranscription of our inner history; these are processes based on newly developed resources of the present moment. Freud did conceive of an idea that has the potential to transform familiar therapeutic factors of psychoanalysis such as transference, resistance and interpretation into a comprehensive theory.[30] This is the concept of *Nachträglichkeit*, a term that Strachey translated as 'deferred action'.[31] What Freud intended to convey by use of that term is that memory is retranscribed as a result of subsequent experiences; a concept which is somehow consonant with the not-so-new thesis of 'subsequentiality' that inspired modern historicism.

The analytic setting has the function of permitting the coexistence of multiple and separate levels of reality. These levels are to be clearly distinguished and are also to be made intercommunicative by means of appropriate 'translations'. In a letter written more than a century ago, Freud says to Fliess 'I should like to emphasise the fact that the successive registrations represent the psychic achievement of successive epochs of life. At the boundary between two such epochs a translation of the psychic material must take place.'[32] The problem is that there is no dictionary to tell us what presentation at one level is the representation of another. Even if there were such a dictionary, it would be of scarce therapeutic value: in fact, dimensions of psychic reality are not different because they are separate, but rather, they are separate because they are 'metabolically' different. They do not mix and intermingle even though they may *appropriately* interact. We should thus recognise that the idea of 'translation' is a timid expression for the intense work to be done. The challenge is that of reconnecting one logic to another hardly commensurable logic, of creating 'connubial' connections, of developing metaphoric links, or of making coexistence possible and profitable; it is not simply an elegant job of translation.[33] As a response to the pressure of unassimilated events, the tendency towards (transference) repetition does not allow us to learn from experience. Because we only 'learn' in the sense that we evolve – rather than repeat – to the extent that life therapy, or psychic therapy, allows us to experience different aspects of our inner reality, and new affects that can interdigitate with old ones. The 'new' affects may then be symbolised and internalised in such a way that they are used to re-evaluate archaic affective experiences. Although our emotions are indispensable to the growth of knowledge, they are not, of course, indisputable. Like all our cognitive resources and theories, they can be misleading, and their contribution always subject to reinterpretation, revision and testing. In this way we allow for an interaction between how we understand our inner world and how we are as people: our responses to our identity change as we conceptualise it differently, while in turn our mutating identity induces further outlooks and insights. From this point of view, the growth of affective functions seems far more challenging and essential than the acquisition of intellectual computational skills which can be conveniently delegated to exosomatic, non-evolving apparatuses.

Throughout his life William James strived to come to terms with the paradox posed by the concept 'self' as it encompasses both a stable sense of identity and a transient consciousness. But the crucial psychic problem is, of course, that of transmuting transient consciousness into a relatively stable identity. At least one of the known strategies to accomplish this vital task is the successful elaboration of past experiences by means of appropriate redescriptions and narratives. The psychic need to engage in these attempts is so acute that perhaps the ubiquitous search for a measure of negotial power could be seen as instrumental in attaining conditions to constantly retell one's stories and experiences. As speaking rights seem to be directly proportional to the changing equilibriums of power, a relational position of force seems to confer the right to be listened to, to reinterpret one's story, and thus to fortify one's own self. If the individual contributes to self-formation by reinterpreting past events through a sequence of narratives, others who are listening seem essential to the process; and one of the lures of power might be seen as increased opportunities to be listened to. Or, more simply, human beings try to talk as much as they can in order to create some sense of their life stories. In a synoptic view we could say that the first person 'I', as a universal element of grammar, becomes vital and stable as it gradually synthesises the subject's identity. The self that we seek to create does not in fact emerge as a definable unity in a particular lapse of linear time, this is usually referred to as 'early development'. The self is constantly re-established as a self through experience and elaboration of its own history. In the language of Henry James, one could say that we relearn about ourselves through 'the terrible *fluidity* of self-revelation'.[34]

Once our inner life begins to exist fear of death and fear of mental collapse, or psychic death, are equally dreaded. 'The need to maintain the continuity and coherence of the self' says Modell 'is a vital urge of no less importance than sexual desire or the need for attachment to others.'[35] Although there is widespread acclaim for mother–infant observation as a path to the affective roots of mental life, we should bear in mind, according to Green, that there is no guarantee that observational procedures can account for the vicissitudes of inner psychic life, especially with regard to attaining continuity and coherence by means of the self-reflective reweaving of past events; the personal reconstruction work operated by the subject with respect to his past is not really open to observation, and is perhaps more clearly discernible through the psychoanalytic relation.[36]

We should also consider that the idea of a constant work of reconstruction may well belong to the cultural heritage of the West; it emerges, for instance, in Plotinus' view of inner life: 'And note that we do not appeal to stored up impressions to account for memory: we think of the mind awakening its powers in such a way as to possess something not present to it.'[37] More recently Hegel also suggests that 'For life, as for the mind, there is no past which is absolutely past; the moments that the mind seems to have behind it are also borne in its present depths.'[38] 'Borne', yes, but also shaped and construed in ways that are a matter of constant concern. Of course if we look back with all the unfazability of retrospection, we can say that because this happened so then that happened too. However, that does not mean that such a 'this' will ever again be followed by such a 'that'; one can never be certain in the domain of psychic life. There is nothing automatic about maturation.

Modell suggests that 'One distinct adaptive advantage conferred upon those organisms who possess a sense of self is the ability to be free of the tyranny of ongoing events in real time. The experience of self enables the individual to model future actions by matching *value-laden* memories of past events with current perceptions.'[39] Thus the sense of self functions as a dominant matrix conferring structure and coherence upon current interaction; this concurs to the clarification of the paradox posed by the continuity of the self in conjunction with the ongoing flux of mental vicissitudes. Thus we cannot think of an inner organisation as independent of the transformational force of affects. We need to think of self identity as emerging from a dynamics of relations, of constant reconstructions and fields of force. We thus need a logic of 'fluidity' suitable to affects, rather than an inclusionary–exclusionary logic, even though it may be mitigated by flexibility. In Battersby's view the self is no fixed entity as it ultimately appears configured by patterns of relations 'as a kind of harmony . . . produced by the intersection of present, future and past'.[40] The affective intensity of the therapeutic experience, in fact, does not 'correct' past empathic failures by means of empathic activity; it does not replace a past deficit. Rather, something new is created in a relationship that alters the intersubjective environment. Past experience is recontextualised in the present, so that a person operates from within a different affective landscape and generates novel attitudes and experiences.[41]

Any reading of so-called reminiscences leaves us with a profound admiration for the human capacity to shape past events to present needs. Not only do facts mutate in accordance with temporal perspectives, but the constructive power of memory with which we create 'a life' necessarily intertwines with the structural demands and assertions of the story which is being generated. According to Maclean[42] any personal narrative is a discursive *mise en scène* in which a self emerges from the shifting interplay of signifiers and utterances.[43] However, not only are the produced stories enmeshed in the dominant myths of the culture, but they can also be the result of a distorting and perverse process of retrospective attribution; indeed they can be fictional and aggravating accounts. The myths produced can be so potent and the narrative structures so compelling that they have real consequences, and personal life may even have to follow a destructive path. Granted that to reach an insight into our personal history, it is necessary to follow mature forms of affective life, for it is the study of maturity which enlightens our appreciation of the origins, the problem remains with regard to the level of 'maturity' itself. Thus the process by which the meanings of maturity are assigned retroactively can lead to different ends; we can in fact interpret or narrate whatever may fit with some sort of current theory or model. However, our current 'immature' theorising or inner perverse paradigms, can distort narrations of past vicissitudes in a pre-emptive way. In this sense, then, we can be both users and victims of our celebrated capacity for retrospective attribution.

NOTES

1. We think of a patient not only as a sufferer but as someone seeking maturation and identity. So we can hypothesise a secret wish to have one's projections disconfirmed, a wish that, paradoxically, proceeds in parallel with a compulsion to repeat and confirm early paradigms; the latter wish, of course, serves the purpose of offering illness benefits through a sense of cohesion and continuity.
2. Ruth Stein, *Psychoanalytic Theories of Affect*, New York: Westport, Connecticut and London: Praeger, 1991, p. 187. These 'gaps in personhood' resonate with Schwaber's suggestion that essential elements in personal history can be silenced unless the analyst can patiently monitor voice tonalities. 'Unspeakable vicissitudes revealed in the subtleties of tonality may otherwise remain a deep-seated and invisible impasse. Such obscured passages might even function as "black holes" in the sense of absorbing and neutralising psychic energies which create an unexplainable tiredness to go about life.' Evelyne Albrecht Schwaber, 'The non-verbal dimension in psychoanalysis: "state" and its clinical vicissitudes', *The International Journal of Psycho-Analysis*, vol. 79, 1998, pp. 667–79. Spezzano remarks that although certain archaic experiences are not amenable to representation, they nevertheless maintain a peremptory presence in psychic life. 'One might say that a category of early affects takes the form of a painful, lonely, enraged, anxious, or depressed mood – an ego state that inhabits the person's psyche. At this archaic stage the affect becomes the world. We may flow in such states inexorably without consciousness, foreknowledge or will.' Charles Spezzano, *Affect in Psychoanalysis. A Clinical Synthesis*, Hillsdale and London: Analytic Press, 1993, p. 225.
3. The investing force of affects is often discussed by André Green in his contributions; see especially 'On discriminating and not discriminating between affect and representation', *The International Journal of Psychoanalysis*, vol. 80, 1999, pp. 277–316.
4. Ibid., pp. 277–316.
5. This issue is extensively explored in Robert Caper, 'A mind of one's own', *The International Journal of Psycho-Analysis*, vol. 78, 1997, part 2, pp. 265–78.
6. Arnold H. Modell, *The Private Self*, Cambridge, MA and London: Harvard University Press, 1996, p. 181.
7. R. Caper, 'A mind of one's own', p. 267.
8. Wilfred Ruprecht Bion, *Experiences in Groups*, New York: Basic Books, 1961, p. 149; quoted in R. Caper, 'A mind of one's own'.
9. R. Caper, 'A mind of one's own', p. 267.
10. See Stefano Bolognini, 'Empathy and "empathism"', *International Journal of Psychoanalysis*, vol. 78, 1997, pp. 279–93.
11. The self-reflectiveness of analysts can be quite resistant and enduring; this same capacity is also at times revealed in profoundly suffering patienty: William Styron

seems to be describing something like this faculty of mind in writing of his deep depression, telling of a sense of being accompanied by a second self – a wraith-like observer who, not sharing the dementia of his double, is able to watch with dispassionate curiosity as his companion struggles. *Darkness Visible. A memory of Madness*, New York: Random House, 1990, p. 64.

12. See Burness E. Moore and Bernard D. Fine (eds), *Psychoanalytic Terms and Concepts*, New Haven and London: The American Psychoanalytic Association and Yale University Press, 1990, p. 67.

13. See R. Caper, 'A mind of one's own', p. 267.

14. Ibid., p. 268.

15. Ibid., p. 277.

16. Ibid., p. 272.

17. Ibid., p. 273.

18. Richard Rorty, *Contingency, Irony and Solidarity*, Cambridge, UK: Cambridge University Press, 1989, p. 27.

19. Wilfred Ruprecht Bion, *Learning from Experience*, p. 97.

20. Ibid., p. 97.

21. Allison M. Jaggar, 'Love and knowledge: emotion in feminist epistemology', in A.M. Jaggar and S.R. Bordo (eds), *Gender/Body/Knowledge: Feminist Reconstructions of Being and Knowing*, New Brunswick, NJ and London: Rutgers University Press, pp. 145–71.

22. R. Caper, 'A mind of one's own', p. 274.

23. Ibid., p. 275.

24. S. Bolognini, 'Empathy and "empathism"', p. 281.

25. R. Caper, 'A mind of one's own', p. 273.

26. S. Bolognini, 'Empathy and "empathism"', p. 286.

27. P.N. Pao, *Therapeutic Empathy in the Schizophrenic. On Empathy II*, London: Analytic Press, 1984; quoted in S. Bolognini, 'Empathy and "empathism"', p. 282.

28. Jacques Lacan, *Ecrits: A Selection*, trans. A. Sheridan, London: Tavistock Publications, 1977, p. 7.

29. Sören Kierkagaard, *Fear and Trembling and the Sickness onto Death* (translated by W. Lowrie), Princeton, NJ: Princeton University Press, 1974, p. 15.

30. This thesis is suggested by Arnold H. Modell in the Introduction to *Other Times, Other Realities. Toward a Theory of Psychoanalytic Treatment*, Cambridge, MA and London: Harvard University Press, 1995, p. 2.

31. Different translations have been proposed by other scholars. The terms 'retrospective attribution' and 'retranscription of memory', for instance are derived from the paper of H. Thomä 'Freud's concept of *Nachträglichkeit* and its translation', presented at the Symposium on Translation and Transition, London, 20–2 April 1989. In a broader interpretation of the term, Modell also uses the notion of 'recategorisation of time'.

32. Jeffrey Masson (ed. and trans.), *The Complete Letters of Sigmund Freud to Wilhelm Fliess*, Cambridge, MA: Harvard University Press, 1985, p. 207, letter dated 6 December 1896.

33. These issues are discussed in Gemma Corradi Fiumara, *The Metaphoric Process. Connections between Language and Life*, London and New York: Routledge, 1995. See for instance the paragraphs entitled 'Interepistemic links', 'The pathology and literalness', 'Notes on the difference between digital and analogic styles', 'Connections between digital and analogic processes', 'The interaction between metaphoricity and literalness', 'Symbolic play and affectual synergies', 'From biological life to dialogic existence'.

34. Henry James, Preface to *The Ambassadors*, S.P. Rosenbaum (ed.), New York: W.W. Norton, 1964, p. 11.

35. A.H. Modell, *The Private Self*, p. 201.
36. Communications presented by André Green at the Standing Conference on Psychoanalytical Intracultural and Intercultural Dialogue of the International Psychoanalytical Association, Paris 27–29 July 1998. The focus of the conference was an exploration of Freud's idea of *Nachträglichkeit*.
37. Plotinus, Third Ennead, Sixth Tractate, *The Enneads*, trans. S. Mackenna, London: Faber and Faber, 1956, p. 203.
38. Georg Wilhelm Friedrich Hegel, 'Vorlesungen über die Philosophie der Geschichte', G. Lasson (ed.), *Hegel's Sammtliche Werke Kritische Ausgabe*, Leipzig: Meiner, 1905. Quoted in Maurice Merlean-Ponty, *The Structure of Behaviour*, trans. A. Fisher, Boston: Beacon Press, 1967, p. 207.
39. A.H. Modell, *The Private Self*, p. 71 (emphasis added).
40. Christine Battersby, *The Phenomenal Woman. Feminist Metaphysics and the Patterns of Identity*, Cambridge and Oxford: Polity Press, 1998, p. 170.
41. See on this topic Daniel Stern, Louis Sander, Jeremy Nahum, *et al.*, 'Non-interpretative mechanisms in psychoanalytic therapy. The "something more" than interpretation', *The International Journal of Psychoanalysis*, vol. 79, 1998, pp. 903–21.
42. Marie Maclean, *The Name of the Mother. Writing Illegitimacy*, London and New York: Routledge, 1994, p. 1.
43. In the discussion of these issues European culture has been greatly influenced by the contributions of Paul Ricoeur. See, for instance, *Time and Narrative*, trans. K. McLaughlin, Chicago: University of Chicago Press, 1984; and also *Oneself as Another*, trans. K. Blamey, Chicago and London: University of Chicago Press, 1992.

Chapter 12

Affects and indifference

The question of indifference

We often seem to move forward under the burden of some intangible indifference that weighs upon the world as something not extraneous to it, but rather as something that humans have engendered. We come to know of everything while there seems to be no way of caring about it. As an attempt to monitor such an unnoticeable advance of indifference, the listening approach cannot possibly be viewed as a form of passivity. Paradoxically, whatever is not attentively listened to is actually submitted to, accepted, and absorbed.[1] We can no more avoid thinking of coming to terms with the biophysical atmosphere surrounding us than we can ignore the myriads of human messages to which we have become indifferent. For what we have become inattentive to reaches us in any case, in ways that may induce psychic apathy or torpid states, and we often try to react with monotonous contentions in favour or against something. Ironically, however, being in favour of or against anything at all can even serve to disguise a chronic state of indifference that only produces competing monologues that deteriorate culture.[2] Like parasites, 'bad' emotional attitudes attach themselves to their hosts, and biologists remind us that anything that damages its supporting environment is known to ultimately destroy itself. The main question, however, is how can we possibly regard as bad anything that gently and silently 'helps' us cope with psychic pain and even annul it? Thus, the creative awareness of this painless temptation to avoid psychic suffering is to be cultivated as a priority; because indeed, the question of premises and preliminaries often determines ultimate conclusions. If we initially accept indifference as an escape from mental pain, we somehow pre-emptively exclude the variegated labours of human creativity. In our 'theologies' of progress we are offered the privilege of grasping or scanning an exciting entire world that is telepresent to us, but somehow too removed from our affects. Far from being simply immobilised, the active-victim or passive-agent, which is the protagonist of our culture, can interact with a screen, or meander along information highways, connecting and disconnecting at leisure. Perhaps only the sufficient attachment to a laborious maturational itinerary can help us manage a cohabitation with the numbing excitements of technology.

Inducing a general impairment in our capacity for enjoyment, indifference also leaves us with the feeling that something is missing from our lives.[3] Of course, the more common ways of dealing with this sense of loss is to attempt to substitute the internal condition of joy with experiences of excitement; from this follows the production of 'thrills' in the most disparate of areas. In this sense, we are all indebted to the nameless and invisible pathology of indifference, for we are all keen on using and fabricating prosthetic sources of excitement in every field. Only novelty and excitement sell well in our culture, and this is probably because of our subservience to the invasive power of apathy, nonchalance, and unconcern.[4]

McDougall describes 'disaffectation' as the mode of psychic survival of those who have the psychic necessity to expel from their consciousness any awareness of drive vicissitudes, or interpersonal relations, and thus create an impassable barrier between affects and the mental representations to which they are linked.[5] In this perspective, the indifferent refusal of dialogue could ultimately be seen as a willed regression to a preverbal level where the psyche is incapable of 'word-presentation', in the language of Freud, and is totally exposed to the violence of what he calls 'thing-presentation'. This, in turn, confirms the desperate urge to extinguish insufferable affective experiences. However, this intangible degradation of mental life does not represent any clear psychopathological solution. In our increasingly affluent culture, the 'pathology' of indifference may become both widespread *and* inconspicuous, devastating *and* unalarming.

Beyond the most disparate forms of pathology, there is a further possible outcome of our fights against psychic pain, or the solution that McDougall defines as 'radical indifference'.[6] Although in opposition to each other, the affects of love and hate are none the less interwoven with a passion for life. In the innumerable forms of struggle against inner suffering, there is an incoercible will to live and cope with affective life, or a life in which cognition and emotion somehow manage to remain connected. In this gaze, then, the ultimate danger is the 'elimination' of all affect and the achievement of indifference. As McDougall suggests, indifference renders the individual omnipotently invulnerable to psychic suffering, while the variety of neurotic and psychotic constructions are strenuous and often desperate attempts to create personal meaning in life; ultimately they are stubborn refusals to break affective links.[7] Psychic conflicts are far removed from the annihilation of meaning and extinction of desire. By contrast the solution of indifference culminates in the disinvestment of any mental presentation capable of mobilising affect and in the annulled awareness of suffering. It is a 'solution' that is unwittingly supported by an increasing number of cultural offers. What may be even worse is that those who cannot suffer pain cannot 'suffer joy' either, in the language of Bion. As he remarks 'People exist who are so intolerant of pain or frustration (or in whom pain or frustration is so intolerable) that they feel the pain but will not suffer it and so cannot be said to discover it.'[8] Only a negative definition usually seems to be attempted regarding the indifferent condition of a person who is trying to avoid psychic pain; but then it is precisely when one cannot manage to experience pain that one cannot even discover the variegated itinerary of joy.

The silent passion for indifference cannot simply be qualified as 'error' or 'pathology' because it actually gravitates towards the lack of any distinction, where no differentiation between right and wrong, sane and insane can be vouched for. In fact the distinction between 'good' and 'evil' only holds as long as even the slightest choice can still be made between them. But the first capacities to fall in the darkness of detachment and affective torpor are precisely the functions of choice, preference, and valuation. Our emotional atrophy may ultimately incline us to entirely surrender to the benumbing pull of nonchalance. Indifference may even latently become a trend that acts finally as both a norm and anesthetising support. An awareness of this ubiquitous and numbing danger may alert us to the risk of allowing feelings of futility or boredom to silently invade us when we share conditions of indifference that are unwittingly conducive to psychic blindness and deafness. To monitor this risk in psychoanalytic work 'may require repeated and violent incursions in our own counter transference attitudes' says McDougall.[9] For, indeed, we should consider that indifference is also an ultimate defence against inner suffering and thus a 'creative' strategy after all. Unless we cultivate this awareness, we might naïvely attempt to simply neutralise painful affects. The annulment of a negative affect, however, can even function as an insult to the other's suffering self, and as something that only serves to emphasise the 'goodness' of the listener. According to McDougall, the therapeutic goal is to liberate the desire to live a mature life in which love and hate, pain and joy are not unbearably dreaded, but can somehow fulfil their life-preserving function.[10]

In a culture that is almost saturated with the din of innumerable messages intent upon instilling codes and priorities for the avoidance of painful affects, the inhibition of our affective lives could be regarded, paradoxically, as a clever maturational option. In order to safeguard authentic emotional resources, one may develop 'non-listening' defences of detachment that tend to protect one's inner self. The person who has not been sufficiently responded to by means of authentic contacts does not seem to be capable of listening vigilantly to our resounding and visual culture, but only of becoming its victim. Perhaps in adhering to some innate self-preserving resource, the person may altogether 'refuse' to listen and feel. It is almost as if the individual tacitly were to say to himself: 'I am trying to find a way of not feeling because I no longer want to feel the emotions of others' or 'I wonder why I should carry on with a life of emotions if these are of no good for myself, but only for some mimetic form of survival.' When the desire to live an affective life still 'vexes' us, it does so in a subtle, unintrusive way: the latent aspects of our more lively self, in fact, can hardly express themselves when immersed in an intersubjective context that is overburdened by a pseudo-language. We should indeed develop expressions for emphasising the potential threat of a linguistic involution that might go so far as to jeopardise the development of meaningful relations at large, or even silently transform them into parasitic, destructive patterns. This is even more menacing than the ecological degradations that we can monitor. In Bion's view, we could conceive of relations as either parasitic or commensal; by commensal he means that any two agents depend on each other for mutual benefit without harm to either one.[11] Where commensality cannot possibly be achieved, and only parasitic prospects are available, indifference can almost appear as a life-preserving defence. The staging of indifferent relations is inevitably associated with a lifeless, invasive language that may only function as a filler. It is a language that can also produce epistemic spaces that are only illusively free from conflicts with our profound motivations; a language charged with the task of nullifying vital relations. This fictitious language seduces us into a deadening perversion which is the most public and concealed of all. When the remnants of our affectivity are dealt with by means of this 'language', there is the risk that words that originally indicated experiences of loss and desire will be used for the almost absurd purpose of denying all loss, longing, or precariousness. Words that have been illusively freed from the burdening complexity of affective bonds only contribute to the staging of an invasive indifference. In a synoptic view of the situation, we could say that the threat of indifference is more dangerous than any other psychic menace, in that it functions as an almost irresistible seduction – it is painless, costless, invisible, and increasingly effective against any suffering.

This ubiquitous and inconspicuous inclination to extinguish affective life and stage fictions, or parodies, may even contaminate the very domain of affects by way of inducing spurious emotions that often reveal themselves in analytic work. When these 'false' affects are not recognised, we may conspire with a sequence of collusions. The unrecognised presence of a false affect induces the complementary absence of authentic responses in the analyst; and if one is unaware of this exasperating possibility that fills the interactive space, while at the same time communicating nothing usable, one may even become collusive and inexplicably angry. It is almost as if everything could be forged and simulated in psychic life – even affects. As Modell[12] clinically illustrates, there are patients who exhibit seductive, sexualised behaviour for the sake of obliquely obtaining relief from a sense of deadness that is too painful to confront; there are individuals who habitually create contexts of crisis for the sake of obtaining the sort of attention that may fill an otherwise empty self; and we are also familiar with attitudes that falsely emotionalise everything they deal with, to the point of inducing a sense of psychic nausea in the interlocutor.[13] Of course, there are organisations, parties, or groups that relieve us from the risky management of genuine affects: they coach us into the 'proper and satisfying' allocation of our emotional forces in such a way that we grossly misrepresent and falsify core affects.

Psychodiversity and co-optosis

These neologisms are used to indicate the risk that our rich variety of psychic modes of survival, or psychodiversity, may be inconspicuously domesticated and absorbed into major homogeneous world views, or even that insufficient appreciation or indifference towards our inner development may induce a desire to always seek admission into dominant systems, or co-optosis. Knowledge is abstractly supposed to belong to every one, but this generality conceals the exclusivity of dominance and the exclusion of diversified aspects of our creativity, ultimately inducing the production of views so constructed as to safeguard detachment and interepistemic indifference.[14] Aspiring to epistemic homogenisation can be a mental narcotic that may even damage psychodiversity if unexpected interrogations, or crises, did not occasionally expose its presumption.

There are numerous attempts, especially at the 'perifery' of culture, to dissolve the binding constraints that tend to combine rationality and domination into a vision of consciousness where differences can only be seen in terms of degrees, or in terms of a descending hierarchical scale of homogeneous constructs. That creatures who are differently rooted in various milieux may find different cognitive processes suited to their particular conditions is rather commonly accepted.[15] Yet, once purposes and values are identified, the issue of efficacy in the service of their authors almost becomes 'natural', or canonic; and paradoxically while purposes and values efface their affective origins, they tend to become statutory and self perpetuating. The thesis is that it is not so imperative to strive for consensus, but it is vital to try to create conditions of interaction whereby persuasions and convictions may be cared for despite (and perhaps even because of) a lack of consensus.[16] At times we appropriately dare to wonder whether the concordance with a repertoire of affects and ideals may stem from a need to appear sufficiently normal in order to be co-optable, and exhibit 'accounts' that maximise chances of approval, adoption, and acceptance. Thus, even the most sincere, heart-rending, and well-meant of inquiries are necessarily influenced by the determination to avoid exclusion, and to be co-opted by the 'best' ones. How much creativity is being smothered in this inclination we do not know. Of course, whenever we are less than totally 'faithful to the record' we run the risk of composing a fictional rendition. But then, why be so keen on veridical details if not moved by the impulse to generate some meaningful presentation that is not only co-optable, but also illuminating?

The idea of truth is a human construct, and as such it can be imbued with logocentric assumptions. We should perhaps revitalise the tendency, which has been silently present all along, to conceive further ways of pursuing knowledge that free us from dualistic, oppositional constraints between truth and untruth. It is a logocentric attitude that conveniently perpetuates the time-honoured style of binarised oppositions such as mind and body, emotion and reason, instinct and intellect, synthetic/a priori, digital/analogic, logic/empirical, literal/metaphoric. As is known, a common argumental move in most situations is to demonstrate that our interlocutor has made an assertion that is not true; this supposedly erases the merits of his position and effaces the speaker from the dialogic scene. This adds to an accumulated burden, for it is hardly ever a question of actual relations and live interdependencies, but rather a sort of dictat that is presented as a preemptive assumption without which no 'real' knowledge could ever be developed. Yet ironically, the not-so-true assertions do not indicate an indifference to the truth, but the seriousness of their dedication to it; it is a seriousness that impels differently situated inquirers into different views and dissensus. Finally, however, the noble winner in the discussion may not altogether proclaim the exclusion of the 'defeated', and may even offer to co-opt anyone willing to recognise the superiority of the winner's system and seek access to it. In the domain of feminist epistemologies, as is known, the issue of gender differences is often presented as yet another way in which men try to maintain their dominance over women.[17] Here, everything is at stake because the capacity of each person to strive to a full human life depends upon opportunities to develop and express the deepest potentials of one's own mind and heart. Of course, however, in a broader outlook, the liberation that the innumerable 'underdeveloped' are seeking is not merely freedom *from* marginalisation and oppression, but rather the capacity *for* self-creation and self-definition in view of the exercise of personhood in every sphere. According to Scheman, as long as we hold on to the ideal of mind as a 'seamless unity', we will necessarily marginalise the patterns of thinking and feeling of a wide variety of individuals for whom unity could only be exhibited at the price of self-betrayal and distortion.[18] What is ironic is that even though classicities tend to actively co-opt heterogeneous patterns of thinking for purposes of domestication, representatives of dissenting attitudes may be secretly seduced by dominant epistemologies, and thus actively seek to be homogenised into the system.

In Rorty's view, by breaking with both Kant's residual Platonism and Nietzsche's inverted Platonism, psychoanalytic culture enables us to perceive both Nietzsche's superman and Kant's common moral consciousness as exemplifying two out of *many possible* forms of psychic survival, or two out of the many strategies for coping with the conditions of one's upbringing.[19] Even Spinoza laboriously sought to explore the puzzling attitude of 'those who prefer to detest and scoff at human affects . . . than to understand them', and he finally remarked: 'I remember indeed that the celebrated Descartes, although he believed that the mind is absolutely master over its own actions, tried nevertheless to explain by their first causes human affects, and at the same time to show the way by which the mind could obtain absolute power over them; but in my opinion he has shown nothing but the acumen of his great intellect.'[20] In this same sense, Descartes is often considered an emblematic figure of our intellectual way of seeking knowledge, in the sense of focusing on the mind and withdrawing from the world (and even ultimately from one's own embodied existence) in order to produce an abstract relation to it; it is a suitable position for generating a self-image of translucid homogeneity, as well as a hierarchised view of all the rest. Thus, only the 'peripheral' areas of inquiry are places still available for the exercise of the 'lesser', affective faculties, while the indifferent core of epistemology is where 'real' knowledge is being produced. Then, however, through a developing psychoanalytic culture, we tend to dissolve traditional distinctions between central and peripheral, higher and lower, and we incline to perceive the self as a tissue of contingencies rather than a cohesive system of faculties.[21]

The logocracy of mainstream knowledge remains unrecognised as such because there is no other sufficiently contextualised knowledge with which it can interact. In Grosz's view, professional philosophers take on the roles of neutral knowers only because they have conveniently ignored their own specific embodied condition, and have repressed all traces of their gender-specificity from the knowledge that they produce.[22] Gender is also just one important human specificness among innumerable others. In appropriating the realm of the mind for themselves, the authors-authorities have none the less required a support and cover for their disavowed affectivity. 'Others' are thus made to function as the bearers of affects at the service of indifferent theorists who may ultimately even agree to train and co-opt them. The reaction to co-optosis moves away from the Platonic tradition that looks for systemic order under the aegis of abstract principles. Rather, it belongs to the Aristotelian tradition that looks to organic balance and to an ecological equilibrium of diversity.[23] Even in our days some inquirers seem to favour the rational uniformity of harmonious consensus and eschew the creative diversity of dissensus. Some of our prestigious thinkers seem to constantly invoke the tidiness of theorising reason and to decry the diversified complexity of our contingent subjectivities. In every inquiry, our judgements rest on some primal experiential basis that differs from one context (or psycho-ecological niche) to another, and which determines the differentiation of outlooks; for the appropriate exploitation of our diverse experiences is bound to lead into different directions. This simple recognition entails a necessary pluralism of rational processes, authorising, or even counselling, that differently situated agents should proceed differently. The psychodiversity that influences the variation of knowing processes is not to be seen as a violation, but rather as a requirement for an integrated and evolving concept of rationality.[24]

According to Battersby, our epistemologies have been developed from the point of view of an identity that was never 'born', that hesitates to think of death, and cannot 'give birth', in the sense that it does not want to see its psychic history.[25] It is a timeless sort of identity whereby birthing is treated as a deviation from the 'normal' models of identity, that is, 'not integral to thinking identity itself'.[26] The fact that attention to psychic ontogeny is rather rare could also be indicated by the virtual absence of 'children' in the trajectory of Western thought; it is an exclusion which might even be the sign of a statutory detachment from life itself, that is being born, giving birth, and dying. In fact, the image of the 'lovely infant' has a relatively recent origin. There was nothing romantic about the infant in our less recent history, not even in literary works. It is possible that because infants were symbols of impotence, incapable of speech, and totally dependent upon others, they had no cultural relevance, and philosophy conveniently disposed of the issue. Notoriously, the theoretical input of 'lesser' patterns of thinking remains frequently unnoticed by mainstream epistemology; it is a situation that nevertheless enhances the ancient mental habit of extrapolation that consists of acquiring whatever may be conveniently imported, processed and recycled as the output of leading world views. Through such opportune transformations, classicities tend to ignore the specific quality of alien *philo*sophical contributions. It is almost as if vital, specific features had to be left behind in order to function within the translucid rational power system into which they are attracted. Co-optation, in fact, seems to invariably entail a measure of homogenising procedures that may denature the original sources.

To the extent that the seductions of epistemic power are resisted by a force of nurturance, listening and empathic knowledge, a special acuity in recognising the richness of affects is maintained. Because of its lesser social relevance, this vast psychic labour of acumen, precision and balanced connections is only rarely acknowledged in the literature that culminates with the construction of dominant epistemologies. Rather, it is imported, processed, and recycled as the creation of mainstream classicity.[27] The increasing frequency of terms such as 'empathy', 'charity' and 'emotion' is quite significant; officially naming these attitudes in the elitist literature confers to them a measure of legitimacy and prestige that they could not have claimed as long as central epistemology had only regarded them as 'natural' responses or 'instinctual' mechanisms of 'lesser', 'subrational' creatures who move about somewhere in the periphery. Pristine originality can be an illusion since germinal ideas may inconspicuously be at work well before a 'legitimate' founder proclaims them with the sufficient persuasive power to elicit recontextualisations. Official innovators may utilise the full implications of the intuitions that precursors lived by, albeit with a scarce grasp of their 'revolutionary' force.[28]

Perhaps our task is to remind ourselves of the complexity, fragility, and uniqueness of our being, and thus strive to repossess our rationality by extracting it from its 'nowhere' place, bringing it somewhere into time and space, and into our history. Any contributions are indeed *local* philosophies, rather than just philosophies, let alone 'pure' thinking. In contemporary academia, the 'dangers' of exclusion are especially 'threatening' for those who insist upon feeling their thinking (or thinking their feeling) in ways that, from the outside, may look too nomadic and coexistential. It is the sort of work that keeps them from being identified within any permanent ideological topography ranging from a superior 'nowhere' position to itinerant, on-the-road inquiry.[29]

The well-known binarised oppositions of our classicities may serve as a source of symbolic expression for a wide range of cultural preoccupations with different issues.[30] As is argued in feminist epistemologies, we tend to see the gender oppositions that are current in our culture in terms of existing essential differences between men and women, or at least in terms of differences attributable to their specific 'natures'. By means of cross-cultural exploration into different epistemologies we could appreciate, with some irony, that the qualities we think of as distinguishing women from men belong to a complex network of metaphors that are unrelated to gender *per se*. At the same time, however, gender differences are injudiciously defined by reference to oppositional attributions. Conversely, those who cannot adhere to the style of adversarial oppositions or seductive co-optations, may often continue to inquire by means of laborious forms of coexistence and irony. Yet the frequent reduction of irony to the either/or model of inversion may lead to oversimplified notions of how ironic discourses come into being.[31] The common view is that irony involves a conscious rejection of literal significance and the substitution of ironic meaning. Hutcheon suggests that the rejection/substitution theory limits the scope of irony by reducing it to a single disparity between the said and the unsaid, between sign and meaning.[32] This oversimplification may be the final result, the *longa manus*, of the adversarial, binarised logic of classicities. The either/or oppositional dyad does not in fact account for the inclusive and simultaneous nature of ironic meanings as an ulterior dimension of our enquiring efforts.

Preliminaries as conclusions

The affective vicissitudes subjacent to any micro- or macro-community constitute the precondition and essential prologue to its subsequent developments. This is not to say that the prelude is some abstract, autonomous construct that is independent from human contingencies, it is rather to emphasise the relevance of the proleptic vicissitudes of affects that greatly influence the subsequent course of human reason. It is almost as if prologues determined achievements. Unless we attend to the emotional origins of our ventures, we may unwittingly make use of 'premises' in automatically fabricating conclusions. Indifference to these issues may enforce the compulsive use of preliminaries, as if they were ultimate goals. To the extent that we unknowingly adhere to this inclination, affects may increasingly function as silent constraints, rather than as a source of energy for flexible and diversified developments. Although the difference between binding constraints and enlivening guidelines is a small one, the equilibrium between the two seems enormously important.

According to Modell, affective categories exist that function as a potential awaiting activation in the sequence of psychic experiences.[33] To the extent that a given affect category represents unassimilated trauma, or central pathogenic fantasy, there will be a propensity to induce corresponding affective responses in others, and thus reactions that may even exhibit self-confirming characteristics. If we regard fantasies as indicators of profound affects, we can perhaps search for prologues in the 'dreams' that animate any individual or collective venture. What is imaginary is not alien to, or outside of, knowledge and culture; it is its subjacent, necessary companion. Even though fantasies shape our experience of the inner and outer worlds to a surprisingly large extent, it is sometimes believed that these psychic processes are of little significance to our lives. According to Person, even though they may be regarded as evanescent, ephemeral, or inconsequential mental presentations that become diffused in the course of our mind's life, they in fact constitute the essential scenarios in which all the other psychic activities unfold and implement their courses, all the way to a full construction of reality.[34] Fantasies, in her gaze, may be seen as catalysts that organise our lives and guide familial and existential goals;[35] thus they are also epistemic and cultural pursuits. Although early psychoanalytic formulations regarded fantasy as providing substitute gratification and a retreat from the external world, in Person's view the weaving of fantasies is a precious creation of the mind, essential in guiding our inclinations and tracing the path on which we travel through life.[36] We are thus striving to become conversant with psychic preliminaries, which might otherwise function as conclusions.

If we turn to the more intersubjective and cultural contexts, we should of course appreciate that it is by virtue of our participation *and* of our individual history that we can each uniquely contribute to the knowledge that is generated in any epistemic community. Yet, what should be specified is that no individual can know what no one else can think of. However singular, creative or exceptional, what a subject knows is probably made possible by affective interactions and master symbols that animate the preludes of any cultural venture. Indeed, the synergy between emotional prologues and epistemic preliminaries can be more constraining than we are commonly prepared to admit. The agents of any micro- or macro-epistemology are not isolated or isolatable, but profoundly interwoven within the emotional pre-history of their communities.[37] The idea that knowers are dispassionate agents whose affective and cultural roots are scarcely relevant to their knowing, functionally coincides with the idea that 'evidence' and 'truth' are definitive, auto-nomous self-evident ascriptions.[38] However, even the standards of evidence are increasingly recognised as historically contingent and as emerging *together* with the processes through which knowledge is generated. Thus, the affective quality of the interpersonal bonds within the epistemic community may be seen as the main factor that influences the knowledge that is produced. In attempting a synoptic view we could say, in the language of Putnam, that 'What counts as the real world depends upon our values',[39] that is upon the ultimate developments of our originary fantasies.

Theories have a core of 'pre-historical' beliefs which cannot be given up without the risk that thinking and feeling fall into disarray.[40] Some theory is essential to us either because it belongs to activities that we cannot perform without it or because it pertains to feeling as such. As is known, simple denial in the face of unwanted or inexplicable circumstances is common enough. Splitting and dissociation may also appear as relatively simple ways of protecting our basic, irrenounceable assump-tions – Bolton and Hill suggest that they may become unsustainable, however, in the face of traumatic events or enduring adverse experiences.[41] One way of coping with undeniable adverse relations involves a variety of insulating measures, in the sense that traumatic experiences, and in particular their apparent meanings, are kept separate from the affective assumptions that are presupposed for action. In this further way of splitting off there is a form of denial that insulates the core of the self and does not allow difficulties to reach and assail our essential preliminaries and irrenounceable prologues. The necessity of 'foundational' premises can be more easily appreciated in the less affective, and more factual, domains. If as '*we assume* that the earth has existed for many years past' says Wittgenstein 'then of course it sounds strange that we should *assume* such a thing. But in the entire system of our language-games it belongs to the foundations. The assumption, one might say, forms the basis of action, and therefore, naturally, of thought.'[42] Hence, the suggestion evolves that the foundations of certainty are what is required for action and thought. These foundations are preliminary assumptions within systems of beliefs that serve as criteria for the interpretation of experience, as clearly distinguished from those beliefs that might tranquilly be overthrown by experience. If these originary assumptions, which tend to coincide with primal affects, were to be questioned, then the entire system of beliefs would be under threat. 'The child learns by believing the adult. Doubt comes *after* belief' says Wittgenstein.[43]

The insufficient familiarity with our inner depths, however, may even mutate our use of preliminary assumptions and definitions in such a way that they come to function as final answers that erase the fact that they have been psychic issues in the first place; their status becomes unshakeable, almost natural, and hardly, if ever, questioned. Only a retrospective 'historical' outlook permits us to identify affects that have influenced a particular development of values: these are as inconspicuous as they are generally shared and are ultimately quite constraining. The prologues, in fact, can make life difficult even for the most creative of hypotheses. Longino remarks that when we focus the discussion on the relation between evidence and hypothesis, rather than on the relation between evidence and theory, it is possible to observe certain modes of reasoning that have not developed a system of explanation comprehensive enough to be called a theory.[44] 'A great deal of contemporary biological research is of this nature and is still structured by background assumptions that mediate inference between data and hypotheses.'[45] The idea is that certain preliminaries can be so binding that they inconspicuously impede the evolution of 'minor' hypotheses into actual theories.

Some very general beliefs are essential to action at large, even though what they amount to may vary between individuals, and between cultures and subcultures. In so far as there are such convictions, however, they maintain psychological order: what lies beyond them inclines to fragmentation.[46] The risks involved in abandoning preliminary assumptions testify to their necessity, and to the importance of defending them at practically any cost. These psychic defences often serve to protect affective prologues that are perceived as necessary for action. If these assumptions are surrendered because of experience itself, or because parental figures have instilled the necessity to relinquish such hopes, the result is that intentionality and projects are perceived as impossible or pointless.[47] Some basic assumptions, moreover, may be given up in order to preserve still other prologues that are somehow perceived as even more essential. Whatever the origin of maladaptive assumptions, they similarly take on the status of principles for the interpretation of experience, or a status as guidelines to be held to with certainty, and even protected from what comes across as apparent counterevidence.

There is less of a desire for the improvement of daily life than for the identification of ideals that are sufficiently magnetic to function as communal fantasies, or as forces that unite and reinforce our individual originary affects. There is an increasing demand for the enlivening of desire by means of dreams that are sufficiently significant in creating a synergy of our efforts, in mobilising unconscious energies, and even in surpassing individual dreams – they are an overwhelming source of seduction. Our more recent cultural dreams include the cohesive phenomena of French-born enlightenment with the promise that no problem or predicament can resist the redeeming power of reason. Communal dreams include the left- and right-wing developments of German-born historicism, with their even more encompassing promises and follies. We could perhaps also enlist contemporary interest in truth conditions, standards of meaning, and logical analysis of language that might lead to full linguistic clarity and total communication. Psychoanalytic culture itself is not immune from preliminary fantasies such as the early idea of 'conquering' the unconscious, while its current dreams are of course more difficult to perceive. Significantly, according to Schmidt-Hellerau, the question is not '*What* did Freud think (or intend)?' but '*How* did he think?'; that is, 'What are the basic assumptions and movements of his theorising, which remained *constant* through all the revisions of his metapsychology?'[48] She also remarks that the metapsychological constructs that follow from his basic assumptions are by no means irrelevant to the practice of psychoanalysis; they are the necessary guidelines towards insight and orientation when it comes to the question of *how* psychoanalysts perceive, think, and arrive at practical or theoretical conclusions.[49] In spite of the adoption of critical distances, metapsychological assumptions may 'influence the analyst even when he believes that he is listening without a trace of prejudice'.[50]

Attention to the cultural archaeology in which theories are generated, rather than to specific theoretical segments, would incline us to greater moderation; if a certain vocabulary enabled us to 'predict' and operate more easily than another, it would not mean that the world, or the mind, would speak in that idiom or be structured in accordance with it. Of course, our actual selves do not have a Freudian, Jungian, Piagetian or Kleinian structure, simply because we systematically use certain assumptions to interpret mental life. But, paradoxically, speaking of interpretation in a psychoanalytic sense seems almost to speak from the 'outside': the attitude acknowledges the role of thinking in the formation of experiences, almost as if one could compare one style of thought to another.[51] Seen from 'within', however, one's originary affective beliefs do not simply 'interpret' experience, but rather they come to define what one's experience is as a complexive view of reality.

NOTES

1. 'Devastation can hunt us everywhere . . . by keeping itself hidden' and the same could perhaps apply to indifference. Martin Heidegger, *What Is Called Thinking?* trans. J.G. Gray and F.D. Wieck, New York: Harper and Row, 1972, p. 30.
2. 'Although people may have no interest in what they are saying' says Pascal 'we must not absolutely conclude from this that they are not lying; for there are some people who lie for the mere sake for lying.' Blaise Pascal, *Pascal's Pensées*, with an introduction by T.S. Eliot; New York: E.P. Dolton, 1958, §108, p. 34.
3. See on this issue Joseph M. Jones, *Affects as Process. An Inquiry into the Centrality of Affects in Psychological Life*, Hillsdale, NJ: Analytic Press, 1995, p. 92.
4. This topic is discussed in Gemma Corradi Fiumara, *The Other Side of Language. A Philosophy of Listening*, chapter 6 'The philosophical problem of benumbment', London and New York: Routledge, 1990, pp. 82–94.
5. See Joyce McDougall, 'Reflections on affect: a psychoanalytical view of alexithymia' in *Theatres of the Mind. Illusion and Truth on the Psychoanalytic Stage*, London: Free Association Books, 1986, pp. 147–79. The alexithymic condition is characterised by poorly differentiated and poorly verbalised affects that do not serve the signal function adequately. Alexithymic subjects tend to think in an operative way and may appear to be superadjusted to reality. In the analytic relation, though, the disturbance becomes apparent as the subject tends to recount dramatic events of daily life with monotonous

detail, in a way that reveals a painful lack of imagination, intuition, empathy, sympathy, especially in relation to fellow human beings. They seem oriented towards things and even tend to approach themselves in thing-like way. Burness E. Moore and Bernard D. Fine (eds), *Psychoanalytic Terms and Concepts*, New Haven and London: The American Psychoanalytic Association and Yale University Press, 1990, p. 11. The term 'alexithymia' was introduced by P.E. Sifneos in 'Problems of the psychotherapy of patients with alexithymic characteristics and physical disease', *Psychotherapy and Psychosomatics*, vol. 26, 1975, pp. 65–70. Viewing the phenomenon as a developmental defence closely allied with denial and splitting, J. McDougall prefers the term 'dis-affectation'; 'The dis-affected patient', *The Psychoanalytic Quarterly*, vol. 53, 1984, pp. 386–409.

6. J. McDougall, *The Many Faces of Eros. A Psychoanalytic Exploration of Human Sexuality*, London: Free Association Books, 1995, p. 242.

7. Ibid., p. 242.

8. Wilfred R. Bion, *Attention and Interpretation. A Scientific Approach to Insight in Psycho-analysis and Groups*, London: Tavistock, 1970, p. 9.

9. J. McDougall, *The Many Faces of Eros*, p. 244.

10. Ibid., p. 244.

11. Wilfred R. Bion, *Learning from Experience*, London: William Heinemann, 1962, p. 90.

12. Arnold H. Modell, *Other Times, Other Realities. Toward a Theory of Psychoanalytic Treatment*, Cambridge, MA and London: Harvard University Press, 1995, p. 104. Also see *Psychoanalysis in a New Context*; Italian translation by Francesca Ortu, *Psicoanalisi in un nuovo contesto*, Milan: Cortina, 1992, 'Affetti spuri e manipolati', pp. 22–4.

13. Ibid., p. 24.

14. 'Accepting the indispensability of appropriate emotions to knowledge means no more (and no less) than that discordant emotions should be attended to seriously and respectfully rather than condemned, ignored, discounted, or suppressed.' Allison M. Jaggar, 'Love and knowledge: emotion in feminist epistemology', in A.M. Jaggar and S.R. Bordo (eds), *Gender/Body/Knowledge*, New Brunswick, NJ and London: Rutgers University Press, p. 163.

15. Long before his involvement with the idea of truth and falsification, Popper argued that 'There is no history of mankind, there is only an indefinite number of histories of all kinds of aspects of human life. The history most of us learn . . . is largely the history of power politics.' Karl Popper, *The Open Society and Its Enemies*, vol. 2, London: Routledge and Kegan Paul, 1962, p. 270.

16. This thesis is developed by Nicholas Rescher in *Pluralism. Against the Demand for Consensus*, Oxford: Clarendon Press, 1995, p. 194. Significantly, the dedication of the book says: 'For (though also against) Jürgen Habermas'. In his view the guiding principle is no longer 'Let us do whatever we can to promote consensus', but rather 'Let us do whatever we can to render dissensus harmless – and even, whenever possible, profitable'. Ibid., p. 193.

17. Feminist epistemologists typically argue that representation of the world is the work of men, and is thus described from their own points of view that they confuse with objectivity. Lorraine Code is among those who critically engage in the epistemology generated by mainstream philosophers; it is an artefact that is articulated, as it turns out, from their points of view, yet upheld as a source of truth about the way the world should be known and represented. Or at least they only conceive of the restricted perspective on demand, and systematically disregard other perspectives. *What Can She Know? Feminist Theory and the Construction of Knowledge*, Ithaca, NY and London: Cornell University Press, 1991.

18. Naomi Scheman, *Engenderings. Construction of Knowledge, Authority and Privilege*, London and New York: Routledge, 1993, pp. 104–5.

19. Richard Rorty, *Contingency, Irony, and Solidarity*, Cambridge, UK: Cambridge University Press, 1989, p. 35.

20. de Spinoza, Benedict, *Ethic. Demonstrated in Geometrical Order* (translated from the Latin of Benedict De Spinoza by W. Hale White; translation revised by A. Hutchison Stirling), London: T. Fisher Unwin, 1894; 'On the origin and nature of affects', third part, p. 105.

21. R. Rorty, *Contingency, Irony, and Solidarity*, p. 32.

22. Elisabeth Grosz, 'Bodies and knowledges: feminism and the crisis of reason', in Linda Alcoff and Elizabeth Potter (eds), *Feminist Epistemologies*, London and New York: Routledge, 1993, p. 204.

23. 'Formerly we thought of a hierarchy of taxa ... We now see a different hierarchy of units – gene-in-organism, organism-in-environment, ecosystems, etc. Ecology, in the widest sense, turns out to be the study of the interaction and survival of ideas and programs (i.e. differences, complexities of differences, etc.) in circuits.' Gregory Bateson, *Steps to an Ecology of Mind*, New York: Ballantine, 1972, p. 483. Mayr distinguished the typologist from the population thinker 'For the typologist, the type (*eidos*) is real and the variation an illusion, while for the populationist the type is an abstraction and only the variation is real.' Ernst Mayr, *Animal Species and Evolution*, Cambridge, MA: Harvard University Press, 1963, p. 5.

24. See N. Rescher, *Pluralism*, p. 101.

25. Christine Battersby, *The Phenomenal Woman. Feminist Metaphysics and the Patterns of Identity*, Cambridge and Oxford: Polity Press, 1998, p. 4.

26. Ibid., p. 4.

27. An attitude vaguely comparable to speaking of English tea, Swiss chocolate or Italian espresso, as if coffee, cocoa and tea had ever grown in these countries.

28. This point is discussed in Gemma Corradi Fiumara, *The Metaphoric Process. Connections Between Language and Life*, London and New York: Routledge, 1995, p. 5.

29. This general outlook is presented in Rosi Braidotti, *Nomadic Subjects. Embodiment and Sexual Differences in Contemporary Feminist Theory*, New York: Columbia University Press, 1996.

30. Antonio Damasio is judiciously concerned with oversimplifications like 'the idea, for instance, that mind and brain are related but only in the sense that the mind is the software program run in a piece of computer hardware called brain; or that brain and body are related, but only in the sense that the former cannot survive without the life support of the latter.' *Descartes' Error. Emotion, reason, and the Human Brain*, London: Papermac-Macmillan General Books, 1996, p. 247. This outlook, which is pre-emptively shaped by binarised oppositions like software and hardware, mind and body, matter and form, ultimately turns into a fictional parody of the human condition.

31. Linda Hutcheon, *Irony's Edge. The Theory and Politics of Irony*, London and New York: Routledge, 1994, p. 61.

32. Ibid., p. 61.

33. A.H. Modell, *Other Times, Other Realities*, p. 65.

34. Ethel S. Person, *The Force Fantasy. Its Roles, Its Benefits, and What It Reveals about our Lives*, London: HarperCollins, 1997, p. 1.

35. Ibid., p. 1.

36. Ibid., p. 1.

37. These issues are extensively discussed by Lynn Hankinson Nelson in 'Epistemological Communities', L. Alcoff and E. Potter (eds), *Feminist Epistemologies*, London and New York: Routledge, 1993, pp. 121–60.

38. Ibid., pp. 121–60.

39. Hilary Putnam, *Reason, Truth, and History*, Cambridge, UK: Cambridge University Press, 1981, p. 137.
40. This is suggested by Derek Bolton and Jonathan Hill, *Mind, Meaning and Mental Disorder. The Nature of Causal Explanation in Psychology and Psychiatry*, Oxford, New York and Tokyo: Oxford University Press, 1996, p. 309.
41. Ibid., p. 309.
42. Ludwig Wittgenstein, *On Certainty – Über Gewissheit*, G.E.M. Anscombe and G.H von Wright (eds), Oxford: Basil Blackwell, 1970, paragraph 411.
43. Ibid., paragraph 160.
44. Helen Longino, *Science as Social Knowledge. Values and Objectivity in Scientific Inquiry*, Princeton, NJ: Princeton University Press, 1990, p. 60.
45. Ibid., p. 60.
46. See D. Bolton and J. Hill, *Meaning and Mental Disorder*, p. 50.
47. Ibid., p. 312.
48. Cordelia Schmidt-Hellerau, 'Libido and lethe: fundamentals of a formalised conception of metapsychology', *The International Journal of Psychoanalysis*, vol. 78, 1997, pp. 683–97.
49. Ibid., pp. 683–97.
50. Helmut Thomä and Horst Kächele, *Psychoanalytic Practice*, vol. 1, *Principles*, trans. M. Wilson and D. Roseveare, Berlin, Heidelberg and New York: Springer-Verlag, 1987, p. 14.
51. See D. Bolton and J. Hill, *Meaning and Mental Disorder*, p. 40.

Bibliography

Adorno, Theodor W. (1982) *Against Epistemology*, trans. W. Domingo, Oxford: Basil Blackwell.

Ahumada, J. (1994) 'What is a clinical fact? Clinical psychoanalysis as inductive method', *The International Journal of Psychoanalysis* 75: 949–62.

Alcoff, L. and Dalmiya, V. (1993) 'Are "old wives' tales" justified?', in L. Alcoff and E. Potter (eds), *Feminist Epistemologies*, London and New York: Routledge, pp. 217–44.

Allison, H.E. (1998) 'Spinoza, Benedict de, 1632–1677', in E. Craig (ed.), *Routledge Encyclopaedia of Philosophy*, London and New York: Routledge, vol. 9, pp. 91–107.

Alston, W. (1967) 'Emotion and feeling', in P. Edwards (ed.), *Encyclopaedia of Philosophy*, New York and London: Macmillan.

Andermatt Conley, V. (1997) *Ecopolitics. The Environment in Poststructuralist Thought*, London and New York: Routledge.

Arbib, M. and Hesse, M.B. (1986) *The Construction of Reality*, Cambridge: Cambridge University Press.

Arendt, H. (1978) *The Life of the Mind*, vol. 1 *Thinking*; vol. 2 *Willing*, San Diego, CA: Harcourt Brace Javanovich.

Arlow, J. (1977) 'Affects and the psychoanalytic situation', *The International Journal of Psychoanalysis* 58: 157–70.

Armon-Jones, C. *Varieties of Affect*, New York and London: Harvester Wheatsheaf, a division of Simon and Schuster International Group; date of publication not indicated. Oxford thesis supervised by Kathleen Wilkes of St Hilda's College and Paul Snowdon of Exeter College, 1991.

Averill, J.R. (1994) 'In the eyes of the beholder', in P. Ekman and R.J. Davidson (eds), *The Nature of Emotion. Fundamental Questions* (series on Affective Science), New York and Oxford: Oxford University Press, pp. 7–14.

Averill, J.R. and Nunley, E.P. (1992) *Voyages of the Heart. Living an Emotionally Creative Life*, New York and Oxford: The Free Press.

Baader, F. von (1982) *Filosofia erotica*. Introduction, trans. and notes by L. Procesi Xella, Milan: Rusconi.

Bain, A. (1875) *The Emotions and the Will*, London: Longman.

Baranger, M. *et al.* (1983) 'Process and non-process in analytic work', *The International Journal of Psychoanalysis* 64: 1–15.

Barker, F. (1984) *The Tremulous Private Body: Essay in Subjection*, London: Methuen.

Bateson, G. (1972) *Steps to an Ecology of Mind*, New York: Ballantine.

Battersby, C. (1998) *The Phenomenal Woman. Feminist Metaphysics and the Patterns of Identity*, Cambridge and Oxford: Polity Press.

Baudrillard, J. (1996) *Il delitto perfetto. La televisione ha ucciso la realtà?*, Milan: R. Cortina Editore.

Beardsley, M.C. (1958) *Aesthetics: Problems in the Philosophy of Criticism*, New York: Harcourt Brace.

Berenstein, I. (1997) 'A child is being beaten and the battered child', in E.S. Person (ed.), *On Freud's 'A Child Is Being Beaten'*, New Haven and London: Yale University Press, pp. 133–56.

Berlin, I. (1990) 'The apotheosis of the romantic will', *The Crooked Timber of Humanity. Studies in the History of Ideas*, London: John Murray.

Berlyne, D.E. (1954) 'A theory of human curiosity', *British Journal of Psychology* XLIV: 180–91.

Bernstein, R.J. (1981) 'Toward a more rational community', in K. Ketner *et al.* (eds), *Proceedings of the C. S. Peirce Bicentennial International Congress*, Lubbock, TX: Texas Tech Press, pp. 115–20.

Bernstein, R.J. (1983) *Beyond Objectivism and Relativism*, Philadelphia: University of Pennsylvania Press.

Bion, W.R. (1961) *Experiences in Groups*, New York: Basic Books.

Bion, W.R. (1962) *Learning from Experience*. London: William Heinemann.

Bion, W.R. (1970) *Attention and Interpretation. A Scientific Approach to Insight in Psycho-analysis and Groups*, London: Tavistock.

Bloor, D. (1976) *Knowledge and Social Imagery*, London: Routledge and Kegan Paul.

Bollas, C. (1987) *The Shadow of the Object: Psychoanalysis of the Unthought Known*, London: Free Association Books.

Bollas, C. (1995) *Cracking Up: The Work of the Unconscious*, New York and London: Routledge.

Bollas, C. (1997) 'Wording and telling sexuality', *The International Journal of Psychoanalysis* 78: 363–7.

Bolognini, S. (1997) 'Empathy and "empathism"', *The International Journal of Psycho-analysis* 78: 279–93.

Bolton, D. and Hill, J. (1996) *Mind, Meaning and Mental Disorder. The Nature of Causal Explanation in Psychology and Psychiatry*, Oxford, New York and Tokyo: Oxford University Press.

Borch-Jacobsen, M. (1991) *Le lien affectif*, Paris: Aubier.

Boulous Walker, M. (1998) *Philosophy and the Maternal Body, Reading Silence*, London and New York: Routledge.

Braidotti, R. (1991) *Patterns of Dissonance. A Study of Women in Contemporary Philosophy*, Cambridge: Polity Press.

Braidotti, R. (1994) 'Body-images and the pornography of representation', in K. Lennon and M. Whitford (eds), *Knowing the Difference Feminist Perspectives in Epistemology*, London and New York: Routledge, pp. 17–30.

Braidotti, R. (1996) *Nomadic Subjects. Embodiment and Sexual Differences in Contemporary Feminist Theory*, New York: Columbia University Press.

Brazelton, T.B. (1980) 'Neonatal assessment', in G. Pollock and S. Greenspan (eds), *The Course of Life*, vol. I, Washington, DC: US Department of Health and Human Services.

Brennan, T. (1992) *The Interpretation of the Flesh*, London and New York: Routledge.

Brodie, R. (1990) *Virus of the Mind: The New Science of the Meme*, Seattle: Integral Press.

Brown, J. (1983) *Affectivity. Its Language and Meaning*, Lanham, MD: University Press of America.

Bruner, J. (1990) *Acts of Meaning*, Cambridge, MA and London: Harvard University Press.

Burke, K. (1969) *A Rhetoric of Motives*, Berkeley: University of California Press.

Burrow, T. (1926) 'The reabsorbed affect and its elimination', *The British Journal of Medical Psychology* VI(3): 211–18.

Butler, J. (1990) *Gender Trouble*, London and New York: Routledge.

Butler, J. (1993) *Bodies That Matter*, London and New York: Routledge.

Butler, J. (1997) *The Psychic Life of Power. Theories in Subjection*, Stanford, CA: Stanford University Press.

Calabi, C. (1996) *Passioni e ragioni. Un itinerario nella filosofia della psicologia*, Milan: Guerini.

Calhoun, C. and Solomon, R. (eds) (1984) *What is an Emotion?*, New York: Oxford University Press.

Caper, R. (1997) 'A mind of one's own', *The International Journal of Psychoanalysis* 78(2): 265–78.

Caputo, J.D. (1987) *Radical Hermeneutics: Repetition, Deconstruction and the Hermeneutic Project*, Bloomington, IN: Indiana University Press.

Churchland, P.M. (1988) *Matter and Consciousness: A Contemporary Introduction to the Philosophy of Mind*, Cambridge, MA: MIT Press.

Cicero (1979) *De Oratore*, trans. E.W. Sutton, Cambridge, MA: Harvard University Press.

Ciompi, L. (1982) *Affektlogik. Über die Structur der Psyche und ihre Entwicklung. Ein Beitrag zur Schizophrenieforschung*. Stuttgart, Germany: Ernst Klett. *Logica affettiva. Una ricerca sulla schizofrenia* (1994) trans. F. Giancanelli and D. Maperna, Milan: Feltrinelli.

Code, L. (1988) 'Experience, knowledge, and responsibility', in M. Griffiths and M. Whitford (eds), *Feminist Perspectives in Philosophy*, London: Macmillan, pp. 157–72.

Code, L. (1991) *What Can She Know?: Feminist Theory and the Construction of Knowledge*, Ithaca, NY and London: Cornell University Press.

Conway, M.A. (1996) 'Autobiographical knowledge and autobiographical memories', in D.C. Rubin (ed.), *Remembering Our Past: Studies in Autobiographical Memory*, New York: Cambridge University Press, pp. 67–93.

Corradi Fiumara, G. (1990) *The Other Side of Language: A Philosophy of Listening*, London and New York: Routledge.

Corradi Fiumara, G. (1992) *The Symbolic Function: Psychoanalysis and the Philosophy of Language*, Oxford, UK and Cambridge US: Blackwell.

Corradi Fiumara, G. (1995) *The Metaphoric Process: Connections between Language and Life*, London and New York: Routledge.

Craig, E. (ed.) (1998) *Routledge Encyclopedia of Philosophy*, vol. 9, London and New York: Routledge.

Damasio, A.R. (1996) *Descartes' Error: Emotion, Reason and the Human Brain*, London: Papermac-Macmillan General Books.

Damasio, A.R. (2000) *The Feeling of What Happens*, London: Vintage.

Davidson, D. (1982) 'Paradoxes of irrationality', in R. Wollheim and J. Hopkins (eds), *Philosophical Essay on Freud*, Cambridge: Cambridge University Press, pp. 289–305.

Davidson, D. (1985) *Inquiries into Truth and Interpretation*, Oxford: Clarendon Press.

Dawkins, R. (1976, 1989) *The Selfish Gene*, Oxford: Oxford University Press.

De Angelis, V. (1997) *La logica della complessità. Introduzione alle teorie dei sistemi*, Milan: Bruno Mondadori.

de Lauretis, T. (ed.) (1986) *Feminist Studies/Critical Studies*, Bloomington, IN: Indiana University Press.

Deleuze, G. (1970) 'Un nouvel archiviste', *Critique* 274: 195–209.

de Man, P. (1969) 'The rhetoric of temporality', in C.S. Singleton (ed.), *Interpretation: Theory and Practice*, Baltimore: Johns Hopkins University Press.

Demos, E.V. (1987) 'Affect in the development of the self: a new frontier', in A. Goldberg (ed.), *Frontiers in Self Psychology*, Hillsdale, NJ: Analytic Press, pp. 27–53.

Dennett, D.C. (1991) *Consciousness Explained*, Boston: Little, Brown and Company.

Dennett, D.C. (1995) *Darwin's Dangerous Idea*, New York: Simon and Schuster.

Descartes, R. (1986) *Cartesio – Opere Filosofiche, I principi della filosofia* vol. III, E. Garin (ed.), trans. A. Tilgher and M. Garin, Rome and Bari: Laterza.

De Sousa, R. (1987) *The Rationality of Emotion*, Cambridge, MA: MIT Press.

Dijkstra, B. (1986) *Idols of Perversity*, Oxford: Oxford University Press.

Dorstal, R. (1987) 'The world never lost: the hermeneutics of trust', *Philosophy and Phenomenolocigal Research* 47: 413–34.

D'Urso, V. and Trentin, R. (eds) (1996) *Psicologia delle emozioni*, Bologna: Il Mulino.

Edelman, G. (1987) *Neural Darwinism*, New York: Basic Books.

Edelman, G. (1992) *Bright Air, Brilliant Fire. On the Matter of the Mind*, London: Allen Lane, The Penguin Press.

Egidi, R. (ed.) (1995) *Wittgenstein: Mind and Language*, Dordrecht, Boston and London: Kluwer Academic Publishers.

Ekman, P. and Davidson, R.J. (eds) (1994) *The Nature of Emotion. Fundamental Questions* (series in Affective Science), New York and Oxford: Oxford University Press.

Elam, D. and Wiegman, R. (eds) (1995) *Feminism Beside Itself*, London and New York: Routledge.

Emde, R. (1999) 'Moving ahead: integrating influences of affective processes for development and for psychoanalysis', *The International Journal of Psychoanalysis* 80: 317–40.

Faimberg, H. (1988) 'The telescoping of generations', *Contemporary Psychoanalysis* 24(1): 99–118.

Felman, S. (1987) *Jacques Lacan and the Adventure of Insight: Psychoanalysis in Contemporary Culture*, Cambridge, MA: Harvard University Press.

Ferrell, R. (1996) *Passion in Theory: Conceptions of Freud and Lacan*. London and New York: Routledge (Warwick Studies in European Philosophy, edited by Andrew Benjamin).

Fimiami, M. (1994) *Paradossi dell'indifferenza*, Rome: Franco Angeli.

Fine, B.D. and Moore, B.E. (1987) *A Glossary of Psychoanalytic Terms and Concepts*, The American Psychoanalytic Association.

Flack, W.F., Jr, and Laird, J.D. (eds) (1998) *Emotions in Psychopathology. Theory and Research*, New York and Oxford: Oxford University Press.

Fludernik, M. (1996) *Towards a 'Natural' Narratology*, London and New York: Routledge.

Fodor, J. (1987) *Psychosemantics*, Cambridge, MA: MIT Press.

Fonagy, P. (1999) 'Guest editorial. Memory and therapeutic action', *The International Journal of Psychoanalysis* 80: 215–223.

Forrester, J. (1990) *The Seductions of Psychoanalysis*, Cambridge, UK: Cambridge University Press.

Foskett, J. (1987) *Meaning in Madness. The Pastor and the Mentally Ill*, London: SPCK Press.

Foucault, M. (1970) *The Order of Things*, London: Tavistock Publications.

Foucault, M. (1972) *The Archaeology of Meaning and the Discourse on Language*, New York: Pantheon.

Foucault, M. (1977) *Discipline and Punish: The Birth of the Prison*, New York: Pantheon.

Foucault, M. (1978) *Histoire de la sexualité 1: Volonté de savoir*, Paris: Gallimard.

Foucault, M. (1980) 'The subject of power' and 'Two lectures', in C. Gordon (ed.), *Power/Knowledge: Selected Interviews and Other Writings, 1927–77*, New York: Pantheon, pp. 78–108.

Fox-Genovese, E. (1991) *Feminism without Illusion: A Critique of Individualism*, Chapel Hill: University of North Carolina Press.

Fox Keller, E. (1985) *Reflections on Gender and Science*, New Haven: Yale University Press.

Fox Keller, E. (1985) *A Feeling for the Organism: The Life and work of Barbara McClintock*, New York: Freeman.

Fréjda, N. (1986) *The Emotions*, Cambridge: Cambridge University Press.

Freud, S. (1905), 'Fragment of an analysis of a case of hysteria', in J. Strachey in collaboration with A. Freud (trans. and ed.), *The Standard Edition of the Complete Psychological Works of Sigmund Freud*, London: The Hogarth Press and the Institute of Psycho-Analysis, 1966, vol. 7.

Freud, S. (1914) 'On narcissism: an introduction', in J. Strachey in collaboration with A. Freud (trans. and ed.), *The Standard Edition of the Complete Psychological Works of Sigmund Freud*, London: The Hogarth Press and the Institute of Psycho-Analysis, 1966, vol. 14.

Freud, S. (1916) 'Anxiety' in 'Introductory lectures on psycho-analysis', in J. Strachey in collaboration with A. Freud (trans. and ed.), *The Standard Edition of the Complete Psychological Works of Sigmund Freud*, London: The Hogarth Press and the Institute of Psycho-Analysis, 1966, vol. 15.

Freud, S. (1920) 'Beyond the pleasure principle', in J. Strachey in collaboration with A. Freud (trans. and ed.), *The Standard Edition of the Complete Psychological Works of Sigmund Freud*, London: The Hogarth Press and the Institute of Psycho-Analysis, 1966, vol. 18.

Freud, S. (1932), 'New introductory lectures on psycho-analysis', in J. Strachey in collaboration with A. Freud (trans. and ed.), *The Standard Edition of the Complete Psychological Works of Sigmund Freud*, London: The Hogarth Press and the Institute of Psycho-Analysis, 1966, vol. 22.

Fricker, M. (1994) 'Knowledge as construct. Theorizing the role of gender in knowledge', in K. Lennon and M. Whitford (eds), *Knowing the Difference. Feminist Perspectives in Epistemology*, London and New York: Routledge, pp. 95–109.

Gallop, J. (1988) *Thinking Through the Body*, New York: Columbia University Press.

Gardner, H. *Frames of Mind. The Theory of Multiple Intelligences*, London: Fontana Press.

Gatti Pertegato, E. (1991) *Dietro la maschera: sulla formazione del sé e del falso sé*, Rome: Franco Angeli.

Gazzaniga, M. (1992) *Nature's Mind: The Impact of Darwinian Selection on Thinking, Emotions, Sexuality, Language and Intelligence*, New York: Basic Books.

Giardini, F. (1999) 'Public affects. Clues towards a political practice of singularity', *European Journal of Women's Studies* 6: 149–59.

Gibbs, R.W. (1984) 'Literal meaning and psychological theory', *Cognitive Science* 8: 275–304.

Gilligan, C. (1982) *In a Different Voice. Psychological Theory and Women's Development*, Cambridge, MA: Harvard University Press.

Glasser, M. (1998) 'On violence: a preliminary communication', *The International Journal of Psychoanalysis* 79: 887–902.

Goellner, E.W. and Shea Murphy, J. (1995) *Bodies of the Text: Dance as Theory, Literature as Dance*, Rutgers, NJ: Rutgers University Press.

Goethe, J.W. (1976) *Goethe' Faust*, trans. R. Jarrell, New York: Farrar, Straus and Girouse.

Goldie, P. (2000) *The Emotions: A Philosophical Exploration*, Oxford: Clarendon Press.

Goleman, D. (1995, 1996) *Emotional Intelligence, Why It Can Matter More than I.Q.*, New York: Bantam 1995, Bloomsbury 1996.

Gordon, R. (1969) 'Emotions and knowledge', *The Journal of Philosophy* 66: 408–13.

Gordon, R. (1986) 'The passivity of emotions', *Philosophical Review* 95: 371–92.

Gordon, R. (1987) *The Structure of Emotions: Investigations in Cognitive Philosophy*, Cambridge: Cambridge University Press.

Gould, S. (1977) *Ontogeny and Philogeny*, Cambridge, MA: Harvard University Press.

Graeme, T. (1997) *Disorders in Affect Regulations*, Cambridge: Cambridge University Press.

Green, A. (1985) 'Réflexious libres sur la représentation de l'affect', *Revue Française de Psychoanalysis* 49: 773–88.

Green, A. (1998) 'The primordial mind and the work of the negative', *The International Journal of Psychoanalysis* 79: 649–65.

Green, A. (1999) 'On discriminating and not discriminating between affect and representation', *The International Journal of Psychoanalysis* 80: 277–316.

Greenberg, J. and Mitchell, S. (1983) *Object Relations in Psychoanalytic Theory*, Cambridge, MA: Harvard University Press.

Greenspan, P. (1988) *Emotions and Reasons: An Inquiry into Emotional Justification*, London and New York: Routledge.

Grene, M. *The Knower and the Known*, New York: Basic Books.

Grinberg, L. (1986) 'Pulsions et affects: des modèles plutôt que des théories', *Psychoanalysis in Europe Bulletin* vols. 26–7.

Grosz, E. (1990) 'Philosophy', in S. Gunew (ed.), *Feminist Knowledge: Critique and Construct*, London and New York: Routledge, pp. 147–74.

Grosz, E. (1993) 'Bodies and knowledges: feminism and the crisis of reason', in L. Alcoff and E. Potter (eds), *Feminist Epistemologies*, London and New York: Routledge, pp. 187–215.

Gunew, S. (ed.) (1990) *Feminist Knowledge: Critique and Construct*, London and New York: Routledge.

Habermas, J. (1990) *Moral Consciousness and Communicative Action,* trans. C. Lenhart and S. Weber Nicholsen, Cambridge, MA: MIT Press.

Hankinson Nelson, L. (1993) 'Epistemological communities', in L. Alcoff and E. Potter (eds), *Feminist Epistemologies*, London and New York: Routledge, pp. 121–60.

Haraway, D. (1988) 'Situated knowledge: the science question', *Feminism and the Privilege of Partial Perspective'*, *Feminist Studies* 14(3): 584–94.

Haraway, D. (1996) *Simians, Cyborgs and Women. The Reinvention of Nature*, London: Free Association Books.

Harding, S. (1986) *The Science Question in Feminism*, Milton Keynes: Open University Press.

Harding, S. (1991) *Whose Science? Whose Knowledge? Thinking from Women's Lives*, Milton Keynes: Open University Press.

Harding, S. (1993) 'Rethinking standpoint epistemology: what is strong objectivity?', L. Aleoff and E. Potter (eds), *Feminist Epistemologies*, London and New York: Routledge, pp. 49–82.

Harris, J. (1994) *Early Language Development. Implications for Clinical and Educational Practice*, London and New York: Routledge.

Harrison, S.M. (1981) 'Peirce on persons', in K.L. Ketner *et al.* (eds), *Proceedings of the C.S. Peirce Bicentennial International Congress*, Lubbock, TX: Texas Tech Press, pp. 217–21.

Heidegger, M. (1972) *What Is Called Thinking?*, trans. J.G. Gray and F.D. Wieck, New York: Harper and Row.

Heim, M. (1993) *The Metaphysics of Virtual Reality*, Oxford and New York: Oxford University Press.

Herzfeld, M. (1982) 'Disemia', in M. Herzfeld and M.D. Lenhart (eds) *Semiotics 1980*, New York and London: Plenum Press.

Hilmy, S. (1995) 'Wittgenstein on language, mind and mythology', in R. Egidi (ed.), *Wittgenstein: Mind and Language*, Dordrecht, Boston and London: Kluwer Academic Press, pp. 235–48.

Holland, N.J. (1990) *Is Women's Philosophy Possible?*, Savage, MD: Rowman and Littlefield.

Hollis, M. (1970) 'The limits of irrationality', in B. Wilson (ed.), *Rationality*, Oxford: Basil Blackwell, pp. 221–39.

Hughes, R. (1992) *The Culture of Complaint*, New York: Oxford University Press.

Huizinga, J. (1936) *The Shadow of Tomorrow*, London: Willian Heinemann.

Hume, D. (1988) *Treatise on Human Nature*, L.A. Selby-Bigge (ed.), Oxford: Clarendon Press.

Hutcheon, L. (1994) *Irony's Edge. The Theory and Politics of Irony*, London and New York: Routledge.

Irigaray, L. (1974) *Speculum de l'autre femme*, Paris: Minuit (*Speculum of the Other Woman*, trans. G.C. Gill, Ithaca, NY: Cornell University Press, 1985).

Irigaray, L. (1990) *Je, tu, nous*, Paris: Grasset-Fasynelle (*Je, tu, nous: Toward a Culture of Difference*, trans. A. Martin, London and New York: Routledge, 1993).

Irigaray, L. (1992) *Elemental Passions*, trans. I. Collie and J. Still), London and New York: Routledge.

Izard, C. (1991) *The Psychology of Emotions*, New York: Plenum Press.

Jacob, F. (1973) *La logique du vivant*, Paris: Gallimand (*The Logic of Life*, trans. B.E. Spielman, New York: Vintage, 1976).

Jacobson, E. (1957) 'Normal and pathological moods', *The Psychoanalytic Study of the Child* 12: 73–113.

Jaggar, A.M. (1989) 'Love and knowledge: emotion in feminist epistemology', in A.M. Jaggar and S.R. Bordo (eds), *Gender/Body/Knowledge: Feminist Reconstructions of Being and Knowing*, New Brunswick, NJ and London: Rutgers University Press, pp. 145–71.

James, W. (1884) 'What is an emotion?', *Mind* 19: 188–204.

James, W. (1892) *Psychology. Briefer Course*, New York: Henry Holt.

James, W. (1912) *A Pluralistic Universe*, New York: Longmans, Green.

James, W. (1950) *The Principles of Psychology* (authorized edition in two unabridged volumes bound as one), New York: Dover Publications.

James, W. (1956) *The Will to Believe and Other Essays in Popular Philosophy*, New York: Dover Publications (also Cambridge, MA and London: Harvard University Press, 1979).

Jones, J.M. (1995) *Affects as Process. An Inquiry into the Centrality of Affect in Psychological Life* (foreword by J.D. Lichtenbeg), vol. 14, Hillsdale and London: Analytic Press.

Kant, I. (1907) *Immanuel Kant's Critique of Pure Reason* 2nd edn, trans. F. Max Müller, New York and London: Macmillan.

Kant, I. (1987) *Political Writings*, H. Reis (ed.), trans. H.B. Nisbet, Cambridge: Cambridge University Press.

Kappeler, S. (1986) *The Pornography of Representation*, Cambridge: Polity Press.

Kaufer, D. (1977) 'Irony and rhetorical strategy', *Philosophy and Rhetoric* 10(2): 90–110.

Keleman, H. (1987) 'On resonant cognition', *International Review of Psychoanalysis* 14: 111–24.

Kemper, T.D. (1987) 'How many emotions are there? Wedding the social and the autonomic components', *American Journal of Sociology* 93: 263–89.

Kenny, A. (1963) *Action, Emotion and Will*, London: Routledge and Kegan Paul.

Kernberg, O. (1979) *Object Relations: Theory and Clinical Psychoanalysis*, New York: Jason Aronson.

Kernberg, O. (1980) *Internal World and External Reality. Object Relations Theory Applied*, New York and London: Jason Aronson.

Kernberg, O. (1995) *Love Relations*, New Haven and London: Yale University Press.

Kernberg, O. (1997) 'Modernity and its discontents. A discussion of the paper by Sergio Paulo Rouanet', *International Psychoanalysis. The Newsletter of the International Psychoanalytical Association* 6(2):.

Ketner, K.L., Rausdell, J.M., Eisele, C., Fisch, M.H. and Hardwick, C.S. (eds) (1981) *Proceedings of the C.S. Peirce Bicentennial International Congress*, Lubbock, TX: Texas Tech Press.

Khan, M. (1974) *The Privacy of the Self*, New York: International Universities Press.

Kierkegaard, S. (1843) *Fear and Trembling*, ed. and trans. H.V. Hong and E.H. Hong, *Kierkegaard's Writings*, vol. 6, Princeton, NJ: Princeton University Press, 1983.

Kitayama, O. (1998) 'Transience: its beauty and danger', *The International Journal of Psychoanalysis* 79: 937–54.

Kohut, H. (1959) 'Introspection, empathy and psychoanalysis', *Journal of the American Psychoanalytic Association* 7: 459–582.

Kosslyn, S.M. and Koenig, O. (1992) *Wet Mind: The New Cognitive Neuroscience*, New York: The Free Press.

Krystal, H. (1988) *Integration and Self-Healing: Affect, Trauma, Alexithymia*, Hillsdale, NJ: Analytic Press.

Kuhn, T.S. (1970) *The Structure of Scientific Revolutions* 2nd edn, Chicago and London: University of Chicago Press.

Lacan, J. (1976) *The Language of the Self. The Function of Language in Psychoanalysis*, trans. with notes and commentary by A. Wilden, Baltimore and London: Johns Hopkins University Press.

Lacan, J. (1977) *Ecrits: A Selection*, London: Tavistock Publications.

Langer, S.K. (1988) *Mind: An Essay on Human Feeling*, abridged edition by G. Van Der Heuval, Baltimore and London: Johns Hopkins University Press.

Langs, R. (1999) *L'evoluzione della mente emotiva*, Rome: Giovanni Fioriti Editore.

Laplanche, J. and Pontalis, J.B. (1967) *The Language of Psychoanalysis*, trans. D. Nicholson-Smith, New York: Norton.

Laplanche, J. and Pontalis, J.B. (1995) *Enciclopedia della psicoanalisi* vols. 1–II, Rome and Bari: Laterza.

Latour, B. (1987) *Science in Action*, Cambridge, MA: Harvard University Press.

Lazarus, R.S. and Lazarus, B.N. (1996) *Passion and Reason. Making Sense of Our Emotions*, New York: Oxford University Press (originally published in 1994).

Lazarus, R.S. and Smith, C.A. (1994) 'Knowledge and appraisal in the cognition-emotion relationship', in P. Eckman and R.J. Davidson (eds), *The Nature of Emotion. Fundamental Questions*, New York and Oxford: Oxford University Press, pp. 281–300.

Le Doeuff, M. (1987) 'Women and philosophy', in T. Moi (ed.), *French Feminist Thought*, Oxford, UK and Cambridge, US: Blackwell.

Le Doeuff, M. (1989) *The Philosophical Imaginary*, trans. C. Gordon, Stanford, CA: Stanford University Press (originally published as *L'imaginaire philosophique*, Paris: Payot, 1980).

Le Doux, J. (1998) *The Emotional Brain. The Mysterious Underpinnings of Emotional Life*, trans. Sylvie Coyaud, *Il cervello emotivo. Alle radici delle emozioni*, Milan: Baldini-Castoldi.

Levi, A.W. (1962) *Literature, Philosophy and the Imagination*, Bloomington: Indiana University Press.

Levins, R. and Lewontin, R. (1985) *The Dialectical Biologist*, Cambridge, MA and London, UK: Harvard University Press.

Lichtenberg, J.D. (1983) *Psychoanalysis and Infant Research*, Hillsdale, NJ: Analytic Press.

Lichtenberg, J.D. (1995) (foreword to J.M. Jones), *Affects as Process. An Inquiry into the Centrality of Affect in Psychological Life*, Hillsdale and London: Analytic Press, pp. xiii–xix.

Lichtenberg, J.D., Bornstein, M. and Silver, D. (eds) (1984) *Empathy*, vols 1–2, Hillsdale and London: Analytic Press.

Lloyd, G. (1984) *The Man of Reason*, London: Methuen.

Loewald, H. (1988) 'Psychoanalysis as an art, and the fantasy character of the psychoanalytic situation', *Papers on Psychoanalysis*, New Haven: Yale University Press.

Lombroso, G. (1923) *The Soul of Woman*, New York: E.P. Dutton.

Longino, H.E. (1990) *Science as Social Knowledge. Values and Objectivity in Scientific Inquiry*, Princeton, NJ: Princeton University Press.

Lopez McAlister, L. (1996) *Hypatia's Daughters: 1500 Years of Women Philosophers*, Bloomington, IN: Indiana University Press.

Lynch, A. (1996) *Thought Contagion. How Belief Spreads through Society*, New York: Basic Books.

Lyons, W. (1980) *Emotion*, Cambridge: Cambridge University Press.

Lyons, W. (1998) 'Philosophy, the emotions, and psychopathology', in W.F. Flack, Jr and

J.D. Laird (eds), *Emotions in Psychopathology. Theory and Research*, Oxford and New York: Oxford University Press, pp. 3–19.

Lyotard, J.-F. (1988) *The Différend: Phrases in Dispute*, trans. G. van Den Abbeele, Minneapolis: University of Minnesota Press (originally published as *Le Différend*, Paris: Minuit, 1983).

Macdonald, C. (1990) *Mind Body Identity Theories*, London and New York: Routledge.

Maclean, M. (1994) *The Name of the Mother. Writing Illegitimacy*, London and New York: Routledge.

Mainong, A. (1972) *On Emotional Presentation*, Evanston, IL: Northwestern University Press.

Malpas, J.E. (1992) *Donald Davidson and the Mirror of Meaning: Holism, Truth, Interpretation*, Cambridge: Cambridge University Press.

Mandler, G. (1975) *Mind and Emotion*, New York: Wiley.

Marchant, C. (1980) *The Death of Nature*, San Francisco, CA: Harper and Row.

Marcuse, H. (1962) *Eros and Civilization*, New York: Vintage.

Marlean-Ponty, M. (1942) *La structure du comportement*, Paris: Presses Universitaires de France, trans. A.L. Fisher, *The Structure of Behavior*, Boston: Beacon Press, 1967.

Masson, J. (ed. and trans.) (1985) *The Complete Letters of Sigmund Freud to Wilhelm Fliess*, Cambridge, MA: Harvard University Press.

Matte Blanco, I. (1981) *L'inconscio come insiemi infiniti. Saggio sulla bi-logica*, introduction and trans. P. Bria, Turin: Einaudi.

McDonald, C. (1995) 'Personal criticism: dialogue of differences', in D. Elam and R. Wiegman (eds) *Feminism Beside Itself*, London and New York: Routledge, pp. 237–60.

McDougall, J. (1984) 'The "dis-affected" patient', *Psychoanalytic Quarterly* 53: 386–409.

McDougall, J. (1990) *Plaidoyer pour une certaine anormalité*, Paris: Editions Gallimard.

McDougall, J. (1995) *The Many Faces of Eros. A Psychoanalytic Exploration of Human Sexuality*, London: Free Association Books.

Meissner, W. (1988) *Treatment of Patients in the Borderline Spectrum*, New York: Jason Aronson.

Mele, A.R. (1992) *Springs of Action: Understanding Intentional Behaviour*, New York: Oxford University Press.

Miller, A. (1984) *For Your Own Good: Hidden Cruelty in Child Rearing and the Roots of Violence*, trans. H. and H. Hannum, New York: Farrar, Straus, and Giroux.

Milroy, J. and Milroy, L. (1997) *Authority in Language. Investigating Language. Standardization and Prescription*, London and New York: Routledge.

Min-ha, T. (1989) *Woman, Native, Other*, Bloomington, IN: Indiana University Press.

Mischel, T. (1974) 'Concerning rational explanation and psychoanalytic explanation', in R. Wollheim (ed.), *Freud: A Collection of Critical Essays*, New York: Anchor, pp. 322–31.

Mitchell, S. (1988) *Relational Concepts in Psychoanalysis*, Cambridge, MA: Harvard University Press.

Mitchell, S. (1993) *Hope and Dread in Psychoanalysis*, New York: Basic Books.

Modell, A.H. (1977) 'Humiliating fantasies and the pursuit of unpleasure', in E.S. Person (ed.), *On Freud's 'A Child Is Being Beaten'*, New Haven and London: Yale University Press, pp. 67–75.

Modell, A.H. (1995) *Other Times, Other Realities. Toward a Theory of Psychoanalytic Treatment*, Cambridge, MA and London: Harvard University Press.

Modell, A.H. (1996) *The Private Self*, Cambridge, MA and London: Harvard University Press.

Moore, B.E. and Fine, B.D. (eds) (1990) *Psychoanalytic Terms and Concepts*, New Haven and London: The American Psychoanalytic Association and Yale University Press.

Muller, J.P. (1997) *Beyond the Psychoanalytic Dyad. Developmental Semiotics in Freud, Peirce and Lacan*, London and New York: Routledge.

Murdoch, I. (1970) *The Sovereignity of Good*, London: Cox and Wyman.

Nietzsche, F. (1910) *Will to Power*, vol. 15 of *Complete Works*, trans. A.M. Ludovici, Edinburgh: T.M. Fowlis.

Nietzsche, F. (1967) *On the Genealogy of Morals* (1887), New York: Random House.

Nozick, R. (1981) *Philosophical Explanations*, Oxford: Clarendon Press.

Nunberg, H. (1960) *Curiosity*, New York: International University Press.

Oatley, K. and Jenkins, J.M. (1996) *Understanding Emotions*, Oxford: Blackwell.

Ornstein, R. and Ehrlich, P. (1989) *New World. New Mind: Moving Toward Conscious Evolution*, Norwalk, CT: Simon and Schuster.

Pally, R. (1998) 'Emotional processing: the mind-body connection', *The International Journal of Psychoanalysis* 79: 349–62.

Pao, P.N. (1984) *Therapeutic Empathy in the Schizophremic. On Empathy II*, Hillsdale and London: Analytic Press.

Park, P. (ed.) (1993) *Voices of Change: Participatory Research in the United States and Canada*, Westport, CT and London: Bergin and Garvey.

Parker, R. (1998) 'Killing the angel in the house: creativity, femininity and aggression', *The International Journal of Psychoanalysis* 79: 757–74.

Pascal, B. (1958) *Pascal's Pensées*, introduction by T.S. Eliot, New York: E.P. Dutton.

Pears, D. (1962) 'Causes and objects of some feelings and psychological reactions', *Ratio* 4: 91–111.

Peirce, C.S., Hartsborne, C. and Weiss, P. (eds) (1931–5, 1958) *Collected Papers of Charles Sanders Peirce*, vols 1–6, Cambridge, MA: Harvard University Press, 1931–5; vols 7–8, A. Burks (ed.), 1958.

Penneker, J.W. (1980) *Opening Up. The Healing Power of Expressing Emotions*, New York and London: The Guilford Press.

Person, E.S. (ed.), (1997) 'On Freud's "A child is being beaten"', *Contemporary Freud: Turning Points and Critical Issues*, New Haven and London: Yale University Press.

Person, E.S. (1997) *The Force of Fantasy. Its Roles, Its Benefits and What It Reveals about our Lives*, London: HarperCollins.

Peters, R.S. (1970) 'The education of the emotions', in M.B. Arnold (ed.), *Feelings and Emotions*, New York: Academic Press.

Pfister, J. and Schuog, N. (eds) (1997) *Inventing the Psychological: Toward a Cultural History of Emotional Life in America*, New Haven: Yale University Press.

Plotinus (1956) *The Enneads*, trans. S. MacKenna, London: Faber and Faber.

Plutchik, R. (1962) *The Emotions: Facts, Theories and a New Model*, New York: Random House.

Plutchik, R. (1994) *The Psychology and Biology of Emotions*, New York: HarperCollins.

Plutchik, R. and Kellerman, H. (eds) (1980) *Emotion Theory, Research and Experience*, vol. I: *Theories of Emotion*, London: Academic Press.

Potter, E. (1993) 'Gender and epistemic negotiation', in L. Alcoff and E. Potter (eds), *Feminist Epistemologies*, London and New York: Routledge, pp. 161–86.

Pugh, G. (1977) *The Biological Origin of Human Values*, New York: Basic Books.

Putnam, H. (1981) *Reason, Truth and History*, Cambridge: Cambridge University Press.

Putnam, H. (1995) *Pragmatism. An Open Question*, Oxford: Blackwell.

Quine, W.V.O. (1960) *Word and Object*, Cambridge, MA: MIT Press.

Quine, W.V.O. (1961) *From a Logical Point of View*, New York: Harper Torchbooks.

Quine, W.V.O. (1969) *Ontological Relativity and Other Essays*, New York: Columbia University Press.

Quintilian (1977) *The Institutio Oratoria*, trans. H.E. Butler, Cambridge, MA: Harvard University Press.

Radden, J. (1985) *Madness and Reason*, London: Allen and Unwin.

Radnitzky, G. (ed.) (1988) *Centripetal Forces in the Sciences*, vol. 2, New York: Paragon House.

Rapaport, D. (1967) 'On the psychoanalytic theory of affects', in M. Gill (ed.) *The Collected Papers of David Rapaport*, New York: Basic Books, pp. 476–512.

Raymond, L.W., and Rosbrow-Reich, S. (eds) (1997) *Inward Eye. Psychoanalysts Reflect on Their Lives and Work*, Hillsdale and London: Analytic Press.

Rescher, N. (1995) *Pluralism. Against the Demand for Consensus*, Oxford: Clarendon Press.

Ricoeur, P. (1992) *Oneself as Another*, trans. Kathleen Blamey, Chicago and London: The University of Chicago Press.

Rorty, A.O. (ed.) (1980) *Explaining Emotions*, Berkeley, CA: University of California Press.

Rorty, R. (1980) *Philosophy and the Mirror of Nature*, Oxford: Blackwell.

Rorty, R. (1989) *Contingency, Irony and Solidarity*, Cambridge: Cambridge University Press.

Rorty, R. (1991) *Objectivity, Relativism and Truth. Philosophical Papers*, vol. I, Cambridge: Cambridge University Press.

Rutter, M. and Rutter, M. (1993) *Developing Minds: Challenges and Continuity Across the Lifespan*, New York: Basic Books.

Sartre, J.-P. (1948) *The Emotions. Outline of a Theory*, New York: Philosophical Library.

Schachtel, E. (1959) *Metamorphosis*, New York: Basic Books.

Schafer, R. (1964) 'The clinical analysis of affects', *Journal of the American Psychoanalytic Association* 12: 275–99.

Schafer, R. (1976) *The Psychoanalytic Life History*, London: H.K. Lewis.

Schafer, R. (1980) 'Narration in the psychoanalytic dialogue', *Critical Inquiry* 7: 29–53.

Schafer, R. (1992) *Retelling a Life*, New York: Basic Books.

Scheler, M. (1972) *The Nature of Sympathy*, trans. P. Heath, Hamden, CT: Anchor Books.

Scheman, N. (1993) *Engenderings. Construction of Knowledge, Authority and Privilege*, London and New York: Routledge.

Schmidt-Hellerau, C. (1997) 'Libido and lethe: fundamentals of a formalised conception of metapsychology', *The International Journal of Psychoanalysis* 78: 683–97.

Schopenhauer, A. (1969) *The World as Will and Representation*, vol. 1, trans. E.F.J. Payne, New York: Dover.

Schore, A.N. (1994) *Affect Regulation and the Origin of the Self: The Neurobiology of Emotional Development*, Hillsdale, NJ: Lawrence Erlbaum.

Schulte, J. (1995) 'Emotion: remarks on Wittgenstein and William James', in R. Egidi (ed.) *Wittgenstein: Mind and Language*, Dordrecht, Boston and London: Kluwer Academic Publishers, pp. 249–62.

Schwaber, E.A. (1998) 'The non-verbal dimension in psychoanalysis: "state" and its clinical vicissitudes', *The International Journal of Psychoanalysis* 79: 667–79.

Shapiro, T. (1999) 'The 41st International Psychoanalytic Congress – Foreword', *The International Journal of Psychoanalysis* 80: 275–6.

Sharpe, R.B. (1959) *Irony in the Drama: An Essay on Impersonation, Shock and Catharsis*, Chapel Hill, NC: University of North Carolina Press.

Sifneos, P.E. (1975) 'Problems of psychotherapy of patients with alexithymia characteristics and physical disease', *Psychotherapy and Psychosomatics* 26: 65–70.

Silverman, K. (1996) *The Threshold of the Visible World*, London and New York: Routledge.

Smith, B.H. (1988) *Contingencies of Value: Alternative Perspectives for Critical Theory*, Cambridge, MA: Harvard University Press.

Smith, P. (1988) *Discerning the Subject*, Minneapolis: University of Minnesota Press.

Smith, S.G. (1992) *Gender Thinking*, Philadelphia: Temple University Press.

Solomon, R.C. (1993) *The Passions: Emotions and the Meaning of Life*, Indianapolis, IN: Hackett Publishing Company.

Solomon, R.C. (1998) 'The nature of emotions', in E. Craig (ed.) *Routledge Encyclopedia of Philosophy*, vol. 3, London and New York, pp. 281–90.

Sorice, M. (1996) *Logiche dell'illogico. Introduzione alle teorie del consumo*, Rome: Edizioni SEAM.

Spence, D.P. (1998) 'Rain forest or mud field? Guest editorial', *The International Journal of Psychoanalysis* 79: 643–8.

Spezzano, C. (1993) *Affect in Psychoanalysis. A Clinical Synthesis*, Hillsdale and London: Analytic Press.

de Spinoza, B. (1894) *Ethic: Demonstrated in Geometrical Order*, trans. from the Latin of Benedict de Spinoza by W. Hale White (translation revised by A. Hutchison Stirling), London: T. Fisher Unwin.

Stein, E. (1970) *On the Problem of Empathy*, trans. W. Stein with a foreword by E. W. Strauss, The Hague: Martinus Nijhoff.

Steiner, C. and Perry, P. (1997) *Achieving Emotional Literacy*, New York: Simon and Shuster.

Stern, D. (1985) *The Interpersonal World of the Infant*, New York: Basic Books.

Stern, D.N., Sander, L.W., Nahum, J.P. *et al.* (1998) 'Non-interpretative mechanisms in psychoanalytic therapy. The "something more" than interpretation', *The International Journal of Psychoanalysis* 79: 903–21.

Stick, S. (1983) *From Folk Psychology to Cognitive Science: The Case Against Belief*, Cambridge, MA: Bradford Books, MIT Press.

Stolorow, R. and Atwood, G. (1992) *Contexts of Being*, Hillsdale and London: Analytic Press.

Strawson, P.F. (1959) *Individuals: An Essay in Descriptive Metaphysics*, London: Methuen.

Stroll, A. (1998) *Sketches of Landscapes: Philosophy by Example*, Cambridge, MA: MIT Press.

Strongman, K.T. (1996) *The Psychology of Emotion. Theories of Emotion in Perspective*, Chichester and New York: John Wiley.

Tavris, C. (1989) *Anger: The Misunderstood Emotion*, New York: Touchstone.

Taylor, P. (1986) 'Dialectical biology as political practice: looking for more than contradictions', in L. Davidow (ed.), *Science as Politics*, London: Free Association Books.

Thalberg, J. (1964) 'Emotion and thought', *American Philosophical Quarterly* 1: 45–55.

Thalberg, J. (1977) *Perception, Emotion and Action*, Oxford: Blackwell.

Thalberg, J. (1980) 'Avoiding the emotion-thought conundrum', *Philosophy* 55: 396–402.

Thomä, H. and Kächele, H. (1987) *Psychoanalytic Practice. vol. 1: Principles*, trans. M. Wilson and D. Roseveare, Berlin, Heidelberg and New York: Springer-Verlag.

Thompson, M.G. (1985) *The Death of Desire*, New York: New York University Press.

Tomkins, S. (1988) *Affect, Imagery, Consciousness*, vol. I, New York: Springer-Verlag.

Toulmin, S. (1990) *Cosmopolis: The Hidden Agenda of Modernity*, New York: Free Press.

Trigg, R. (1970) *Pain and Emotion*, Oxford: Clarendon Press.

Varela, F. Thompson, E. and Rosch, E. (1992) *The Embodied Mind*, Cambridge, MA: MIT Press.

Warnock, M. (1994) *Imagination and Understanding*, Oxford: Blackwell.

Weinberg, A.M. (1988) 'Values in science: unity as a value in administration of pure science', in G. Radnitzky (ed.), *Centripetal Forces in the Sciences*, vol. 2, New York: Paragon House.

Weissman, D. (1993) *Truth's Debt to Value*, New Haven and London: Yale University Press.

Whitford, M. (ed.) (1991) *The Irigaray Reader*, Oxford, UK and Cambridge, US: Blackwell.

Whitford, M. (1991) *Luce Irigaray: Philosophy in the Feminine*, London and New York: Routledge.

Wieland-Burston, J. (1992) *Chaos and Order in the World of the Psyche*, London and New York: Routledge.

Wilson, E.O. (1992) *The Diversity of Life*, Cambridge, MA: Harvard University Press.

Wilson, J.R.S. (1972) *Emotion and Object*, Cambridge, UK: Cambridge University Press.

Wisdom, J. (1965) *Paradox and Discovery*, Oxford: Basil Blackwell.

Wittgenstein, L. (1958) *The Blue and Brown Books* (edited and with a preface by R. Rhees), Oxford: Basil Blackwell.

Wittgenstein, L. (1961) *Tractatus Logico-Philosophicus*, trans. D.F. Pears and B.F. McGuinness, London: Routledge and Kegan Paul; New York: Humanities Press.

Wittgenstein, L. (1963) *Philosophical Investigations*, G.E.M. Anscombe (ed.), Oxford: Basil Blackwell.

Wittgenstein, L. (1967) *Remarks on the Foundations of Mathematics*, G.H. von Wright, R. Rhees and G.E.M. Anscombe (eds), Cambridge, MA: MIT Press.

Wittgenstein, L. (1970) *On Certainty*, G.E.M. Anscombe and G.H. von Wright (eds), Oxford: Basil Blackwell.

Wittgenstein, L. (1980) *Bemerkungen über die Philosophie der Psychologie. Remarks on the Philosophy of Psychology*, vol. I, G.E.M. Anscombe and G.H. von Wright (eds), trans. G.E.M. Anscombe, Oxford: Basil Blackwell.

Index